NATO's New Mission

NATO's New Mission

Projecting Stability in a Post–Cold War World

Rebecca R. Moore

PRAEGER SECURITY INTERNATIONAL
Westport, Connecticut • London

Library of Congress Cataloging-in-Publication Data

Moore, Rebecca R.
    NATO's new mission : projecting stability in a post–Cold War world / Rebecca R. Moore.
        p. cm.
    Includes bibliographical references and index.
    ISBN 0–275–99296–9 (alk. paper)
1. North Atlantic Treaty Organization. 2. World politics—21st century. 3. National security—Europe. I. Title.
    UA646.3.M66 2007
    355′.031091821—dc22   2006038659

British Library Cataloguing in Publication Data is available.

Library of Congress Catalog Card Number: 2006038659
ISBN-10: 0–275–99296–9
ISBN-13: 978–0–275–99296–5

First published in 2007

Praeger Security International, 88 Post Road West, Westport, CT 06881
An imprint of Greenwood Publishing Group, Inc.
www.praeger.com

Printed in the United States of America

The paper used in this book complies with the
Permanent Paper Standard issued by the National
Information Standards Organization (Z39.48–1984).

10 9 8 7 6 5 4 3 2 1

Copyright Acknowledgments

The author and publisher gratefully acknowledge permission to use material from Rebecca Moore, "NATO's Mission for the New Millennium: A Value-Based Approach to Building Security," *Contemporary Security Policy* 23, no. 1 (2002): 1–34. http://www.tandf.co.uk

Chapter 3 is adapted from Rebecca Moore, "The New NATO: An Instrument for the Promotion of Democracy and Human Rights?" in *International Intervention in the Post-Cold War World: Moral Responsibility and Power Politics,* ed. Michael C. Davis, Wolfgang Dietrich, Bettina Scholdan, & Dieter Sepp (Armonk, NY: M.E. Sharpe, 2004). Copyright © 2004 by M.E. Sharpe, Inc. Used by permission

For my daughter, Meghan

Contents

Preface

Forecasts of NATO's imminent demise have been plentiful since the waning days of the Cold War, and they persist. Indeed, for NATO's skeptics, the events of September 11 and subsequent intra-alliance tensions over the Bush administration's wars in Afghanistan and Iraq offered only further reason to question NATO's relevance to the post–Cold War world. Indeed, as the analysis that follows concedes, there are good reasons to be concerned about NATO's future. As it has since the early 1990s, the Alliance continues to face significant challenges in adjusting to life in a world absent the Soviet threat.

Ultimately, however, this is not a pessimistic account of NATO's future. Rather, I believe there is a success story to be told here. It is a story that begins in 1990 when NATO declared its intention to construct a new security order in Europe, an order whose essence U.S. Presidents George H. W. Bush and Bill Clinton attempted to capture with the phrases "Europe whole and free" and "an undivided, democratic and peaceful Europe." Today, Europe is unquestionably more democratic and more united than at any point in its history.

The story does not end here, however. In the wake of September 11, it soon became clear that security could no longer be conceived in purely regional terms. Since then, NATO has gradually abandoned the essentially Euro-centric focus of the 1990s in favor of a more outward-looking perspective, exemplified in military missions in Afghanistan, Iraq, and the Darfur region of Sudan, as well as new or enhanced partnerships throughout the Caucasus and Central Asia, the Mediterranean region, and the Middle East. These initiatives reflect a desire to "project stability" well beyond Europe and a shift away from the largely Euro-centric perspective that had prevailed within NATO during the 1990s. "Projecting stability," NATO Secretary General Jaap de Hoop Scheffer has pronounced, is now the "precondition for [the Allies'] security." Importantly, however, this shift lies, not in the *nature* of NATO's post–Cold War mission, but, rather, in its *scope*. What NATO skeptics have failed to recognize is the extent to which NATO laid the foundation for its post–September 11 initiatives in 1990 when the Allies declared that NATO's mission was no longer to defend an existing order but, rather, to construct a new one—an order ultimately grounded on the liberal democratic values enshrined in the preamble to the original NATO treaty: democracy, individual liberty, and the rule of law.

The analysis that follows is largely an exploration of the evolution of NATO's political dimension since the end of the Cold War with a particular emphasis on what is an essentially values-based and increasingly less Euro-centric conception of security. In telling this story, I seek to highlight the continuity or common thread that runs through NATO's immediate post–Cold War and post–September 11 transformations. Indeed, rather than proving NATO's irrelevance—as some critics contend—the events of September 11 actually served to reinforce the logic underpinning a 1990 decision to enhance NATO's political dimension and the new political institutions, partnerships, and other initiatives that sprang from it. That decision, itself, was inspired by a lesson learned in both the immediate post–Cold War and post–September 11 periods: namely, that NATO territory will not be secure as long as instability reins along its periphery.

NATO's survival, however, is not inevitable. Indeed, while the Alliance has been responding to the challenges of the post–September 11 world by adapting and building on many of the same tools that were used to project stability to the east during the 1990s, it has yet to articulate a clear strategic vision that goes beyond the completion of Europe whole and free. While that mission remains an important one, it will not prove sufficient to sustain the Alliance in what NATO Secretary General Jaap de Hoop Scheffer has termed a world of "globalised insecurity." What NATO needs now is a more comprehensive strategic vision. Indeed, I suggest in the pages that follow that NATO's survival will ultimately hinge as much on the Allies' success in articulating a new political mission as it will on efforts aimed at transforming the Alliance militarily. NATO's capabilities must, as they have in the past, be put in the service of a larger political purpose.

Acknowledgments

Much of the research for this project was facilitated by a NATO-EAPC Fellowship, which I held from 2001 to 2003. I gratefully acknowledge this financial support. I am also indebted to the many members of NATO's international staff, as well as diplomatic and military personnel who gave so generously of their time during my research visits to NATO Headquarters in Brussels. Virtually all of these individuals remain anonymous in the pages that follow. Without their support, however, this project would not have been possible. This is also true of the many scholars, government officials, diplomats, and military personnel with whom I met during trips to Washington D.C., Prague, and Garmisch, Germany. Again, most remain anonymous here, but I owe them my sincere gratitude.

I owe special thanks as well to Ryan Hendrickson, Sean Kay, James Moore, Richard Rupp, Joseph Vorbach, and Sonja Wentling. All gave generously of their time and energy to read and comment on drafts of the manuscript, in part or in its entirety. The book is better for their input. Any flaws remaining are my responsibility alone. I am also grateful for the consistent support of Hilary Claggett and other members of the Praeger Security International team who worked on the book.

To Kenneth W. Thompson, my principal mentor at the University of Virginia, I will remain forever indebted. There truly could be no better role model. Last but not least, I am grateful to my parents for their love and support over the years and to my daughter, Meghan, who inspires me every day with her fierce determination, boundless energy, and endless curiosity. A true gift.

Introduction

NATO's New Mission

During a visit to Mainz, West Germany, following NATO's fortieth anniversary summit in May 1989, former President George H. W. Bush declared NATO's "new mission" to be the achievement of a Europe "whole and free." Twelve years later in Warsaw, President George W. Bush would echo that phrase, proclaiming that his father's vision was "no longer a dream," but rather "the Europe that is rising around us." "A new generation," he declared, "makes a new commitment: a Europe and an America bound in a great alliance of liberty—history's greatest united force for peace and progress and human dignity."[1]

NATO had, in fact, declared in 1990 that it intended to become "an agent of change." Its principal new political mission was the construction of a new security order in Europe—an order grounded on the liberal democratic values embodied in the preamble to the 1949 Washington Treaty—"democracy, individual liberty, and the rule of law"—and encompassing territory outside NATO's traditional sphere of collective defense.[2] Indeed, the declaration issued at NATO's 1990 summit in London asserted that changes in the Soviet Union and Eastern Europe would allow NATO to "help build the structure of a more united continent, supporting security and stability with the strength of our shared faith in democracy, the rights of the individual and the peaceful resolution of disputes."[3]

Although the preservation of liberal democratic values had long been central to NATO's larger mission, developments within the Alliance between 1989 and 1991 marked an important expansion of that mission. No longer would the Allies be content to preserve and promote NATO values chiefly by safeguarding NATO territory. Rather, they had effectively committed themselves to developing the means necessary to encourage the growth of their values outside of NATO's borders. As Secretary General Lord George Robertson later stated it, NATO's task was now "to build the Euro-Atlantic security environment of the future—where all states share peace and democracy, and uphold basic human rights."[4] Notably, this new enterprise constituted a principally *political* rather than military mission.

At the outset, NATO had no clear strategy in place for constructing Europe whole and free, but over the course of the 1990s the Alliance would pursue this vision by developing a variety of essentially political tools intended to shape a European security order favorable to the flourishing of the values enshrined in the preamble to the 1949 treaty. These tools, which ultimately extended to enlarging the Alliance itself, also encompassed new partnerships and institutions, including the Euro-Atlantic Partnership Council, the Partnership for Peace, the NATO-Russia Permanent Joint Council (later reconstituted as the NATO-Russia Council), and the NATO-Ukraine Commission. NATO also adopted new strategic concepts in 1991 and 1999, which set the stage for new military missions in Bosnia, Kosovo, and Macedonia. While the Allies remained committed to the collective defense of their territory, these new initiatives reflected a broader understanding of security than had prevailed during the Cold War.

Indeed, the mission of Europe whole and free reflected an evolving concept of security underpinned by a considerable faith in the pacifying effect of shared democratic institutions and values. "NATO," former Supreme Allied Commander Europe George A. Joulwan explained in 1997, "is now more than ever a political alliance, but as a military man that suits me fine. We represent shared ideals, not just tanks and soldiers. We want our values to take root in other countries because that is the best way we know to prevent conflicts from exploding into war."[5] Security was now to be constructed on the basis of shared liberal democratic values, making it an almost tangible commodity. Rather than relying principally on military means simply to defend NATO territory, the Alliance had committed itself to projecting stability beyond its borders. Indeed, former NATO Secretary General Lord Robertson described NATO's transformation in 1999 as that of an alliance that had "evolved from a passive, reactive defence organization into one which is actively building security right across Europe."[6]

The Impact of September 11

Ultimately, however, the project of constructing Europe whole and free was an essentially inward-looking one, and just months after Bush's 2001 address in Warsaw, the terrorist acts carried out in the United States on September 11, 2001, revealed clearly that, despite new institutions and partners, NATO was not fully prepared for the security challenges it now confronted. Although NATO's unprecedented invocation of Article 5 (NATO's collective defense clause) on September 12 marked a remarkable display of solidarity on the part of the Allies, new tensions would also emerge within the Alliance over the Bush administration's wars in

Afghanistan and Iraq, prompting predictions of NATO's impending demise reminiscent of those issued in the waning days of the Cold War.

Although NATO had withstood such predictions throughout the 1990s and even hung together during its first war in Kosovo in 1999, the debate over whether to intervene militarily in Iraq—a dispute that, at times, pitted Germany, France, and Belgium against the United States and its supporters within the Alliance—reignited the debate over NATO's ability to survive the loss of the common external threat that inspired it. Critics pointed, in particular, to the persistent and growing military capabilities gap between the United States and Europe as evidence of NATO's declining relevance as a military alliance. In fact, despite NATO's invocation of Article 5 following the events of September 11, the Bush administration largely shut the Alliance out of its war in Afghanistan, having deemed it of insufficient military value to justify the frustrations associated with conducting a war in accordance with NATO's tradition of consensus-based decision making. Perhaps the most devastating development fueling the debate over NATO's future was the dispute that occurred in early 2003 when France, Belgium, and Germany blocked the initiation of defensive measures aimed at protecting Turkey against potential spillover from the war in Iraq. What was clearly an attempt to frustrate the Bush administration's war planning appeared to many Allies—especially NATO's newest members—to be at odds with the Article 5 commitment that has long been NATO's bedrock.

Taking note of the schism revealed by this dispute, Henry A. Kissinger submitted that the rift and challenges to NATO's framework by France and Germany had deeper causes than diplomatic missteps on the part of the Bush administration. This "diplomatic revolution" could not have taken place, he insisted, "had not the traditional underpinnings of the Alliance been eroded by the disappearance of a common threat, aggravated by the emergence into power of a new generation that grew up during the Cold War and takes its achievements for granted." Kissinger further suggested that, if the trend were to continue, it would "fundamentally" alter the international system. "Europe will split into two groups defined by their attitude towards cooperation with America. NATO will change its character and become a vehicle for those continuing to affirm the transatlantic relationship."[7] In an even gloomier assessment published in the *Financial Times* just prior to NATO's 2002 summit in Prague and well before the dispute over Turkey, Charles A. Kupchan argued that the seven aspirants receiving invitations to join NATO at the summit would "be entering a western alliance that is soon to be defunct." He concluded that while "pronouncements emanating from Prague" would "no doubt affirm that the Atlantic Alliance is in the midst of rejuvenation," in fact the summit would "merely postpone NATO's inevitable demise." Kupchan did not, however, base his conclusion principally on Europe's military weakness. Rather, he argued that the United States and Europe were "drifting apart politically" due to the unilateralist bent of the Bush foreign policy.[8] Kupchan was not alone in his analysis. In a much-discussed essay first published in *Policy Review* in the summer of 2002, Robert Kagan had also pronounced that the United States and Europe no longer viewed the world in the same way, although he attributed the divergent perspectives primarily to the military capabilities gap. In his words,

> [Europe] is moving beyond power into a self-contained world of laws and rules and transnational negotiation and cooperation. It is entering a post-historical paradise of peace and relative prosperity, the realization of Immanuel Kant's "perpetual peace." Meanwhile, the United States remains mired in history, exercising power in an anarchic Hobbesian world where international law and rules are unreliable, and where true security and the defense and promotion of a liberal order still depend on the possession and use of military might.[9]

A More Global NATO

Given NATO's almost singular focus during the 1990s on enhancing its political component, there is considerable irony associated with the state of transatlantic relations today. However, NATO pessimists and even some optimists have been too quick to dismiss NATO's initial post–Cold War transformation as irrelevant or inconsequential to the threats and challenges of the post–September 11 era. This book contends that NATO laid the foundation for a post–September 11 transformation during the 1990s, beginning as early as 1989 when the Allies first recognized that their own security ultimately depended on reaching out to the east and addressing the many potential sources of instability skirting NATO's borders. The events of September 11 served to reaffirm that NATO territory cannot be secure if instability reins along NATO's periphery, in addition to broadening the Allies understanding of that periphery. Indeed, the events of that day proved critical in moving NATO toward the more global role that many Allies had resisted during the 1990s, beginning with NATO's assumption of command responsibility for the International Security Assistance Force in Afghanistan in August 2003. NATO agreed to take over responsibility for the force from Germany and the Netherlands on April 16, 2003, just two months after the effort by France, Germany, and Belgium to block NATO preparations for the defense of Turkey. A little over a month later on May 21, 2003, NATO also agreed to provide logistical support to Poland, in order that it might assume command responsibility for a peacekeeping sector in central Iraq. These decisions were significant in that they appeared to confirm NATO's resolution of the "out-of-area" debates that had divided the United States and

Europe during the 1990s. As former NATO Secretary General Lord Robertson put it in late 2002, NATO's new security environment does "not afford [the Allies] the luxury of fighting theoretical battles about what is 'in' and what is 'out-of-area.'" Rather, he stressed, NATO "will have to be able to act wherever our security and the safety of our people demand action."[10]

Decisions taken at NATO's 2004 Istanbul Summit, aimed at enhancing NATO's partnerships with the states of Central Asia and extending the partnership concept to the Greater Middle East, also reflected a belief on the part of at least some of the Allies that NATO must now seek to project stability well beyond Europe and, therefore, a shift away from the largely Euro-centric perspective that had prevailed within NATO during the 1990s. As former Ambassador to NATO R. Nicholas Burns characterized it, "NATO's past was focused inward, on Cold War threats directed at the heart of Europe. NATO's future is to look outward to the Greater Middle East to expand security in that arc of countries from South and Central Asia to the Middle East and North Africa—where the new challenges to global peace are rooted."[11] NATO's latest outreach initiatives remain consistent with the essentially values-based conception of security that NATO embraced during the 1990s. Indeed, the notion of "projecting stability" continues to be inextricable from the promotion of liberal democratic values. As NATO Secretary General Jaap de Hoop Scheffer declared at Istanbul, the Allies are now "committed to defend[ing] and to promot[ing] our common values and shared interests, in the Euro-Atlantic area and beyond."[12]

This is not to suggest that there have been no divisions among the Allies as to the scope and nature of NATO's activities in the post–Cold War, post–September 11 world. Indeed, some Allies have expressed concern that NATO is becoming overextended or even putting at risk its own integrity by engaging with governments that do not share its values. Tensions stemming from the wars in Afghanistan and Iraq also continue to generate significant and legitimate questions as to whether the Allies are sufficiently united to pursue a political mission that extends beyond the construction of Europe whole and free. What is perhaps most troubling about recent assessments of NATO's health are suggestions that the Alliance suffers, not only from the loss of a single, commonly agreed-upon threat and outdated military capabilities, but also from a values or cultural gap that is serving to erode the Alliance's foundation as a community of states committed to defending liberal democratic values.[13] Can these values, which were so frequently invoked as NATO's foundation during the 1990s, continue to sustain the Alliance well into the twenty-first century? At the core of this study are questions about the very essence of NATO. Does NATO continue to exist as a genuine political community, bound together by a common vision of the future and a consensus on the meaning of security in the twenty-first century? Or will the dissolution of the Soviet threat ultimately prove fatal as some realist scholars forecast during the early and mid-1990s?

Structure of the Work

Chapter 1 explores the mission of Europe whole and free through the lens of NATO's Cold War experience. The chapter argues that, contrary to realist assumptions that NATO existed during the Cold War as a one-dimensional military alliance, the reality of NATO's essence was always more complicated. Indeed, virtually all of the new initiatives that NATO adopted during the 1990s stemmed from a firm belief that one of NATO's greatest successes during the Cold War was the creation of a Kantian-like federation of liberal states that had pledged peace to one another. NATO's new vision of a Europe whole and free required that the "pacific federation" established in Western Europe now be extended eastward.

Chapter 2 explores the essentially values-based conception of security that has underpinned NATO's mission of Europe whole and free. It directly challenges realist critics who have reproached NATO for allegedly acting on behalf of its values rather than its interests. Such critics have failed to appreciate the extent to which genuine security as conceived by the new NATO is an almost tangible entity. The security order to which the Allies aspired during the 1990s appeared a strikingly Kantian one—an expanding pacific federation, informed by a common commitment to democratic principles and embedded in an increasingly integrated Euro-Atlantic area. Although the events of September 11 shifted NATO's attention outside of Europe and illuminated its deficiencies with respect to new challenges posed by terrorism and weapons of mass destruction, the trend toward a more global NATO, including initiatives designed to improve NATO's capacity to address out-of-area threats does not alter the Allies' basic premise emphasized repeatedly during the 1990s: namely, that true peace and stability ultimately depend upon the triumph of liberal democratic ideas.

Also central to the book is an analysis of whether NATO actually has the capacity to promote the liberal democratic values underpinning its post–Cold War conception of security. Chapter 3 therefore explores and evaluates the various initiatives by which NATO has sought to foster liberal democratic values in Central and Eastern Europe. It challenges the analysis of realist scholars who concluded during the 1990s that NATO has had little, if any, influence on the region. Such scholars have largely ignored the complex processes by which NATO, through its own mechanisms and interactions with other European institutions, has helped to generate norms for the whole of Europe that appear to have influenced the way in which the states of Central and Eastern Europe perceive their own identity and interests and, consequently, their behavior at home and abroad. Indeed, the record of reform in Central and Eastern Europe since the early 1990s supports the notion that NATO's identity as an alliance that has built the political and military means to defend the democratic values its members hold in common constitutes an important part of its appeal and, therefore, a source of its capacity to influence the behavior of prospective members. Chapter 3, however, also poses a question that is explored further in Chapter 6: namely, whether the appeal of NATO's identity and values extend beyond Europe into Central Asia and the Greater Middle East—two regions in which NATO now seeks to "project stability."

Chapter 4 assesses the impact of September 11 on NATO and, in particular, the enlargement decisions taken during the 2002 Prague Summit. It concludes that those states who aspired to join the Alliance at Prague were ultimately assessed in terms of their ability and willingness to contribute to the war on terror in addition to formal NATO criteria and that the United States, in particular, approached enlargement with the objective of a more outwardly focused and militarily robust NATO. Yet, an assessment of the Prague Summit also suggests that the commitment to Europe whole and free remained alive and well. A deeply held belief that security can ultimately be constructed on the basis of shared democratic values ensured that NATO would not abandon its efforts to influence the domestic affairs of those states who aspired to full membership in the Alliance.

Chapter 5 explores the impact of the wars in Afghanistan and Iraq on NATO's political dimension. It concedes the legitimacy of questions about NATO's continued viability, but also argues that the core concern is not so much whether NATO remains credible as a military alliance, although this is certainly a relevant and important question. The more difficult and pressing issue is whether NATO continues to exist as a genuine political community bound together by a common vision for the future. Completing Europe whole and free remains a key strategic objective, but in the wake of September 11, it no longer suffices as NATO's larger political mission. The events of that day revealed clearly that, in an increasingly globalized world, security can no longer be understood in purely regional terms. As the Allies moved toward the 2004 Istanbul Summit, it became increasingly evident that NATO was now in need of an enlarged political mission designed to address new threats posed, not simply by terrorism and weapons of mass destruction, but also by the political and economic conditions beyond the borders of Europe that are often understood to fuel terrorist activity and potentially threaten the very civilization that NATO was designed to preserve.

   Chapter 6 focuses on the prospects for a new political mission aimed at projecting stability beyond the Euro-Atlantic area to Central Asia, the Caucasus, and especially the Middle East. Given the latter region's strategic significance and the tensions it has generated in transatlantic relations, it is now widely believed on both sides of the Atlantic that NATO's future will be decided in the Middle East. This chapter addresses three questions vital to any comprehensive assessment of NATO's future relevance. The first concerns whether NATO can function as the principal vehicle for formulating a common strategy aimed at advancing democracy beyond Europe. Second, given the strategic importance of the Middle East, in particular, what are the implications for NATO if the United States and Europe fail to agree on a common strategy? Finally, does NATO have the capacity to promote its values in geographic areas not traditionally considered part of the "West"?

   Importantly, NATO's military component is not isolated from its political dimension in this analysis. In fact, the two dimensions are inextricably linked. As former NATO Secretary General Lord Robertson stated repeatedly during his tenure at NATO, competent military capabilities to which all Allies contribute constitute a key part of the "political glue" that holds the Alliance together.

   At the same time, however, the Allies must recognize that NATO survived the Cold War, not simply because it retained secondary functions that were not specific to the Soviet threat. NATO survived, and even thrived, due to a concerted effort to enhance NATO's political dimension through the adoption of what was an essentially *political* rather than military mission: namely, the creation of Europe whole and free. The debate over whether NATO can be resuscitated militarily therefore should not obscure the successes of the 1990s and the relevance of the initiatives adopted during that period to the post–September 11 era. And, yet, in a post–September 11 world, the mission of Europe whole and free is no longer sufficient as NATO's principal strategic objective. NATO's capabilities must now be put in the service of a larger political purpose. While NATO's new institutions, partnerships, and military missions represent positive first steps in the quest to project stability beyond Europe, it is not yet clear that they are guided by a comprehensive strategic vision— one that encompasses those issues that are of greatest importance to both the United States and Europe. Whether the Allies will ultimately coalesce around such a vision remains an open question, but the analysis that follows is ultimately an optimistic one, fueled in part by the experience of the 1990s and the relevance of NATO's initial post–Cold War transformation to its ongoing evolution. NATO defied its skeptics during the early post–Cold War years, and there is no reason to believe that it cannot do so again, but success in this endeavor will require considerable political will on both sides of the Atlantic.

CHAPTER 1

A New Mission for NATO: Constructing Europe "Whole and Free"

NATO: A Principally Political or Military Alliance?

Though widely considered the most successful military alliance in history, NATO throughout the Cold War was thought to be just that—a one-dimensional military alliance, aimed principally at deterring a Soviet attack on Western Europe. Consequently, many commentators did not expect NATO to outlive the threat that inspired it. In a widely read article published in *International Security* in the summer of 1990, John J. Mearsheimer offered a scenario of the post–Cold War order predicated upon the assumption that NATO had lost its raison d'etre and it, along with the Warsaw Pact, would dissolve. In his words, "The Soviet Union is the only superpower that can seriously threaten to overrun Europe; it is the Soviet threat that provides the glue that holds NATO together. Take away that offensive threat and the United States is likely to abandon the Continent, whereupon the defensive alliance it has headed for forty years may disintegrate." Mearsheimer allowed that both NATO and the Warsaw Pact might "persist on paper," but neither in his view would continue to "function as an alliance."[1] Taking a slightly different but equally pessimistic perspective, Owen Harries argued in 1993 that proposals for a "new NATO" were "based on a most questionable premise: that 'the West' continues to exist as a political and military entity." Indeed, Harries asserted that "the political 'West' is not a natural construct but a highly artificial one." As he put it, "It took the presence of a life-threatening, overtly hostile 'East' to bring it into existence and to maintain its unity. It is extremely doubtful whether it can now survive the disappearance of that enemy."[2]

Although NATO has now survived the end of the Cold War by over a decade and a half, during that time taking in new members, adopting new missions, and, for the first time ever, invoking Article 5 in response to the terrorist attacks of September 11, bleak predictions reminiscent of those issued in the early 1990s have reappeared—some prompted by tensions within NATO over the Bush administration's determination to launch a war against Iraq in 2003 even in the face of significant European opposition. NATO, Robert A. Levine pronounced in an op-ed piece published in the *International Herald Tribune* in May 2003, had become "irrelevant: a bureaucracy whose time has passed."[3] Just prior to NATO's 2003 summit in Prague, Charles Kupchan similarly argued that a loss of interest in NATO by the United States was producing "a military pact that is hollowing out and of diminishing geopolitical relevance."[4] And Richard E. Rupp, having concluded that NATO was already "in decline prior to 9/11" and that "transatlantic tensions and disputes in the wake of the attacks" had "only increased pressures on the Alliance," asserted in early 2006 that "NATO's best days are in the past."[5]

Historically, however, there exists an alternative view of NATO, one that has never presumed NATO's integrity to depend on the Soviet threat alone. Its proponents emphasize NATO's role in integrating Western Europe and the common values shared by its members. Indeed, from this perspective, the Alliance has served to ameliorate the effects of anarchy among its members, ultimately producing unprecedented stability in Western Europe during the Cold War years and beyond. As John Duffield explained it in 1994, "By damping the security dilemma and providing an institutional mechanism for the development of common security policies, NATO has contributed to making the use of force in relations among the countries of the region virtually inconceivable.[6] Indeed, for NATO optimists, the Alliance has remained relevant in the post–Cold War, post–September 11 world precisely because of its evolution during the Cold War years "from a traditional military alliance for collective defense into a political-military organization for security cooperation with an extensive bureaucracy and complex decision-making process."[7] NATO skeptics, one such scholar observed, have failed to appreciate NATO's continued relevance because they "adopted too narrow a perspective on NATO's function and history, focusing too much on NATO's military functions and geographic limitations."[8]

From the optimists' perspective, NATO's success in pacifying Western Europe can be explained both by the liberal nature of the states that comprise it and the mechanisms developed to promote cooperation among them.[9] Robert O. Keohane, for example, has asserted that both the European Union (EU) and NATO were important sources of stability during the Cold War period because "the nature and strength of international institutions are...important determinants of expectations and therefore state behavior." When "states regularly follow the rules and standards of international institutions," he suggests "they signal their willingness to continue patterns of cooperation, and therefore reinforce expectations of stability." Whether a peaceful post–Cold War Europe was sustained, Keohane therefore predicted would depend greatly on "whether the next decade [was] characterized by a continuous pattern of institutionalized cooperation."[10]

Democratic peace theorists locate the source of Western Europe's stability during the Cold War in a belief that liberal democratic states are unlikely to go to war with each other. Here both structural and normative explanations come into play. While structural accounts look to the institutional constraints within democracies as a cause of peace, normative theories focus on democratic values themselves.[11] Observing that "a pacific union, has been maintained and has expanded" in Western Europe "despite numerous particular conflicts of economic and strategic interest," Michael W. Doyle argues that a liberal peace emanates from the mutual respect that exists between states that respect individual rights, as well as from the domestic constraints on going to war inherent in democratic societies.[12] The liberal peace is rooted in a sense of community ultimately grounded on a moral foundation, the essence of which has been well captured by Thomas Risse-Kappen.

> In sum liberal theory argues that democracies do not fight each other because they perceive each other as peaceful. They perceive each other as peaceful because of the democratic norms governing their domestic decision-making processes. For the same reason, they form pluralistic security communities of shared values. Because they perceive each other as peaceful and express a sense of community, they are likely to overcome obstacles against international cooperation and to form international institutions such as alliances.[13]

NATO, according to Risse-Kappen, constitutes just such an institution. Given their shared values and perceptions of each other, the Allies constituted a community that did not depend on the emergence of the Soviet threat, but, rather, preceded it. Ultimately, they came to construe the Soviet Union as a threat because its ideology, coupled with an effort to dominate Central and Eastern Europe, constituted an assault on their shared values, but "it did not create the community in the first place."[14]

Notably, Risse-Kappen's conception of NATO's origins is consistent with social constructivist approaches to the study of international relations in which the concept of identity, inspired in part by ideas or values, is a key factor shaping the way in which states perceive, and therefore interact, with each other. A belief that the Soviet Union embraced a set of values fundamentally different than their own inspired not only a sense of collective identity among the Allies, but also the perception of a threat. The essence of that threat derived, not simply from Soviet power, but also from an ideology the Allies viewed as threatening to their core values. Former NATO Secretary General Lord Robertson gave voice to this view in September 2001 in observing that "NATO's members shared common values...at a time when those basic values were under threat virtually all around the world." NATO "provided a structure for its members to defend values for their citizens...overcome historical ghosts of division, and instead build a cooperative, peaceful future."[15]

Former U.S. Secretary of State Madeleine K. Albright used a similar argument in making the case for NATO enlargement in the mid-1990s. In her words, "NATO defines a community of interest among the free nations of North America and Europe that both preceded and outlasted the Cold War. America has long stood for the proposition that the Atlantic community should not be artificially divided and that its nations should be free to shape their destiny. We have long argued that the nations of Central and Eastern Europe belong to the same democratic family as our allies in Western Europe."[16] As Ian Thomas has observed, U.S. Secretary of State Dean Acheson also relied heavily on the notion that NATO was "an affirmation of the moral and spiritual values which we hold in common" in his effort to build support for NATO at the time of its inception. NATO, in Acheson's words, "did not create something new as much as it recorded a basic reality—a unity of belief, of spirit and of joint interest which was already felt by the nations of the North Atlantic community."[17] British Foreign Secretary Ernest Bevin saw this community in much the same way. In pushing for a transatlantic alliance after World War II, he had urged that "political and indeed spiritual forces must be mobilized in our defense."[18] Indeed, Sean Kay suggests that, while the "primary reason for NATO's founding was the Soviet challenge in Eastern Europe," this fact was "insufficient to understanding why the states chose the particular institutional form that emerged in April 1949." "The negotiators," he says, "recognized that if a peacetime alliance were to withstand the ebbs and flows of the Cold War, it would have to reflect a broader purpose than collective defense."[19]

In the post–Cold War era, perhaps no one has articulated more forcefully and more eloquently the notion that NATO's identity and its purpose are ultimately rooted in its members' shared democratic values than former Czech dissident and later President Václav Havel. NATO, Havel wrote in 1997, "should urgently remind itself that it is first and foremost an instrument of democracy intended to defend mutually held and created political and spiritual values. It must see itself not as a pact of nations against a more or less obvious enemy but as a guarantor of Euro-American civilization."[20] Former NATO Secretary General Manfred Wörner also emphasized that NATO did not need to invent a political role for itself in the post–Cold War order. As he put it in May 1990, NATO has "always been a community of values and a community of destiny among free nations."[21]

Indeed, longtime NATO international staff member Nicholas Sherwen suggested in 1990 that one of the challenges that NATO faced at the end of the Cold War was "to correct the public image of an organization which has been, from the very outset, a political tool created for a political purpose enshrined in a political treaty." "Throughout the post war years," Sherwen wrote, "the Alliance ha[d] been distracted from its underlying political purpose by the paramount need to contain the implicit threat of a militarily unstable imbalance of forces which, as Moscow now admits, could not but give the NATO Allies legitimate concerns regarding Soviet intentions."[22] Sherwen is not alone in suggesting that NATO's raison d'etre was, from the beginning, multidimensional. Perhaps no expression of the multiple tasks for which the Alliance was created has been quoted more than that of Lord Ismay, NATO's first secretary general, who bluntly stated that NATO was designed "to keep the Russians out, the Americans in, and the Germans down." In practice, keeping the Germans down meant integrating Germany into Western Europe—politically and economically—with NATO supplying the reassuring counterweight of U.S. military power.[23] Lt. General William Odom explained it in testimony before the U.S. House of Representatives' Committee on International Relations in 1996 as follows:

> We set up NATO for a set of rationales best articulated by Robert Schuman and Jean Monnet, the conceivers, the architects of European economic integration. They realized that Germany was the problem and that quarrels among the Germans, the British, and the French would prevent cooperation and rapid reconstruction after the war. They knew they needed a substitute for a supra-national authority there, and they asked the United States to provide it in the form of our military political presence in NATO, and we did.[24]

Moreover, European integration rested on the principles enshrined in the preamble to the 1949 Washington Treaty. As Kay has observed, NATO was tasked from the beginning with strengthening and expanding "an international community based on democratic principles, individual liberty, and the rule of law" and then with building the "institutional structures" necessary to aid in the achievement of these goals.[25] Indeed, the Allies pledged through Article 2 of the original Washington Treaty not only to safeguard their shared values, but also to "contribute toward the further development of peaceful and friendly international relations by strengthening their free institutions, by bringing about a better understanding of the principles upon which these institutions are founded, and by promoting conditions of stability and well-being." They further agreed to "seek to eliminate conflict in their international economic policies and encourage economic collaboration between any or all of them."[26]

As David S. Yost has observed, throughout the Cold War, the Allies also "repeatedly declared their interest in pursuing positive political change in

Europe while avoiding war" as exemplified in part by the 1967 Harmel Report—a document in which NATO explicitly recognized a political as well as a military mission. In addition to maintaining its traditional mission of collective defense, NATO would now commit itself to pursuing détente with the Soviet bloc.[27] Adopting this essentially political function, the report suggested, would allow the Allies to work "towards a more stable relationship in which the underlying political issues [could] be solved."[28]

Though certainly among the better known statements of NATO's political strategy, the Harmel Report was not the Allies' only attempt to fulfill their Article 2 pledges and strengthen the sense of political community between them. As early as 1956, NATO established a Committee of Three to advise the North Atlantic Council on ways to improve cooperation in nonmilitary fields and to "develop greater unity within the Atlantic Community."[29] In much the same spirit, NATO convened an Atlantic Convention in 1962, tasking the delegates—citizens of NATO member states—with making recommendations for achieving closer cooperation among the Allies and fostering a "true Atlantic community." As Jamie Shea has observed, those in attendance "urgently request[ed]" that their governments "reinforce and develop the North Atlantic Treaty Organisation as a political centre."[30] Far more recently, the Allies have sought to focus on the continuity underpinning their collective political mission, observing in NATO's 1999 Strategic Concept that the Alliance had "striven since its inception to secure a just and lasting peaceful order in Europe," based on common values of democracy, human rights and the rule of law.[31]

The London Declaration

If one accepts that NATO does indeed constitute a political community that preceded the Cold War, with political tasks that are of at least as much importance as those associated with its military component, then the destruction of NATO as a political entity does not necessarily follow from the dissolution of the Soviet threat. Indeed, NATO's principal political mission, namely, the defense and promotion of the democratic values that were central to the way in which the individual Allies conceived their interests, was every bit as relevant during the 1990s as it had been during the Cold War—if not more so. "What unites us are shared interests, not shared threats," former NATO Secretary General Javier Solana insisted in 1999. "This is why the alliance has remained so strong beyond the end of the Cold War."[32]

In fact, as Cold War tensions began to dissipate in the late 1980s, President George H.W. Bush recognized that the anticipated collapse of Soviet power necessitated moving NATO's political dimension to the fore.

NATO now required a new mission, a mission he declared in a speech delivered in Mainz, West Germany, in May 1989, to be the creation of Europe "whole and free."[33] At NATO's fortieth anniversary summit in Brussels that same month, the Allies observed that changes throughout the former Soviet bloc were bringing closer the "vision of a just, humane and democratic world" that had "always underpinned" NATO's political strategy, and they declared their desire to shape "a new political order of peace in Europe."[34] Approximately six months later, U.S. Secretary of State James Baker told the Berlin Press Club that the desired security structure was "one in which the military component is reduced and the political one enhanced." "That," he declared, was "NATO's first new mission."[35]

Acting on an initiative put forward by the United States at NATO's July 1990 London Summit, the Allies declared that "security and stability do not lie solely in the military dimension" and affirmed their intention "to enhance the political component of the Alliance as provided for by Article 2" of the Washington Treaty.[36] Casting NATO as an organization that was becoming increasingly political in nature served in part to soften the blow to the Soviet Union of Germany's impending reunification and entry into NATO.[37] The Bush administration was committed to German unification and the preservation of NATO, but it sought to accomplish these aims without jeopardizing the process of continued reform in the Soviet Union. According to Robert L. Hutchings, then director for European affairs at the National Security Council, the former president "did not want Russia any more than Germany to be 'singularized' or isolated in the emerging order." Efforts to address Soviet security concerns during the 1990s were thus aimed not only at facilitating German reunification, but also at creating conditions that would permit the Soviet Union to assume a strong and secure place in the international community.[38] "Integrating the Soviet Union into the community of nations" was, in fact, among the goals Bush had outlined in a commencement address at the U.S. Coast Guard Academy in May 1989.[39] In his own memoirs, Baker recalls that he had informed then Soviet Foreign Minister Eduard Shevardnadze that the administration was conscious of the political constraints the Russians faced and was thus "proposing the adoption of a declaration at the London NATO Summit that would highlight the alliance's adaptation to a new, radically different world."[40]

At the same time, the Bush administration was determined to preserve NATO as a vehicle for continued U.S. involvement in Europe. "No idea," says Hutchings, "was more strongly and deeply held in the upper levels of the administration than the core conviction that the American presence was indispensable to European stability and therefore to vital American interests."[41]

Bush, himself, recounts in his memoirs a conversation with François Mitterand during which he told the French president that he "could not keep the United States in Europe if NATO did not adapt to a new role."[42] Bush's vision of a new European security order, with NATO as its centerpiece, was not immediately shared by U.S. allies, however. France, Russia, and, initially, even Czechoslovakia, under the leadership of Václav Havel, advocated a system built around the CSCE (Conference on Security and Cooperation in Europe). To its favor, CSCE constituted a more comprehensive entity than NATO, but it also lacked any independent military capability. From the Bush administration's perspective, U.S. military power remained a necessary counterweight to a potentially resurgent Soviet Union as well as a force for general stability in Europe, particularly given fears of a newly unified Germany and the power vacuum rapidly materializing in Central and Eastern Europe.

Equally important was the determination of both the Bush administration and Secretary General Wörner that NATO could act as a catalyst for democratic political reform to its east. Wörner, in fact, believed firmly that it was not only NATO's responsibility, but its "destiny," "to support the countries of Central and Eastern Europe in their efforts to build democracy." Without NATO's help, he asserted in May 1990, "they stand no chance."[43] Indeed, the declaration issued at the 1990 London Summit asserted that, while NATO had "done much to bring about the new Europe," it must now "be even more an agent of change" by helping to "build the structure of a more united continent, supporting security and stability with the strength of [the Allies'] shared faith in democracy, the rights of the individual and the peaceful resolution of disputes."[44]

As an initial step in this direction, the Allies extended a hand at London to their former Warsaw Pact adversaries by inviting the governments of Czechoslovakia, Hungary, Poland, Bulgaria, and even the Soviet Union to establish diplomatic liaisons to NATO. The decision to reach out to these states had effectively been made during a NATO foreign ministers' meeting at Turnberry, Scotland, approximately one month prior to the London Summit. There, Baker had called on NATO "to accelerate the alliance's ongoing process of reassessment and renewal" and "to look beyond the narrower task of preventing war to the broader one of building the peace."[45] NATO foreign ministers concluded the meeting by issuing a "Message from Turnberry" which extended "to the Soviet Union and to all other European countries the hand of friendship and cooperation."[46] As Hutchings later observed, NATO had "set as its new political mission the development of cooperation and partnership with former adversaries."[47]

To some degree the inspiration behind NATO's outreach efforts stemmed from continued concern in the United States about Mikhail Gorbachev's vision of a "common European home"—a home in which there was little room for the United States. Baker, in fact, observes in his memoirs that reaching out to Central and Eastern Europe constituted one means by which the Bush administration sought to counter Soviet efforts to divide NATO. "We needed to be 'playing offense' by pushing liberalization in Europe," he explains, citing a phrase used by Robert Zoellick, then a principal adviser to Baker at the State Department. "If Gorbachev was going to try to split our alliance, we should certainly be working to play off the Eastern Europeans against Moscow."[48]

The fact that one of NATO's first priorities was to ensure that its values prevailed throughout the former Soviet bloc also bore witness to a deeply rooted conviction among the Allies that shared democratic values were the key to their success in stabilizing Western Europe. During their 1989 Brussels Summit, NATO members had reaffirmed that the peace and prosperity they enjoyed were "the fruits of a partnership based on enduring common values and interests, and on unity of purpose."[49] Focusing on these shared values, Bush asserted at the time, would provide the West with "both an anchor and a course to navigate for the future."[50] In Prague in 1990, Bush again spoke of his vision of "a Europe that reaches its democratic destiny." "Europe's celebration of freedom brings with it a new responsibility," he declared. "Now that democracy has proven its power, Europe has both the opportunity and the challenge to join us in leadership—to work with us in common cause toward a new commonwealth of freedom...a moral community united in its dedication for free ideas."[51]

The challenge, however, was not simply a moral one. It ultimately derived from the desire to enlarge the zone of stability constructed in Western Europe during the Cold War years. Without "democratic consolidation," Hutchings explains, "no amount of 'architectural' innovation or conflict resolution mechanisms among European institutions would have had any prospect of success." Extending democracy to Central and Eastern Europe was "*the* pre-eminent security issue for post–Cold War Europe." It was also a challenge, Hutchings observes, "for which Western policies and institutions were ill-prepared."[52]

Although the preservation of liberal democratic values had long been central to NATO's larger mission, developments within the Alliance between 1989 and 1991 marked an important expansion of that mission. No longer would the Allies be content to preserve and promote NATO values chiefly by safeguarding NATO territory. In so explicitly enhancing NATO's political dimension, they were effectively committing themselves to encouraging the growth of democratic values beyond NATO's borders. Reaching out to former adversaries constituted one essentially political means of building the more unified and democratic Europe the Allies desired. Although NATO had no clear blueprint for such an ambitious new political mission, these early partnership efforts would ultimately constitute a first step in the construction of a new European security architecture, which by the late 1990s would encompass virtually the whole of Europe and comprise multiple overlapping institutions and partnerships.

Initially, the commitment to greater cooperation with NATO's former adversaries produced a host of bilateral contacts, including significant military-to-military exchanges between individual NATO members and former adversaries. In 1992, the United States also took the lead in establishing the George C. Marshall European Center for Security Studies in Garmisch, Germany.[53] Run jointly by the U.S. and German governments, the center was designed to facilitate democratic reforms in the militaries of Central and Eastern Europe and promote greater military cooperation by offering seminars, workshops, and conferences for both civilian and military officials from throughout the former Soviet bloc. NATO also invited Central and Eastern European military officers to train at NATO defense schools. As Stephen J. Flanagan observes, these various liaison efforts were fully consistent with the Allies' Article 2 commitment to developing "peaceful and friendly international relations by strengthening their free institutions" and to "bringing about a better understanding of the principles upon which these institutions are founded."[54]

A Role for CSCE

Enlarging the community of states that embraced those principles was not to be NATO's mission alone, however. During the same 1989 address in which he had proclaimed NATO's new mission to be the achievement of Europe whole and free, Bush had called upon the CSCE to "promote free elections and political pluralism in Eastern Europe" as a means of encouraging continued political reform in the region.[55] Meeting in Brussels that same month, the NATO Allies stated their intention to develop the CSCE process further "in all its dimensions, and to make the fullest use of it" in an effort to "bring all Eastern countries to enshrine in law and practice the human rights and freedoms agreed in international covenants and in the CSCE documents, thus fostering progress toward the rule of law."[56]

These efforts underscored the centrality of democracy and respect for human rights to NATO's post–Cold War mission, but they also reflected a recognition that NATO would have to look to overlapping European institutions to achieve a new, democracy-based security order. No single institution, Baker observed in December 1989, could realize the vision of Europe "whole and free."[57] Meeting in June 1991, NATO foreign ministers also asserted that their "common security" could "best be safeguarded through the further development of a network of interlocking institutions and relationships, constituting a comprehensive architecture in which the Alliance, the process of European integration, and the CSCE are key elements."[58] Months later, at their November 1991 Rome Summit, the Allies again acknowledged that the changes they faced in Europe could not be "comprehensively addressed by one institution alone, but only in a framework of interlocking institutions tying together the countries of Europe and North America." NATO would therefore work "toward a new European security architecture in which NATO, the CSCE, the European Community, the WEU [Western European Union] and the Council of Europe complement each other."[59]

The North Atlantic Cooperation Council

Even before the Allies could assemble in Rome, however, various developments threatened to undermine NATO's vision of Europe whole and free. An attempted coup in the Soviet Union in the fall of 1991, coupled with the ultimately bloody breakup of Yugoslavia, heightened concerns about the development of a security vacuum in Central and Eastern Europe following the collapse of the Warsaw Pact in 1991. Recognizing the need to adapt to this new threat environment, NATO issued a new Strategic Concept at Rome in 1991. Designed to improve the Alliance's ability to respond to new post–Cold War challenges, including those arising from ethnic rivalries, territorial disputes, and other political and economic difficulties, the new Strategic Concept served to broaden NATO's security policy to include "dialogue" and "cooperation" in addition to the "maintenance of a collective defense capability." In essence, the new Strategic Concept affirmed NATO's new political mission and explicitly recognized that "the opportunities for achieving Alliance objectives through political means [were] greater than ever." Of the four fundamental security tasks it set forth, the first was "to provide one of the indispensable foundations for a stable security environment in Europe, based on the growth of democratic institutions and a commitment to the peaceful resolution of disputes, in which no country would be able to intimidate or coerce any European nation or to impose hegemony through the threat or use of force."[60]

NATO then moved to institutionalize its new liaison relationships with former adversaries by inviting them, along with the three Baltic states, to join the North Atlantic Cooperation Council (NACC), a newly created institution designed to promote consultation and cooperation on political and security matters and encourage democratic development throughout the whole of Europe.[61] The NACC stemmed from several proposals advanced just a month earlier by Baker and German Foreign Minister Hans-Dietrich Genscher regarding NATO's relationship with its neighbors to the east. One such proposal entailed formalizing NATO's new liaison relationships through the creation of a council that would meet regularly at the ambassadorial level. Liaison participation would also be invited in the meetings of some NATO committees, including the Committee on the Challenges of Modern Society. The new council constituted one effort to prevent the renationalization of security to NATO's east—a serious concern given the virulent nationalism driving the war in the Balkans.[62] The NACC, Baker argued, constituted the kind of integrating structure that could help stem the devolution of the nation-state and the danger of further disintegration. Indeed, the establishment of the NACC, which would be succeeded in 1997 by the Euro-Atlantic Partnership Council (EAPC), reflected NATO's belief that genuine security was best achieved on the basis of shared values and in a community that included the whole of Europe. In Baker's words, it represented "NATO's initial effort to leave the Cold War behind and to plant the seeds of post–Cold War institutions by reaching out to the East to expand the community of democratic nations."[63] "For forty years," he observed during the first meeting of the NACC in 1991, "we stood apart from one another as two opposing blocs. Now, history has given us the opportunity to erase those blocs, to join together in a common circle built on shared universal and democratic values."[64]

Not long after the NACC's inception, however, the Allies recognized the new institution's limits in terms of facilitating practical cooperation between NATO and the states of Central and Eastern Europe. The NACC was also unable to serve as a new overarching security institution because it excluded European states that had not been aligned with either NATO or the Warsaw Pact (i.e., Sweden, Finland, Ireland, Austria, and Switzerland). At the same time, the mere existence of the NACC appeared to diminish the importance of CSCE—an institution to which these states did belong. As Hutchings put it, "If the NACC...was to meet regularly at foreign minister level to discuss matters of European security, what role did that leave for the CSCE?"[65] Neither institution, however, was prepared to address Central and East European security concerns stemming from the collapse of the bipolar order. NATO responded only belatedly to the war in the Balkans that began following the secession of the Slovene and Croatian republics from Yugoslavia in mid-1991. The Bush administration had called as early as 1990 for these developments to be discussed both within NATO and at the upcoming November 1990 CSCE summit in Paris, only to have the proposed consultations rejected by the French, who according to former Bush administration officials argued that NATO was "over dramatizing" the situation.[66] The administration, which had its own concerns about U.S. military involvement in the Balkans, later opted to defer to the nascent European Union, which viewed the conflict as an opportunity to formulate and exercise the common foreign and security policy envisioned in the 1991 Maastricht Treaty. "This is the hour of Europe," Jacques Poos, the president of the European Council, famously remarked on behalf of the European community at the outbreak of the Yugoslav crisis: "If one problem can be solved by the Europeans it is the Yugoslav problem. This is a European country and it is not up to the Americans."[67]

In retrospect, the U.S. decision to defer to the Europeans proved disastrous. Europe failed to respond decisively, and war spread quickly from Slovenia and Croatia to Bosnia where it raged until 1995. Although NATO did ultimately intervene by launching limited air strikes against the Bosnian Serbs in 1994 and 1995 and eventually establishing a peace-keeping/stabilization mission to enforce the terms of the 1995 Dayton Peace Accord, the fact that several hundred thousand people had died in the former Yugoslavia before the end of 1995 only furthered a growing perception that NATO was not equipped for the post–Cold War world and was fast becoming irrelevant. In part, NATO's difficulties stemmed from a lack of political will, which was itself a product of internal discord. At the same time, it was becoming increasingly clear that the emphasis on enhancing NATO's political dimension had not been accompanied by a parallel effort to prepare the Alliance's military dimension for the new strategic environment, even though NATO's 1991 Strategic Concept had expressly noted that threats to the Allies' security were now "less likely to result from calculated aggression against the territory of the Allies" than from "the adverse consequences of instabilities" arising from "economic, social and political difficulties, including ethnic rivalries and territorial disputes."[68] Przemyslaw Grudzinski, Poland's deputy foreign minister during NATO's first round of post–Cold War enlargement and later Poland's ambassador to the United States, observed with Peter van Ham in 1999 as follows:

> The well-intentioned and widespread desire to see military force eliminated as a means of settling international disputes has proved to be realistic only for a part of Europe, but certainly not for Europe as a whole. Some of the rhetoric of turning the European continent into a "zone of peace" in which democratic countries would thrive economically has been very useful as a political programme. But we have to take into account that the rhetoric of a "Europe whole and free" blossomed particularly at a time of war in the former Yugoslavia, during military clashes in Moldova, and civil wars in Georgia as well as in Chechnya. In all those instances, the "international community" refused to adopt policies and take action to effectively end those conflicts.[69]

Hutchings also suggests that NATO's "acute ambivalence" with respect to security threats in Eastern Europe led to what he calls a "Fortress Transatlantica" mentality. "Preserving NATO," he observed, "took precedence over adapting it or answering the hard question of how we propose to use it."[70]

The Enlargement Question

No rethinking of NATO's relationship with Central and Eastern Europe, however, could ignore the question of whether NATO should open its door to new members. Although enlargement would not become a reality until 1994, as early as October 1991 Czech President Václav Havel had let it be known that Czechoslovakia desired full membership in NATO. Havel's appeal to NATO stemmed not so much from the fear of a resurgent Russia as it did from concern that, in the absence of a firm security foundation, the region faced a more general threat of growing political and economic instability, especially given the war in Yugoslavia. Poland, though equally desirous of membership, was initially less vocal about its ambitions, in part, because the United States had warned the Polish government not to "bang on NATO's door." Given the continued presence of Soviet troops on Polish soil, the Polish leadership was also reluctant to take any action that might delay or disrupt the withdrawal of those troops.[71] Still, Polish President Lech Wałesa shared Havel's concern that a security vacuum had developed across the region, even telling the NATO Allies during a July 1991 visit to Brussels that the people of Central and Eastern Europe "resolutely reject any ideas of 'gray' or buffer zones." "They imply a continued division of the continent," Wałesa warned. "Without a secure Poland and a secure Central Europe, there is no secure and stable Europe."[72]

The desire for reintegration with Western Europe also prompted the leaders of Poland, Hungary, and the Czech Republic to come together at Visegrád, Hungary, in February 1991 in what would ultimately become known as the Visegrád group, to pledge political and security cooperation aimed at advancing their prospects for integration into Western political and security institutions.[73] As Ronald D. Asmus notes, the attempted coup against Gorbachev in the Soviet Union in August 1991 only furthered the desire of Central and East Europeans for such integration by highlighting the region's vulnerability and the absence of "any meaningful security guarantees." Less than a year later on May 6, 1992, Havel, Wałesa, and Hungarian Prime Minister József Antall, together in Prague, officially declared their intention to seek full membership in NATO.[74] Security in Central and Eastern Europe was now increasingly understood to depend on NATO's willingness to embrace its neighbors to the east.

In the United States, however, divisions within the Bush and, later, Clinton administrations ensured that a decision on enlargement would not come quickly. Although Secretary of Defense Richard Cheney had reportedly told the Polish defense minister following the 1992 election that he favored NATO admission for the Visegrád states,[75] his view was not shared by others in the Bush administration. Some at the State Department resisted enlargement out of a fear that, once begun, there would be no logical endpoint to the process.[76] Deputy Secretary of State Lawrence Eagleburger granted during a NATO meeting in June 1992 in Oslo that enlargement might, at some point, be in NATO's future, but he also stressed that it was not part of the administration's current agenda. Key Bush advisers were also unable to agree on whether the notion of enlargement warranted inclusion in a speech the President delivered in Warsaw on July 5, 1992.[77] In the end, no mention of it was made. As one former Bush administration official explained it, any talk of opening NATO's door to new members was "purely theoretical."[78]

As Central and East Europeans rightfully suspected, the reluctance to grant serious consideration to enlarging NATO stemmed in good part from concerns about the potential impact of such a move on Russia.[79] Despite Boris Yeltsin's declaration at the first meeting of the NACC in late 1991 that NATO membership was "a long-term aim" of Russia,[80] the Bush administration had worried that moving too quickly on enlargement could jeopardize the reforms taking place in both the Soviet Union and Central and Eastern Europe.[81] The decision to enlarge would thus be left to Bill Clinton, whose administration—at least initially—was also hesitant to open NATO's door. Again, fears of antagonizing Russia and setting back the reform process dominated the debate over how to proceed. As has now been well documented, key figures in the administration were, if not unequivocally opposed to enlargement, nevertheless leery of its implications, including Secretary of State Warren Christopher, Secretary of Defense Les Aspin, and Strobe Talbott, who served the administration initially as a special adviser on Russia and later as Deputy Secretary of State. Clinton, himself, was more favorably disposed as was his National Security Adviser, Anthony Lake.[82]

Support for enlargement also existed within the U.S. Department of State's Policy Planning Staff. As Principal Deputy Director of the Policy Planning Staff, Hans Binnendijk, together with Associate Director Stephen Flanagan, had raised the issue in mid-1993, ultimately making the case for enlargement within the government with support from Under-Secretary of State for Arms Control and International Security Affairs Lynn Davis, despite opposition from the State Department's Bureau of European and Eurasian Affairs. Binnendijk, in fact, had published an op/ed in the *International Herald Tribune* in late 1991, while serving as the director of Georgetown University's Institute for the Study of Diplomacy, in which he had argued that the principal issue confronting NATO in the 1990s would be "how and in what circumstances to expand so as to protect new democracies in the East."[83]

Outside of the administration, enlargement was also strongly supported by Germany's Minister of Defense, Volker Rühe, who recognized in the post–Cold War world the potential for instability along Germany's eastern border and looked to NATO enlargement as one means of assisting Central and Eastern Europeans in consolidating their fledgling democracies and integrating Europe as a whole.[84] In the United States, U.S. Senator Richard Lugar, another early proponent of enlargement, agreed that, if NATO was to outlive the Cold War and Europe was to be whole and free, the Allies would need to project eastward the security order they had constructed among themselves after World War II. NATO would, in his words, need to "go out of area or out of business."[85] Ultimately, Rühe and Lugar both looked to three RAND Corporation analysts—Ronald D. Asmus, Richard L. Kugler, and F. Stephen Larrabee—to help make the case for enlargement.[86] Asmus, Kugler, and Larrabee had published an article in *Foreign Affairs* in the fall of 1993 which argued that the Allies should develop a strategy for integrating the Visegrád states into NATO. It was time, they suggested, to "transform NATO from an alliance based on collective defense against a specific threat into an alliance committed to projecting democracy, stability, and crisis management in a broader strategic sense."[87]

Clinton also continued to face pressure for enlargement from both Havel and Wałesa, who met with him while in Washington for the opening of the U.S. Holocaust Memorial Museum in April 1993. Havel was particularly distressed that the West had allowed a security vacuum to open in Central and Eastern Europe, which, he would argue throughout the 1990s, permitted instability and local conflicts fostered by nationalism or ethnic rivalries (e.g., Bosnia) to easily spread.[88] "If the West does not stabilize the East," he warned, "the East will destabilize the West."[89] Indeed, Havel chided the West for not moving quickly enough to consolidate a liberal order in Europe.[90] In his view, enlargement was about securing democracy in Central Europe and, ultimately, ensuring that liberal democratic values took hold even farther east.[91]

Wałesa, on the other hand, emphasized the threat still posed by Russia. "If Russia again adopts an aggressive foreign policy," he told the President, "that aggression will be directed against Poland and Ukraine." The Polish leader also attempted to speak to the administration's concerns about the impact of enlargement on Russia by emphasizing that democratic reform in Russia would first require the stabilization and integration of Central Europe.[92]

Although Clinton was reportedly impressed by the arguments made, his administration remained divided on the issue and no decision on enlargement was taken by the Allies until the NATO summit in Brussels in January 1994. Rather, the Clinton administration proposed in October 1993 a new initiative designed to promote political and military cooperation across Europe, which would come to be known as the Partnership for Peace (PfP). Although the program ultimately served as a sort of proving ground for those seeking admission to NATO, at the time it appeared to prospective members to be a poor substitute for enlargement given the absence of any security guarantees.

By January 1994, however, Clinton had made the decision to support NATO enlargement, at least in principle. The Partnership for Peace, he declared at the NATO summit in Brussels that month, would set "in motion a process that leads to the enlargement of NATO." The President added that NATO had "always looked to the addition of new members who shared the alliance's purposes and who could enlarge its orbit of democratic security." Enlarging NATO therefore constituted a means of realizing "NATO's original vision."[93] In fact, the Alliance alerted aspirants to the fact that "active participation" in PfP would be a factor in determining how the enlargement of NATO would evolve.[94] The President, however, provided no indication as to when the process might begin or to whom invitations might be extended.[95] His administration still faced the problem of reconciling the enlargement decision with worries about Russia, and key allies, including Britain and France, were also reluctant to move quickly. Yet, the process had now begun. A little over three years later at NATO's Madrid Summit in 1997, the Allies issued three membership invitations. Despite some intra-alliance divisions over who should be admitted during this first phase of enlargement, the recipients were, as the Clinton administration desired, Poland, Hungary, and the Czech Republic.[96]

The Case for Enlargement

Although the Clinton administration's case for enlargement certainly benefited from a belief held by some members of Congress that NATO was still needed as a hedge against a potentially resurgent Russia, that was not the essence of the case Clinton and key administration officials made on behalf of enlargement.[97] In fact, by most accounts, the President's support for enlargement stemmed from a strongly held belief that enlarging NATO would serve to extend eastward the democratic values and practices on which NATO had secured peace in Western Europe.[98] Noting in Brussels in January 1994 that the Allies had been "granted an opportunity without precedent," Clinton declared that they now had "the chance to recast European security on historic new principles: the pursuit of economic and political freedom."[99] Indeed, the Clinton administration repeatedly declared that "NATO can do for Europe's East what it did for Europe's West: prevent a return to local rivalries, strengthen democracy against future threats and create the conditions necessary for prosperity to flourish."[100] Ultimately, integration of the states of Central and Eastern Europe into NATO constituted a means of enlarging the space in which "wars simply do not happen."[101]

Administration officials also consistently portrayed NATO as a community of states committed to consolidating and preserving shared values of democracy, respect for human rights, and a commitment to the rule of law. "Those who ask 'where is the threat?' mistake NATO's real value," Secretary of State Madeleine Albright insisted before the Senate Foreign Relations Committee in 1997.

> The alliance is not a wild-west posse that we trot out only when danger appears. It is a permanent presence, designed to promote common endeavors and to prevent a threat from ever arising. That is why current allies still need it and why others wish to join. NATO does not need an enemy. It has enduring purposes.[102]

The new NATO was no longer targeted at Russia or anyone else; its mission was "to help build an undivided, democratic, and peaceful Europe."[103] Although the Clinton administration had opted for slightly different language to characterize NATO's new charge, the goal was fully consistent with the mission George H. W. Bush had articulated in 1989. Enlargement would constitute yet another stage in the process of constructing Europe whole and free.

In fact, the arguments advanced by the Clinton administration rested on an important assumption: namely, that the lure of NATO membership would be sufficiently appealing to prospective members to encourage them to make the requisite political, economic, and defense reforms. Although NATO has published no specific membership criteria, it did release an internal study on enlargement in September 1995, which concluded that the enlargement process would serve to enhance security and stability in Europe by "encouraging and supporting democratic reforms," fostering in new members "patterns and habits of cooperation and consultation and consensus-building," and "promoting good neighborly relations."[104] The study served to notify prospective members that only those states that demonstrated a commitment to democratic values and practices would be considered for membership. This would include resolving ethnic and external territorial disputes by peaceful means and establishing "appropriate democratic and civilian control of their defense forces." Clinton also stated publicly that "countries with repressive political systems, countries with designs on their neighbors, countries with militaries unchecked by civilian control or with closed economic systems need not apply."[105]

In effect, the enlargement process became a way of rewarding those Central and Eastern Europeans who had made the political and economic reforms essential to NATO's vision of a Europe whole and free. It was, as Sean Kay has suggested, a "fundamentally political act rather than a military one."[106] In fact, Strobe Talbott observed in an article published in the *New York Review of Books* in August 1995 that, while "military and geographical considerations" had been the principal determinants of NATO decisions during the Cold War, the new era was one in which "other, nonmilitary, goals [could] and should help shape the new NATO."[107]

Notably, the administration also declined to place limits on the scope of enlargement or foreclose the possibility of Russia becoming a member. To do so, Talbott observed in 1997 "would be to draw a new line on the map and betray the President's vision of an undivided, increasingly integrated Europe."[108] Similarly, Albright insisted in 1998 that it would be in NATO's interest to welcome any European country that had been deemed important to the Allies' security and which had demonstrated that it was ready "politically, economically, and militarily" to contribute to their security.[109] Indeed, NATO assured prospective members after the first round of invitations was issued in 1997 and again following the accession of those states to the Alliance in 1999 that NATO's door remained open.

Notably, nothing about the decision to enlarge was inevitable. At the same time, however, it was a choice that followed logically from the decision taken at the 1990 London Summit in favor of enhancing NATO's political dimension. As Stephen Flanagan observed, if NATO was increasingly to be understood as "an alliance of democracies with historical ties and common values, what is the basis for excluding other such countries in Europe who request membership?"[110] Building security now meant enlarging the community of states that embraced liberal democratic values and established peace with one another on the basis of those values.

Yet, the Clinton administration never suggested that NATO's boundaries must circumscribe the entire community of states committed to democracy, human rights, the rule of law, and free markets. "To the extent that societies reflect these values—whether it be Russia, Lithuania, the United States, or Norway—," former U.S. Ambassador to NATO Alexander Vershbow explained in 1998, "then we have an inherent interest in working together, in being at peace with one another, in fostering trade and economic growth, and in helping others to share these same benefits. This is what we mean when we talk about increasing the space in Europe where wars simply do not happen. This is our vision of Euro-Atlantic integration."[111]

Indeed, enlargement was only one piece of a larger effort aimed at integrating Europe politically, economically, and militarily. Toward this end, NATO had already begun constructing a series of new, overlapping institutions designed in part to foster liberal democratic values beyond NATO territory. This new Euro-Atlantic security architecture began with the NACC and PfP, but by 1997 had grown to include a Mediterranean Dialogue established in 1994 with six Mediterranean states, the NATO-Ukraine Commission, and the NATO-Russia Permanent Joint Council—the latter created in 1997, in part, to soften the blow of enlargement for

Russia and make clear that NATO also sought to integrate Russia into the evolving security architecture.[112] NATO also replaced the NACC in 1997 with the EAPC, which now numbers 46 members and encompasses virtually the entire Euro-Atlantic area, including the former Soviet republics and the non-NATO EU states.

"Out of Area or Out of Business"

NATO's new mission of Europe whole and free and the partnerships and institutions it generated did not, however, reflect a consensus within the Alliance as to the proper scope of NATO's activities, particularly with regard to NATO's military missions in the Balkans and later Afghanistan. Indeed, NATO's 1990 decision to reach out to the states of Central and Eastern Europe set the stage for what became known as the "out-of-area" debates. Arguably, NATO has experienced two distinct, yet interconnected, out-of-area debates since the early 1990s: the first over enlargement and the second over the proper scope of NATO's military activities. This second debate can be understood as comprising two phases: the first concerned NATO's responsibility for the Balkans as war raged in the former Yugoslavia, followed by a second debate over the question of whether NATO should act militarily outside of Europe.

Those who first called on NATO to go out of area (e.g., Richard Lugar and Manfred Wörner), however, were not focused so much on new military missions, as they were appealing for NATO to adopt a strategy aimed at projecting stability eastward and integrating Central and Eastern Europe with the West. As Lugar explained in 2002, he had used the phrase "out of area or out of business" in the 1990s to express his belief that NATO must "switch from thinking about defending the Fulda Gap in the heart of Germany to assuming responsibility for the defense of Europe as a whole, including the eastern half of the continent."[113] In fact, NATO had already ventured out of area simply by proclaiming as its new mission the construction of Europe whole and free and seeking to influence political developments to the east. As Wörner observed in 1993, in light of the relations established with the states of Central and Eastern Europe through the NACC as well as NATO's engagement in crisis management beyond its borders, the slogan "out of area—or out of business" was already "out-of-date." "We *are* acting out-of-area and we very much are in business," he pronounced. At the same time, Wörner called on NATO to open a discussion on enlargement in addition to developing further the "alliance's capabilities for crisis management, peacekeeping and peacemaking."[114]

Indeed, the war in Bosnia between 1991 and 1995 forced the Allies to consider the question of NATO's military responsibility for territory outside of its traditional defense perimeter, and it was one over which they were deeply divided. The issue was complicated by the fact that several European allies, including both Britain and France, had put troops on the ground in Bosnia as part of a United Nations Protection Force (UNPROFOR) deployed in 1993 to provide security for humanitarian relief efforts. Given the desire of the Europeans to maintain the neutrality of the UN operation and the fact that their forces would be at risk in any military intervention, the Clinton administration initially found key allies opposed to NATO air strikes against the Bosnian Serbs—generally seen by the United States as the aggressors—despite the fact that the UN force on the ground was ill-equipped for its mission. Only after Bosnian Serb forces had threatened "safe zones" established by UNPROFOR to protect Bosnian civilians did NATO finally agree to employ airpower against the Bosnian Serbs, and even then the strikes were carried out only with UN approval. It ultimately took a brutal Bosnian Serb attack in July 1995 on the UN "safe area" at Srebrenica in which 8,000 men and boys were executed and women and children were raped and tortured and a subsequent Serb mortar attack on a Sarajevo marketplace before NATO agreed to engage in massive air strikes over a period of 22 days.[115]

As the Allies had belatedly recognized, any talk of constructing Europe whole and free rang hollow given the horrors unfolding next door in Bosnia. "A gap," Manfred Wörner observed in the fall of 1993 has "emerged between our vision of a new peaceful order in Europe and our appreciation of the price we must pay to bring it about." "Shall we renounce our goal of a new, more democratic, just and peaceful European order?" he asked. "Shall we just leave the world to the forces of disorder and limit ourselves to safeguarding our own national borders and security?"[116] Indeed, NATO's failure to respond decisively raised legitimate and significant questions about its relevance to the post–Cold War world. As Stanley R. Sloan framed the issue, "if NATO was not going to be used to deal with this crisis in Europe, would it simply become an insurance policy, ceasing to be an important vehicle for the future management of Euro-Atlantic relations?"[117] NATO could not "afford such passivity," declared Wörner, because it was at odds with not only NATO's values, but also its interests. "In the world today," he insisted, "you simply cannot live in security surrounded by chaos."[118] Ironically, NATO's early outreach efforts to Central and Eastern Europe had stemmed from a belief that NATO territory could not be secure if instability reined along NATO's periphery—a lesson that was applied only belatedly in the case of Bosnia. By 1995, however, it had become clear that the mission of Europe whole and free could not be a purely political project.

NATO ultimately sustained a series of peacekeeping/stabilization missions in Bosnia, beginning in early 1996 with an Implementation Force (IFOR), authorized by the UN Security Council and comprised of 60,000 troops drawn from within and outside the Alliance, including PfP members. Its principal mission was to permit implementation of the peace accord signed at Dayton, Ohio, in late 1995. Given the need for a sustained NATO presence in the region, the Alliance then deployed a Stabilisation Force (SFOR) in late 1996 following the expiration of the IFOR mandate. SFOR remained in Bosnia until December 2005, after being replaced by a European Union Force deployed in late 2004.

As is discussed further in Chapter 2, the Allies were also divided over how to wage a second conflict in the Balkans in 1999 following Serbian leader Slobodan Milosević's rejection of a peace proposal aimed at resolving diplomatically a conflict between the Serbian regime and the ethnic Albanian majority in Kosovo, a formerly autonomous region of Serbia. Reports of ethnic cleansing in Kosovo at the hands of Serbian forces in 1998 had prompted NATO's involvement, but it was not until March 1999 that NATO began an air campaign in Serbia and Kosovo intended to force Milosević to agree to the removal of Serbian forces from Kosovo and the deployment of a NATO-led peacekeeping mission known as Kosovo Force (KFOR). Less controversial this time, however, was the intervention itself. Again, a conflict had erupted that threatened both the stability of the region and therefore NATO's vision of Europe whole and free. In this case, the Allies agreed to act even in the absence of a UN Security Council resolution, recognizing that Russia and China would invariably veto any resolution authorizing what was in essence a humanitarian intervention. What they did not agree on, however, was how to wage the war, which was ultimately confined to a 78-day air campaign, due to the reluctance of many Allies to put forces on the ground. Although NATO prevailed in the end, hundreds of thousands of ethnic Albanians were driven from their homes during the NATO air campaign, again raising questions about NATO's willingness to undertake risks in pursuit of its vision of Europe whole and free.

Moreover, the Kosovo war did not culminate in a resolution of NATO's out-of-area debates. The NATO interventions in Bosnia and Kosovo had ultimately confirmed the Allies' willingness to undertake a non-Article 5 mission outside of its territory, but the issue remained as to whether the Alliance would act militarily outside of Europe. The debate was triggered in part by the Clinton administration's view that NATO should play a role in addressing common interests outside of Europe, including stemming the proliferation of weapons of mass destruction, terrorism, and preventing disruptions to the flow of oil.[119] Indeed, Ronald Asmus, who served as Deputy Assistant Secretary of State for Europe from 1997 to 2000, suggests that underpinning the Clinton administration's support for NATO enlargement was a belief that "by locking in peace and security on the continent once and for all, the U.S. could create precisely the kind of stability in Europe that would better allow it to address new challenges elsewhere. This would in turn allow the U.S. and its European allies to focus on the new challenges they needed to confront together in the years and decades ahead in a globalized world."[120] The idea that NATO would take on global responsibilities, however, confronted considerable resistance within the Alliance, and the Clinton administration made little progress during its tenure in moving the debate forward. Yet, there was no ignoring the issue after September 11. Indeed, the events of that day simply reaffirmed that threats to the security of the Euro-Atlantic area were now more likely to materialize beyond, rather than within, the borders of Europe. Referencing his earlier assertion that NATO must go "out of area or out of business," Richard Lugar observed in 2002 that "in a world in which terrorist 'Article 5' attacks on our countries can be planned in Germany, financed in Asia, and carried out in the United States, old distinctions between 'in' and 'out of area' have become meaningless." "NATO," he argued, "must be able to act beyond Europe...if it is going to fulfill its classic mission today."[121]

NATO's assumption of responsibility for the International Security Assistance Force in Afghanistan in August 2003 appeared finally to confirm resolution of this second out-of-area debate. Indeed, NATO has since taken further steps in the direction of a more global role, including the establishment of a training mission in Iraq in 2004 and a logistical support mission begun in June 2005 in Darfur, Sudan, to assist African Union peacekeepers in combating a pattern of mass killings, labeled a genocide by the U.S. Department of State in 2004. NATO's more global face also extends to new partnerships in the Middle East and possibly even Asia. Although NATO Secretary General Jaap de Hoop Scheffer has resisted suggestions that this ever-widening circle of partnerships means that NATO is becoming a "global alliance," he has noted the need for "global partners" in a world in which "the threats and challenges are of a global nature."[122]

Conclusion

Indeed, NATO's latest initiatives are indicative of an effort to project stability well beyond Europe and a shift away from the largely Eurocentric perspective that prevailed within NATO during the 1990s. Yet, as I further argue in subsequent chapters, these new initiatives are also fully consistent with the course that NATO pursued, beginning at its 1990 summit in London when the Allies declared that they intended for NATO to become an "agent of change." No longer would NATO seek to defend an existing order. Rather, it had embarked on an effort to construct a new one, grounded on liberal democratic values and incorporating areas outside of its traditional sphere of collective defense. Constructing a new European security order, however, required that NATO develop new tools with which to promote the liberal democratic values on which the new system was to be grounded. Over the course of the next decade NATO would develop a series of new institutions aimed at fulfilling that mission—including PfP, the EAPC, the NATO-Russia Council, and the NATO-Ukraine Commission. It would also open its door to new members as an essentially political means of projecting stability eastward.

NATO skeptics have generally failed to acknowledge the extent to which NATO has been approaching its new out-of-area missions with many of the same political tools it developed during the 1990s in pursuit of a Europe whole and free. Moreover, as I argue in the following chapter, the conception of security underpinning these latest initiatives is fully consistent with the essentially values-based understanding of security that drove NATO's first post–Cold War transformation. This is not to suggest that the events of September 11 did not turn attention to NATO's long-neglected military capabilities. In fact, the need for new capabilities was well recognized by many in the aftermath of the war in Kosovo and then reinforced by the events of September 11. Yet, the events of that day also bolstered rather than undermined the view that securing both NATO territory and values requires projecting stability beyond Europe through political as well as military means.

CHAPTER **2**

"Security...Is What We Make of It"

Despite the solidarity demonstrated by NATO members in the immediate aftermath of September 11, the events of that day served to reinvigorate the debate about NATO's post–Cold War relevance. NATO, it appeared, was ill-equipped to address the threats posed by terrorism and weapons of mass destruction, even though these threats had been recognized in the Alliance's 1999 Strategic Concept. NATO's lack of capacity in this regard was perhaps most vividly demonstrated by the Bush administration's rebuff of NATO offers of support as it prepared for war in Afghanistan in late 2001. For some at the Pentagon, the principal lesson of the 1999 Kosovo conflict was that NATO had few military capabilities that would warrant another war in which U.S. military strategy would require the blessing of the North Atlantic Council—NATO's principal decision-making body.

Indeed, the trend at NATO during the 1990s was to regard security as increasingly a political rather than a military task. Dialogue, cooperation, and partnership, ultimately grounded on shared values, were proclaimed the key to peace in the coming century. Although NATO remained committed to its collective defense mission, constructing new political institutions took precedence over developing new military capabilities, and NATO's focus remained essentially Euro-centric, despite appeals from the Clinton administration for further transformation aimed at equipping NATO for more global threats.[1]

September 11, however, largely resolved this second "out-of-area" debate, namely, the question of whether NATO should undertake military missions outside of Europe. As former NATO Secretary General Lord Robertson observed in late 2002, the new security environment no longer afforded the Allies "the luxury of fighting theoretical battles about what is 'in' and what is 'out-of-area.'"[2] In seeking to improve NATO's capacity to address new threats stemming from beyond Europe, the Allies broadened the agenda for NATO's 2002 summit in Prague—which had originally been characterized as an enlargement summit—to encompass not only new members, but also new partners and new capabilities. With the need for military as well as political transformation now readily apparent, the Allies also agreed at Prague to establish the NATO Response Force—a rapid response force designed to allow NATO to project force quickly to wherever it might be needed—in addition to renewing earlier commitments to improve defense capabilities.[3]

While intra-alliance divisions remain over the *extent* to which NATO should pursue a global agenda, the Alliance has demonstrated its willingness to act outside of Europe in new military missions in Afghanistan, Iraq, and Sudan. NATO's political transformation has continued as well. In addition to taking in additional new members in 2004, NATO agreed during the Istanbul Summit that same year to enhance its partnerships with the Central Asian and Caucasus states and extend the partnership concept to the Greater Middle East. With these new initiatives, NATO embarked on an effort to ''project stability'' well beyond Europe—an objective NATO Secretary General Jaap de Hoop Scheffer has pronounced ''the precondition for [the Allies] security.''[4] These efforts also represent a shift away from the Euro-centric perspective that prevailed within NATO during the 1990s. The trend does not, however, entail a fundamental shift in the essentially values-based conception of security embraced by NATO during the 1990s. Indeed, the events of September 11 and subsequent developments within NATO have not altered the Allies' basic premise, emphasized repeatedly during the 1990s: that genuine peace and stability ultimately depend upon the triumph of liberal democratic values.

In short, it is not the nature of NATO's post–Cold War mission that has changed, but rather its scope. As September 11 vividly demonstrated, security must now be constructed in a global rather than a regional context. However, the brand of stability that NATO seeks to project remains inextricably linked to the promotion of democratic values. This chapter explores the evolution of this essentially values-based conception of security, including both its origins and the various ways in which it has influenced NATO's post–September 11 transformation. Indeed, NATO's most recent initiatives suggest that, despite the post–September 11 emphasis on developing new military capabilities, security remains as much a political task as a military one.

A Liberal Security Order

Bidding farewell to NATO in the fall of 1999, former NATO Secretary General Javier Solana expressed optimism about the Alliance's ability to transform the nature of security in Europe. In his words, ''The future can be shaped if there is a common vision, the means, and the solidarity to implement it." "Security," Solana declared, "is what we make of it."[5] No longer would NATO be content to maintain the status quo. European security had come to be understood as an almost tangible entity that was to be actively constructed, not simply defended. The Alliance, former NATO Secretary General Lord Robertson observed in 1999, had "evolved from a passive, reactive defence organization into one which is actively building security right across Europe."[6] The new security order to which the Allies aspired appeared a strikingly Kantian one—an expanding pacific federation, informed by a common commitment to liberal democratic principles, and embedded in an increasingly integrated Euro-Atlantic area. Although NATO remained committed to the collective defense of its territory, this new concept of security was less state-centric, less deferential to the Westphalian principle of nonintervention, and tightly linked to the notion of individual rights. Indeed, as evidenced by virtually all of the Alliance's new ventures—including peacekeeping missions in the Balkans, new partnerships, and the decision to admit new members—security for the new NATO not only encompasses the rights of the individual; it ultimately accords preference to the sovereignty of the individual over that of the state. The liberal democratic values that NATO safeguarded during the Cold War are now understood to be norms that should govern the whole of Europe and even areas well beyond its borders.

The realist critique of NATO's initial post–Cold War transformation has tended to reject any presumed link between NATO's values and its interests. Critics such as Michael Mandelbaum, for example, have argued that NATO's intervention in Kosovo was a "failure" because "NATO waged the war not for its interests but on behalf of its values."[7] For Mandelbaum and others, the war served only to jeopardize U.S. relations with Russia and China, both of which vehemently opposed the war. This critique, however, fails to appreciate not only the extent to which NATO has, from the beginning, understood the values enshrined in its preamble to be central to its mission, but also the extent to which those values assumed even greater importance in NATO's post–Cold War conception of security.

As suggested in the preceding chapter, NATO's post–Cold War transformation and the notion of security driving it were profoundly influenced by NATO's internal experiences during the Cold War—above all, the Allies' success in constructing a "pacific federation" much like that imagined by Immanuel Kant in *Perpetual Peace,* a community of states that have *established* peace with one another.[8] Extending this community eastward was central to the new European security order envisioned by George H.W. Bush as the Cold War waned. In a commencement address at the U.S. Coast Guard Academy on May 24, 1989—just one week prior to his pronouncement that NATO's new mission was the creation of Europe "whole and free"—Bush spoke of "a growing community of democracies anchoring international peace and stability, and a dynamic free-market system generating prosperity and progress on a global scale." "The economic foundation of this new era," he asserted, "is the proven success of the free market—and nurturing that foundation are the values rooted in freedom and democracy."[9]

By June 1990 when the Conference on Security and Cooperation in Europe (CSCE) held its Copenhagen Summit, revolution had swept across Europe bringing with it far-reaching democratic reforms and the potential to fulfill Bush's vision. CSCE member states now unanimously adopted the administration's earlier proposal calling for free elections and political pluralism and declared their commitment "to build democratic societies based on free elections and the rule of law." Pluralistic democracy and the rule of law, they agreed, were "essential for ensuring respect for human rights and fundamental freedoms."[10] As Thomas Buergenthal observed at the time, the Copenhagen conference constituted an important step in moving CSCE beyond the practice of merely protesting human rights violations toward a concerted effort to create the democratic institutions that would best ensure respect for human rights.[11]

At a second summit in Paris in November 1990, CSCE members reaffirmed their intentions "to build, consolidate, and strengthen democracy as the only system of government of [their] nations."[12] Evoking the premise of the CSCE Final Act signed at Helsinki in 1975, the Charter of Paris for a New Europe recognized the inalienability of "human rights and fundamental freedoms" and declared that "their observance and full exercise are the foundations of freedom, justice and peace."[13] In order to facilitate the democracy promotion activities consistent with this new commitment, CSCE subsequently established several new institutions, including an Office for Free Elections in Warsaw (later renamed the Office of Democratic Institutions and Human Rights).

Shared democratic values, not territory or the balance of power, were the foundation of the security order envisioned by the Charter of Paris and supported by NATO. As former U.S. Ambassador to NATO Robert Hunter observed in 1995, this understanding of security differed appreciably from that associated with earlier balance of power experiments: "For the first time," he wrote,

> Europe has a chance to found continent-wide security on a basis other than the balance of power with its associated risk of a catastrophic clash of arms. This experiment centers on an attempt to move Eastward one of the most thrilling achievements of the past half century: the abolition of war itself, among the states of Western Europe.[14]

As Timothy Garton Ash also noted, the new order "explicitly legitimated the interest of participating states in each other's internal affairs."[15]

Indeed, the NATO Allies sought to operationalize CSCE principles in June 1992 when they agreed in Oslo "to support, on a case-by-case basis ...peacekeeping activities under the responsibility of the CSCE." Making explicit reference to the initiatives they had taken since 1990 to "reinforce the CSCE and its ability to contribute to a Europe in which change takes place in conformity with CSCE principles," the Allies argued that strengthening "the means available to the CSCE for conflict prevention and crisis management" would be essential to maintaining "peace and prosperity" in Europe.[16] The significance of this decision, as Rob de Wijk has noted, was that CSCE could now "evolve from an institution which only determined norms and standards of behavior of the participating states into a more operational organisation."[17] Six months later, NATO also agreed to support "on a case-by-case basis," peacekeeping operations authorized by the UN Security Council.[18] These 1992 decisions marked the beginning of an evolutionary process within NATO, culminating in the adoption of a second new Strategic Concept in 1999, which formally added conflict prevention and peacekeeping activities to NATO's military mission. The Allies' assumption of these new military responsibilities reflected the growing importance of political, economic, social, and environmental factors in the new security order they envisioned,[19] as well as a growing conviction among them that their own security was "inseparably linked to that of all other states in Europe."[20]

Enlarging the European "Civil Space"

The decision to enhance NATO's political dimension and increasingly cast security in terms of shared values would also have important implications for the size of the alliance. Building security across Europe effectively meant enlarging the community of states that embraced NATO values, and one means of achieving that goal was enlargement of the Alliance itself. As NATO made clear in its 1995 Study on Enlargement and emphasized repeatedly thereafter, new members were expected to be producers and not simply consumers of security.[21] For the aspirants this meant actually implementing democratic principles and practices, including respect for minority rights, striving for peaceful resolution of conflicts with neighbors, and working toward meeting all of NATO's military obligations. "We do not need security consumers," but rather states who can bear the full responsibility of membership, former NATO Secretary General Willy Claes explained in 1996. An anonymous NATO official put it more bluntly: "We don't need any more Frances, Spains, Greeces, or Turkeys."[22]

The tools with which NATO sought to construct a new European security order were not limited to enlargement, however. Committing itself in the early 1990s to the construction of "a common security space from Vancouver to Vladivostok," the Alliance also strongly emphasized the need for "partnership" with states and institutions beyond NATO's borders. "No single transatlantic institution [could meet] the varied security requirements of North America and all of Europe."[23]

NATO's initial attempt to institutionalize the partnership concept was the North Atlantic Cooperation Council (NACC). Originally designed as a forum for political consultation and practical cooperation on security issues with former Warsaw Pact members, the NACC [renamed the Euro-Atlantic Partnership Council (EAPC) in 1997] now encompasses virtually the entire OSCE (Organization for Security and Co-operation in Europe) area, including the traditionally nonaligned states of Austria, Finland, Ireland, Sweden, and Switzerland. The EAPC's membership also essentially parallels that of the Partnership for Peace (PfP) established in 1994. Although PfP was to some extent a consequence of the Clinton administration's initial reluctance to enlarge NATO, the partnership also stemmed from a recognition that true cooperation with NATO's former adversaries required more than just the dialogue facilitated by the NACC. Ultimately, PfP created a framework for military cooperation which promoted interoperability and training with NATO forces and allowed for participation by nonmember states in NATO's post–Cold War peacekeeping/stabilization missions. Given the role of nonmember states in NATO's military mission in Bosnia in the mid-1990s, NATO also moved in 1997 to create a political-military framework for NATO-led PfP operations, thereby permitting nonmembers to play an active political and military role in the planning and execution of non-Article 5 crisis response operations.

By providing opportunities for political and military cooperation with NATO, PfP also served to soften the line between NATO and non-NATO members as have NATO partnerships with Russia, Ukraine, and the seven states that constitute the Mediterranean Dialogue (Egypt, Israel, Mauritania, Morocco, Tunisia, Jordan, and Algeria).[24] First established in 1994, the Dialogue was designed to promote mutual understanding with NATO's neighbors in the Mediterranean region. After September 11, the initiative assumed greater importance as reflected in various measures taken during the Prague Summit to enhance the dialogue, giving it both a political and a practical dimension. At its Istanbul Summit in 2004, NATO went a step further, elevating the Mediterranean Dialogue to the level of a genuine partnership aimed at promoting "stronger practical cooperation," including enhanced political dialogue, interoperability, defense reform, and joint efforts to fight terrorism.[25]

NATO also used the summit to focus attention on its partnerships with the states of Central Asia and the Caucasus—a region that assumed far greater strategic significance after September 11—and to unveil the

Istanbul Cooperation Initiative, a new program aimed at developing practical bilateral security cooperation between NATO and the states of the greater Middle East.[26] These partnership initiatives, which are explored further in Chapter 6, reflect both the perceived success of NATO's PfP and the extent to which the Allies today understand security to be necessarily a cooperative endeavor, requiring dialogue and cooperation among states and other institutions, including the OSCE, the European Union, and the United Nations. As expressed in NATO's 1999 Strategic Concept, the "aim is to build a European security architecture in which the Alliance's contribution to the security and stability of the Euro-Atlantic area and the contribution of these other international organisations are complementary and mutually reinforcing, both in deepening relations among Euro-Atlantic countries and in managing crises."[27]

Characterizing NATO as "an essential pillar of a wider community of shared values and shared responsibility," the Allies pledged during their 1999 Washington Summit to intensify "contacts and co-operation with other international organisations with a role to play in consolidating democracy and preserving peace in the Euro-Atlantic area."[28] Indeed, the advancement of democratic values has been a stated goal of all of NATO's partnerships. The Partnership for Peace Framework Document, for example, declares the "protection and promotion of fundamental freedoms and human rights" to be "shared values fundamental to the Partnership," and partners are expected to reaffirm their obligations under the UN Charter, the Universal Declaration of Human Rights, the Helsinki Final Act, and all subsequent CSCE documents.[29] PfP's objectives also include the achievement of transparency in national defense planning and budgeting processes and the consolidation of democratic control over defense forces, making the partnership a central player in the pursuit of a Europe whole and free. As former U.S. Ambassador to NATO Robert Hunter put it, "Both the Partnership and NATO's expansion are part of a grand experiment that has no precedent in a thousand years of trying to create something better than the balance of power. We are doing nothing less than trying to extend the European Civil Space eastward—one cautious step after another."[30]

Within the context of NATO's relationships with Russia and the Ukraine as well, the advancement of democracy has always been an explicitly stated objective. The NATO-Russia Founding Act adopted in 1997, for example, states that "NATO and Russia will work together to contribute to the establishment of common and comprehensive security based on the allegiance to shared values, commitments and norms of behavior in the interests of all states."[31] Although strategic interests have been a key factor driving these relationships, the fact remains that they exist in the context of a values-based conception of security. As one NATO official, well versed in the NATO-Ukraine agreements, explained it, democracy promotion is a "defacto reality" within the context of the relationship "simply because of the way in which NATO defines security and because all NATO members stress Alliance values in their interactions with Ukraine."[32]

Indeed, NATO's relations with Ukraine have warmed considerably since late 2004, due largely to the victory of prodemocracy candidate Viktor Yushchenko in Ukraine's contested and tumultuous presidential election in September. Prompted by indications that Ukraine was seeking closer relations with NATO, the Allies had already agreed in 2002 to a new NATO-Ukraine Action Plan designed to deepen and broaden the relationship by allowing for a more intense dialogue on political, economic, and defense issues. Yushchenko's victory then provided an enormous boost to Ukraine's prospects for actual NATO membership and prompted the Allies to launch an "Intensified Dialogue" with Ukraine in April 2005, which included a series of measures designed to assist Ukraine in making democratic reforms and meeting NATO's "standards and values."[33] Although Ukraine's prospects for NATO membership have been less clear since Yushchenko's opponent in 2004, Viktor Yanukovych, was named prime minister in August 2006, NATO affirmed during its Riga Summit in late 2006 that the Intensified Dialogue with Ukraine would continue.

Not all of NATO's partners have sought membership, but for NATO aspirants and nonaspirants alike, partnership offers an opportunity to demonstrate the ability to serve as a security producer rather than a mere consumer of NATO assistance. Indeed, partners have participated in significant numbers in NATO's peacekeeping missions in the Balkans, Afghanistan, and Iraq. Even Russia and Ukraine contributed forces to NATO's Kosovo Force mission in Kosovo, despite Russia's vehement opposition to the war.

Since September 11, NATO has also sought to intensify political dialogue and practical cooperation within the EAPC, beginning with the Partnership Action Plan against Terrorism issued during the 2002 Prague Summit. The "first issue-specific" mechanism for cooperation between NATO and its partners, the Plan called for partners to intensify political consultations and information sharing, enhance preparedness for combating terrorism, and impede support for terrorist groups, among a variety of other measures.[34] NATO launched a second PAP at Istanbul in 2004. Directed at the Central Asian and Caucasus states, the Partnership Action Plan on Defence Institution Building focuses on defense reform and, in particular, the need to bring defense institutions under firm civilian and democratic control.[35] In short, NATO has sought to expand opportunities for practical cooperation by enhancing political dialogue with partners throughout the Euro-Atlantic area and, increasingly, beyond it.

NATO's vision of a common security space has not been confined to political and military cooperation, however. Economic and social integration also remain integral to the achievement of a space that NATO characterized during its 1999 Washington Summit as "a community where human rights and fundamental freedoms are upheld, where borders are increasingly open to people, ideas and commerce, where war becomes unthinkable."[36] NATO might even be said to sit at the core of a growing cosmopolitan society, which also serves to facilitate cooperation with states outside the Alliance.

Promoting such a society does not constitute a new objective for NATO. From the beginning, NATO sought to provide the basic military security necessary to support economic recovery and ultimately the establishment of a liberal economic order in Western Europe. NATO also deliberately cultivated a "social dimension" within the Alliance as early as 1969 when it established the Committee on the Challenges of Modern Society to address shared environmental concerns by combining the expertise and technology of member countries.[37] NATO opened the committee to participation by members of the NACC beginning in 1992, and later the Mediterranean Dialogue, as part of its effort to promote cooperation and integration with non-NATO members. Such initiatives reflect a recognition that integration of the broader security community on multiple levels is essential to achieving both NATO's political and military goals. As John Gerard Ruggie has observed, Karl Deutsch and colleagues concluded in 1957 that purely military alliances constituted "a relatively poor pathway" toward integrated security communities unless they were—in Ruggie's words—"embedded in a broader process of political, economic, and social integration."[38] In fact, Deutsch suggested that policy makers working toward integration should "be aware of considering NATO as a purely military alliance" and look "beyond the glare of the Soviet headlights and into the dark area behind, at a future time when the Soviet threat may not furnish the cohesive force which it did in 1949."[39] Today, globalization in the form of global markets and information technology is assisting the integration of the Euro-Atlantic area by facilitating not only the exchange of goods, but also the exchange of ideas at both the state and societal levels.

Linking Security to Democracy and Human Rights

At the core of the values on which NATO's post–Cold War conception of security has been founded are the rights of the individual. Although the defense of democracy and individual liberty has always been fundamental to NATO's mission, concern for individual rights now plays an increasingly prominent role in NATO's conception of security and, consequently, both its political and military activities. This shift derives from a variety of factors, one of which has to do with the nature of the threats confronting NATO since the end of the Cold War. Indeed, the vast majority of post–Cold War conflicts have been civil rather than traditional interstate conflicts. This new reality prompted NATO's issuance of two new Strategic Concepts during the 1990s—one in 1991 and the other in 1999—both of which observed that security threats were now "less likely to result from calculated aggression against the territory of the Allies" and more likely to stem from instabilities precipitated by ethnic and religious rivalries, territorial disputes, failed reform efforts, human rights abuse, and the dissolution of states.[40] Similarly, the OSCE's 1999 Istanbul Charter recognized that threats to security "can stem from conflicts within states as well as from conflicts between states" and that these conflicts "have often resulted from flagrant violations of OSCE norms and principles."[41] That point had been vividly demonstrated in the Balkans throughout the 1990s. Indeed, Václav Havel expressed considerable concern in the early 1990s about the potential for ethnic or nationalist conflicts, like that unfolding in Bosnia, to spread.[42]

The fact that the region's conflicts stemmed at least in part from blatant disregard for individual and minority rights also served to highlight the disconnect between the fate of individual human beings and the security of the state, thereby giving rise to an alternative perspective for thinking about security labeled "human security."[43] As former Canadian Foreign Minister Lloyd Axworthy puts it, human security "establishes a new measure for judging the success or failure of national and international security policies, namely: do these policies improve the protection of civilians from state-sponsored aggression and civil, especially ethnic, conflict?" The individual rather than the state becomes the principal referent in thinking about security. Axworthy further suggests that NATO's intervention in Kosovo in 1999 stands as "a concrete expression of this human security dynamic at work."[44] Indeed, the Allies defended the Kosovo intervention by declaring that they "remained determined to stand firm" against those "who violate human rights" as well as those who "wage war and conquer territory."[45]

Security as conceived by NATO was now inextricably linked to notions of individual rights, as reflected in the transatlantic security strategy issued by the U.S. Department of Defense in December 2000. "Grave violations of human rights in the Balkans or elsewhere" challenge U.S. values and security, the document asserted. "The security of the Euro-Atlantic Community must spring from the consent of free peoples and must be built upon shared purposes and values that can be defended when the need arises."[46] As Richard Cohen has also observed, human security—or what he terms "individual security"—"stands at the center of any real international security system built around liberal democratic ideals."[47]

The Impact of Globalization

As suggested earlier, NATO's vision of a new European security order stemmed in part from NATO's own internal experiences during the Cold War, as well as from the nature of the threats confronting the Allies during the 1990s. Additionally, the demise of communism, evolving global norms of democracy and human rights, global markets, and information technology have all influenced, or at least reinforced, the conception of security that has guided NATO's evolution over the past decade and a half. Indeed, growing numbers of international relations scholars and practitioners now conclude that, in an age of globalization marked by increasingly permeable state borders, security can no longer be conceived in purely state-centric terms.[48] Security must now be understood to comprise the fate of the individual, as well as that of the state. Not all states secure the rights of their citizens, and those that do not are increasingly regarded as sources of instability and are therefore perhaps no longer owed the traditional presumption of sovereignty.

The increased permeability of state borders and the heightened public awareness fostered by modern-day communications technology have also made it virtually impossible in practice to separate values from basic security interests as realists have long prescribed. Coupled with the nature of post–Cold War conflicts, the effects of globalization have served to reinforce the view that egregious human rights violations in any given state have potential implications for the system as a whole. Speaking before the Chicago Economic Club in April 1999, British Prime Minister Tony Blair gave voice to this view when he directly linked NATO's intervention in Kosovo to the phenomenon of globalization.

> Twenty years ago we would not have been fighting in Kosovo. . . . The fact that we are engaged is a result of a wide range of changes—the end of the Cold War; changing technology; the spread of democracy. But it is larger than that. I believe the world has changed in a more fundamental way. Globalisation has transformed our economies and our working practices. But globalisation is not just economic. It is also a political and security phenomenon. We live in a world where isolationism has ceased to have a reason to exist. By necessity we have to co-operate with each other across nations . . . We are all internationalists now, whether we like it or not. We cannot refuse to participate in global markets if we want to prosper. We cannot ignore new political ideas in other countries if we want to innovate. We cannot turn our back on conflicts and the violations of human rights within other countries if we still want to be secure.[49]

As Blair recognized, in an increasingly interconnected world, conflicts deriving from the abuse of human rights are rarely confined within any one state. Rather, they are likely to draw in neighboring states or create refugee crises, with inevitable consequences for the surrounding region.

Given the prevalence of such conflicts in the 1990s, NATO stood little chance of remaining relevant in the post–Cold War world if it did not adapt its mission and its tools accordingly. As Axworthy observed in a 1998 speech to the OSCE,

> To be sure, the old realities of power persist. Classic interstate conflicts and their consequences remain an unfortunate feature of the global landscape. But let there be no mistake: At the end of the 20th century, the humanitarian agenda is no side show. On the contrary, it is rapidly becoming the main event of global affairs.[50]

NATO's new military missions and its willingness to abridge state sovereignty in the name of human rights should not be interpreted to suggest that traditional state-centric notions of security have suddenly become irrelevant. Indeed, from a liberal perspective, the state, properly constituted, remains essential to the preservation of human rights. However, the conflicts in Bosnia and Kosovo, coupled with the increasing permeability of state borders, underscored the view that not only are the security of the individual and the security of the state not necessarily synonymous, but human rights violations anywhere in Europe have at least the potential to threaten the security of the community as a whole. Accordingly, NATO's post–Cold War transformation encompassed the adoption of a broader conception of security than that which guided the Allies during the Cold War. The new concept, as Axworthy has suggested, should be understood as "a continuum, comprising both state and individual concerns."[51]

Emerging Global Norms of Democracy and Human Rights

The end of the Cold War not only fostered a new understanding of security; it also opened up new opportunities for NATO to encourage the growth of democratic values using both political and military means. From a military perspective, the withdrawal of Soviet forces from Eastern Europe beginning in the late 1980s removed a key obstacle to the use of force in the region, including on behalf of humanitarian objectives. At the same time, the collapse of communism in both Eastern Europe and the former Soviet Union was at least equally, if not more, crucial in shaping NATO's increasingly interventionist agenda. As one scholar has observed,

> Ideological differences of opinion between the two superpowers constituted the most important obstacle to interventions. Any intervention could, after all, be construed by the other camp as an attempt to increase their sphere of influence and could therefore be interpreted as a *casus belli*. As a result of this there was no legal basis for military interventions in the internal affairs of

other countries. Once the ideological differences of opinion had been removed, the former opponents worked together to promote peace and security, which resulted in an enormous increase in the number of peace operations since 1989.[52]

While the end of Cold War did not produce an international consensus as to the conditions under which interventions might be deemed permissible, the apparent triumph of democratic ideas in Central and Eastern Europe as well as in parts of Latin America, Africa, and Asia, prompted numerous commentators to greet the new era by proclaiming the emergence of global norms of democracy and human rights. NATO's increasingly proactive and values-based approach to security thus coincided with a greater willingness over the past decade on the part of governments, international institutions, nongovernmental organizations, and scholars to assert a positive relationship between the global expansion of democracy and a more peaceful international system. As the OSCE's 1999 Charter for European Security put it, "Peace and security in our region is best guaranteed by the willingness and ability of each participating State to uphold democracy, the rule of law and respect for human rights." Several years earlier, former UN Secretary General Boutros Boutros-Ghali had stated in his 1996 *Agenda for Democratization* that "democracy contributes to preserving peace and security, securing justice and human rights, and promoting economic and social development."[53] His successor, Kofi Annan, has been even bolder, declaring in his Nobel Peace Prize acceptance speech in 2001 that states which "undermine the rule of law and violate the rights of their individual citizens become a menace not only to their own people, but also to their neighbors, and indeed the world." "What we need today is better governance, " Annan asserted, "legitimate, democratic governance that allows each individual to flourish, and each state to thrive."[54]

Such statements reflect a growing belief that international peace and security are linked to respect for the rights of the individual *and* that only liberal democracy can ultimately guarantee respect for human rights. One of the more remarkable expressions of this emerging, albeit far from universal, consensus is the UN Human Rights Commission's passage of resolutions in 1999 and 2000 affirming a fundamental link between democracy and human rights and appealing to member states to sustain and expand programs aimed at promoting and consolidating democracy around the globe.[55] Even within the academic and human rights communities, which for many years resisted linking human rights and democracy, this trend became increasingly apparent during the 1990s.[56]

Although the challenge of cultural relativism persists, notions of democracy and human rights once regarded as essentially "Western" ideas are now widely understood to be global norms of responsible state behavior. As Thomas Risse has observed, "states that want to be members of international society 'in good standing' increasingly realize that they have to respect basic human rights and meet some minimum standards of behavior toward their citizens...Dictators can no longer claim 'interference in internal affairs' when confronted with gross violations of human rights. This is a profound change in the principles of international society."[57]

Importantly, these trends have roots, not only in the collapse of communism, but also in the foreign policies of U.S. Presidents Reagan, George H.W. Bush, and Clinton, all of whom embraced essentially Wilsonian ideas in arguing repeatedly that the United States would be more secure in an international community that shared its liberal democratic values. Although Jimmy Carter had actively supported congressional efforts to put human rights on the U.S. foreign policy agenda, his administration had been reluctant to use the language of democracy in the implementation of its policy.[58] However, Ronald Reagan proclaimed a worldwide "campaign for democracy" in mid-1982, and both Presidents George H.W. Bush and Bill Clinton subsequently made democracy promotion an explicit component of their human rights policies.[59] Understood in this context, NATO and the CSCE process were tools that could be employed in the service of a U.S. democracy promotion agenda.

At the same time, NATO's own success in establishing peace in Western Europe during the Cold War period lent credence to the notion of the liberal peace and thereby contributed to the evolution of global norms of democracy and human rights. These emerging norms, in turn, have served to support NATO's efforts to construct a liberal security order and its underlying premise: that human rights are a legitimate concern of international politics. Indeed, an examination of the nexus between NATO's post–Cold War initiatives and the burgeoning popularity of democratic ideas on a global scale reveals an interactive process. NATO's own success in establishing a democratic security order during the Cold War has made the Alliance a principal contributor to the evolution of democracy and human rights. Those norms have, in turn, assisted and legitimized NATO's post–Cold War and even post–September 11 efforts to promote a more values-based conception of security. As former NATO Secretary General Lord Robertson observed in September 2001, NATO had been presented with a "historic" opportunity because its values were "now coming to be shared more broadly across the continent." As he framed the opportunity at the time, "Democracy has swept across Central, Eastern, and Southern Europe. Market economies are increasingly the norm, rather than the exception. And basic human rights are being protected, both in law and reality. NATO's mission as we enter the 21st century is to nourish that common culture."[60]

Rethinking State Sovereignty

The end of the Cold War and the evolution of global norms of democracy and human rights have also had far-reaching implications for the Westphalian principle of nonintervention, which are reflected in NATO's post–Cold War missions. Human rights activists have long regarded the state and the presumption of sovereignty it enjoys to be a principal obstacle to respect for human rights. Yet, despite a number of international human rights agreements, including the Universal Declaration of Human Rights and the 1968 United Nations human rights covenants, not until the late 1970s did human rights truly come to be recognized as a legitimate topic of international politics, and even then, this trend was primarily a Western phenomenon. During the 1990s, however, growing numbers of scholars and policy practitioners began to challenge the presumptive legitimacy of states, even to the point of suggesting that states legitimately derive their sovereignty only from the freely expressed consent of their citizens. Understood from this perspective, sovereignty resides ultimately in the individual rather than the state.

As former German Defense Minister Volker Rühe observed in 1993, "During the Cold War, the policy of non-intervention was an important political principle. Now, however, there is a growing international consensus that suppression of ethnic minorities and violations of human rights within state borders can no longer be tolerated."[61] Similarly, Richard Cohen argued that "the Westphalian concept of the absolute right of states to act as they see fit within their own territories is no longer accepted by liberal democratic states nor, increasingly, by nations within international organizations such as the United Nations."[62]

Indeed, Annan expressed this sentiment clearly when he told the UN Human Rights Commission during NATO's 1999 bombing of Kosovo: "Emerging slowly, but I believe surely, is an international norm against the violent repression of minorities that will and must take precedence over concerns of sovereignty."[63] Although Annan ultimately expressed concern that NATO's action had occurred in the absence of a Security Council mandate, he also seemed to imply that the international community had a duty, based on UN principles, to act in such cases. "When we read the [UN] charter today," he argued in September 1999, "we are more than ever conscious that its aim is to protect individual human beings, not to protect those who abuse them." An international commission established in 2000 in response to Annan's appeals that the international community reach consensus on the subject of humanitarian intervention agreed. Sovereignty implies a "responsibility to protect," the International Commission on Intervention and State Sovereignty asserted in a report issued in late 2001. If a state fails to meet that obligation with respect to its own citizens, the responsibility then falls to the international community, which might include an obligation to intervene militarily. As the Commission put it, "Where a population is suffering serious harm as a result of internal war, insurgency, repression or state failure…the principle of non-intervention yields to the international responsibility to protect."[64]

Although Annan, himself, acknowledged deep divisions within the international community regarding the practice of humanitarian intervention, he also insisted that this new norm should be "welcome[d]" because, "despite all the difficulties of putting it into practice, it does show that humankind today is less willing than in the past to tolerate suffering in its midst, and more willing to do something about it."[65] Czech President Václav Havel delivered an even more impassioned defense of humanitarian intervention in an address before the Canadian Parliament during the Kosovo war.

> This war gives human rights precedence over the rights of states. The Federal Republic of Yugoslavia has been attacked without a direct United Nations mandate for NATO's action; but NATO has not acted out of license, aggressiveness, or disrespect for international law. On the contrary, it has acted out of respect for the law—for the law that ranks higher than the protection of the sovereignty of states. It has acted out of respect for the rights of humanity as they are articulated by our conscience as well as by other instruments of international law.[66]

By initiating military action against a sovereign state that had attacked no NATO member, the Alliance had effectively accorded the rights of the Kosovar Albanians primacy over the sovereignty of a rights-abusive, nondemocratic state. Such action, Havel seemingly implied, was fully justified on the basis of universal moral principles, even if those principles were not fully codified in international law.

The Logic of Kosovo

Not surprisingly, the absence of a clear legal basis for NATO's action prompted many commentators to suggest that the Allies had unilaterally challenged the United Nations Charter—traditionally read to prohibit interference in other states' internal affairs—while advancing in its place a new norm in favor of humanitarian intervention.[67] Yet, NATO's intervention in Kosovo was not necessarily an affront to accepted principles of international politics. As suggested earlier, the trend over the past half century—and particularly the past decade—has been unmistakably toward a qualified conception of state sovereignty. As Robert Keohane and Joseph Nye put it in 2000, "Sovereignty is up for grabs in a way that has not been the case since the seventeenth century."[68] Although humanitarian intervention remains among the most controversial issues in international politics today, it can also be said that NATO's role in Kosovo, coupled with its larger efforts to construct a values-based security order in Europe, reflects not only the Alliance's own internal transformation, but also the growing prominence of human rights discourse in international politics and a growing recognition that conflicts within states now have potentially far-reaching implications for international security

Moreover, the end of the Cold War had inspired considerable hope that, after years of paralysis, the United Nations would finally be able to respond effectively to a new generation of conflicts.[69] As Stanley Hoffman has observed,

> Between 1991 and 1993—from the end of the 1991 Gulf War to the misfortunes of the UN in Somalia and Yugoslavia—a kind of euphoria about collective action for good causes, leading to a new and better world order, built up around what the French champion of humanitarian intervention Bernard Kouchner had called the *droit d'ingerence*—a right to intervene for humanitarian reasons that overrides sovereignty. Traditional interpretations of international law and of the UN Charter that denied the legality of such forcible intrusions were declared obsolete partly because of the new salience of human rights, partly because the newly favored intrusions were presented as collective ones, authorized by the UN, rather than unilateral resorts to force.[70]

The UN, however, ultimately failed to avert a series of humanitarian tragedies in Somalia, Rwanda, and Bosnia. By 1995, the organization appeared, at best, incompetent in terms of enforcing even its own resolutions. Indeed, one member of NATO's international staff suggested that the war in Kosovo should be viewed as a contribution to an evolving process in favor of intervention, undertaken largely because the UN had failed to act and, at the time, no other organization possessed either the will or capacity for a successful operation in Kosovo.[71] Notably, NATO itself had a poor track record with respect to earlier humanitarian crises, especially in Bosnia, but those failures ultimately appear to have roused NATO into action by generating regrets and legitimate concerns about the Alliance's continued viability. Indeed, some commentators have suggested that NATO's intervention in Kosovo stemmed in part from the Allies' own sense of shame for their inaction in Bosnia.[72]

It is also worth noting that not all scholars have judged the Kosovo war an "unambiguous violation of international law." Adam Roberts, for example, argued that NATO's action was legally justifiable on two primary grounds. First, there were the requirements of the UN Security Council resolutions passed prior to the intervention. The Security Council had voted unanimously in favor of a series of resolutions, which ultimately declared that the Federal Republic of Yugoslavia had committed gross and systematic violations of human rights against Albanians living in Kosovo and demanded a cessation of these actions.[73] The second piece of Robert's defense of NATO hinges on general international law since 1945. Agreements such as the Geneva Conventions of 1948 and 1949 may be understood to provide grounds for intervention even if it is not explicitly provided for in the treaties themselves. "It cannot be right," he says, "to tolerate acts which violate widely supported legal norms just because the charter does not explicitly provide for military action in such circumstances, or because a veto on the Security Council makes UN-authorised action impossible."[74] Richard Falk also observes that, while the UN failed to endorse NATO's intervention in Kosovo, it also resisted "censuring that intervention" and "even appeared to ratify the outcome by agreeing to play such a pivotal role in the post-war administration of Kosovo." Furthermore, NATO's decision to intervene in Kosovo "helped build political support for a UN humanitarian peacekeeping mission undertaken immediately thereafter for the sake of the people of East Timor."[75]

Although NATO Secretary General Robertson later defended the legality of the Kosovo intervention using arguments similar to those presented above, at the time of the war, NATO members chose to rely principally on moral and practical arguments to justify their action.[76] The crisis then unfolding in Kosovo, as the Allies explicitly recognized in a statement issued during the 1999 Washington Summit, represented "a fundamental challenge to the values for which NATO has stood since its foundation" and on which it sought to construct a new security order.[77] British Prime Minister Tony Blair, in particular, stressed the moral concerns underpinning NATO's action. "This is a just war, based not on any territorial ambitions but on values," he insisted in a speech before the Chicago Economic Club in April 1999. "We cannot let the evil of ethnic cleansing stand."[78] Outlining what ultimately came to be called the "Blair Doctrine" he asserted that, while the principle of noninterference was not one "we would want to jettison too readily," it must be "qualified" because "acts of genocide can never be a purely internal matter." "When oppression produces massive flows of refugees which unsettle neighbouring countries," Blair concluded, "then they can properly be described as 'threats to international peace and security.'"[79] The security and stability of NATO territory as well as the Allies' values were therefore at stake in Kosovo.

Still, some commentators argued that NATO intervened in Kosovo because it needed a new raison d'etre.[80] Indeed, NATO did need to demonstrate its relevance in the post–Cold War era, particularly given its delinquent response to the war in Bosnia. However, NATO was not in need of a new mission. The mission of a Europe whole and free had yet to be realized. And it could not be achieved without confronting the situation in Kosovo. As Solana put it, had NATO not acted in Kosovo, "the entire logic of turning Europe into a common political, economic, and security space would have been invalidated."[81] Bill Clinton made essentially the same argument, writing in the *New York Times* in late May 1999: "We are in Kosovo with our allies to stand for a Europe, within our reach for the first time, that is peaceful, undivided and free. And we are there to stand against the greatest remaining threat to that vision: instability in the Balkans, fueled by a vicious campaign of ethnic cleansing."[82] Southeastern Europe was, in the words of Madeleine Albright, "the critical missing piece in the puzzle of a Europe whole and free." NATO's vision could not be fulfilled if it "remain[ed] divided and wracked by conflict."[83]

In part, the crisis threatened the vision of Europe whole and free because, as Blair had suggested in his Chicago speech, it threatened "to further destabilise areas beyond the Federal Republic of Yugoslavia (FRY)." Perhaps the most alarming scenario was that the conflict would spread to the south, ultimately drawing in both Greece and Turkey. The Clinton administration also expressed concern for the "small and struggling democracies" surrounding Kosovo that were "being overwhelmed by the flood of refugees."[84] Indeed, the potential for the conflict to destabilize an even larger swath of southeastern Europe made it a significant security concern for all NATO members. As Blair explained it, the simple fact of "the mass expulsion of ethnic Albanians from Kosovo demanded the notice of the rest of the world," but it also mattered that these events were "taking place in such a combustible part of Europe."[85] As one NATO official described it, Kosovo was a case in which NATO's "self-interest curve" came to intersect with a "morality curve" that had been rising steadily in the realm of international politics.[86]

To ask whether NATO's actions in Kosovo were undertaken on behalf of its values or on behalf of its interests is therefore to set up a false dichotomy. The reality was that NATO now defined its interests in such a way that they could not be fully separated from its values. As Adam Roberts has suggested, NATO's operation in Kosovo served to further the "trend towards seeing certain humanitarian and legal norms inescapably bound up with conceptions of national interest."[87] Building security, as NATO had come to define it, required taking seriously those values on which it was to be grounded. Intervening in Kosovo, Solana subsequently wrote, "sent a strong signal that in our Atlantic community, values have a meaning."[88]

Even so, NATO officials cautioned against interpreting what happened in Kosovo as a precedent-setting event. NATO's actions there, Robertson suggested, "represented a unique circumstance."[89] Indeed, while no Ally formally broke ranks during the war, disputes arose over its conduct, including the question of whether ground forces should be introduced. NATO officials also acknowledge that Kosovo raised expectations about the Alliance's future role—expectations which might not be met. "We've witnessed the growing permissibility of intervention," one NATO international staff member noted in December 2001, "but not necessarily a growing willingness to intervene."[90]

Additionally, NATO's justification of the intervention in terms of moral principles exposed the Alliance to charges of hypocrisy regarding its conduct. UN High Commissioner for Human Rights Mary Robinson, for example, pronounced NATO's humanitarian objectives in Kosovo a failure because the air strikes had produced civilian casualties.[91] The human rights monitoring organization, Human Rights Watch, also issued a report in February 2000, concluding that NATO had "violated international humanitarian law," citing in particular NATO's use of cluster bombs in populated areas; air attacks on "targets of questionable military legitimacy"; and NATO's alleged failure to verify adequately that military targets did not contain high concentrations of civilians. The organization further claimed that the number of civilian casualties was three to four times higher than had been acknowledged by U.S. defense officials.[92]

Regardless of whether such criticism was warranted, it is true that the Allies demonstrated little willingness to assume any substantial risk to their own soldiers during the course of the intervention. The bombing missions over Kosovo—flown largely by U.S. pilots—were conducted at high altitudes, thereby reducing the danger to NATO pilots, but placing the Kosovar Albanians, whose lives they were purportedly trying to save, at greater risk. Additionally, some NATO members—including the United States—openly resisted any talk of putting NATO troops on the ground. Such tactics prompted former U.S. National Security Advisor Zbigniew Brzezinski to assert that "the high-tech standoff war was waged as if its underlying premise was that the life of even one American serviceman was not worth risking in order to save the lives of thousands of Kosovars."[93] NATO's aversion to casualties also cast some doubt on claims that the Allies had important interests at stake in Kosovo. As Carl Cavanaugh Hodge has written, "There was no inherent virtue in seeking to sacrifice NATO soldiers for the lives of Kosovars, but in light of the mission *as it was articulated* there was an inherent moral imperative in being willing to *risk* their lives for the same."[94]

Still, NATO did not retreat from the concerns that drove the Kosovo intervention. When ethnic hostilities in Macedonia threatened to spread beyond the borders of the state, the Allies opted for early intervention coupled with diplomacy. Ultimately, they launched a series of three operations (Essential Harvest, Amber Fox, and Allied Harmony) designed to facilitate the implementation of an agreed peace plan. The European Union took responsibility for the latter mission, Operation Allied Harmony, in the spring of 2003.

Despite its delinquent involvement in Bosnia, NATO's missions there (Implementation Force and Stabilisation Force) ultimately proved

successful in stabilizing the country, permitting it to be turned over to the
European Union, beginning in late 2004. NATO continues to maintain a
headquarters in Sarajevo to assist with defense reform, carry out counterterrorism operations, and assist the International Criminal Tribunal for
the former Yugoslavia (ICTY) with the apprehension of indicted war
criminals who remain at large in the region. NATO also remains committed to integrating the region into Euro-Atlantic institutions. The Allies
have repeatedly insisted that NATO's door remains open to new members, encouraging NATO aspirants Albania, Croatia, and Macedonia to
continue with the reforms necessary for membership. Indeed, NATO
announced during its Riga Summit in late 2006 that it intended to extend
membership invitations at its next summit in 2008 to "those countries
who meet NATO's performance based standards and are able to contribute to Euro-Atlantic security and stability." Notably, the Allies also
extended invitations at Riga to Bosnia/Herzegovina, Montenegro, and
Serbia to join NATO's PfP and EAPC, although they stressed that the Alliance expected Serbia and Bosnia/Herzegovina's full cooperation with the
ICTY and would closely monitor their respective efforts in this regard.[95]
Given the region's vulnerability to threats such as drug smuggling, terrorism, and human trafficking, NATO also continues to sponsor efforts
aimed at improving border security throughout southeastern Europe.
Indeed, the events of September 11 have served only to reinforce a belief
that NATO territory cannot be secured if instability prevails along its
periphery.

Conclusion

   In the wake of September 11, NATO did not abandon its vision of a
Europe, whole, free, and at peace. To the contrary, that vision remains, in
the words of former U.S. Ambassador to NATO, Nicholas Burns, NATO's
"greatest strategic objective."[96] This continuing commitment, however,
should not be construed as an indication that the Alliance remains mired
in the 1990s. In the aftermath of September 11, NATO moved forward
with its plans for further enlargement and moved to focus even more
attention on its partnership efforts. Yet, the context for conceptualizing
and implementing these various post–Cold War initiatives had changed
dramatically. No longer could NATO afford the insular Euro-centric focus
that had prevailed during the 1990s. In an ever more globalized world,
instability, even well beyond Europe's borders, threatened the vision of
Europe whole and free, as evidenced by NATO's willingness to take on
new missions in Afghanistan, Iraq, and Darfur. The role of partners and
even new members was also fundamentally altered by the events of
September 11. As is discussed in Chapter 5, it became abundantly clear
in the months prior to NATO's 2002 Prague Summit that the NATO

aspirants would now be assessed in terms of their ability to contribute to the war on terror. Even nonaspirant partners would be expected to help construct security in an increasingly global context. Indeed, NATO was now committed to using its partnerships as a means of projecting stability well beyond Europe.

In no way, however, has this less Euro-centric focus led NATO to abandon the essentially values-based conception of security that it came to embrace during the 1990s. As is discussed in Chapters 5 and 6, while the events of September 11 did lead NATO to deem as necessary cooperation with nonliberal democratic states, the brand of stability that NATO seeks to project remains inextricably linked to liberal democratic values. Just as it was during the 1990s, NATO's chief political goal is to enlarge the space in which conflicts are resolved peacefully and in accordance with NATO values. NATO's vision of Europe whole and free therefore has not been abandoned, but rather enlarged.

Although September 11 did lead to a new focus on NATO's military capabilities—a subject discussed in later chapters—security for the new NATO continues to be understood as a task that is as much political as it is military in nature. NATO is now in the business of projecting stability, utilizing and building on a host of essentially political tools developed during the 1990s in pursuit of Europe whole and free. This is not to suggest that whether NATO develops an effective capacity for projecting force to its south and east is irrelevant to its future. NATO's military capabilities were indeed sorely neglected during the 1990s. Many NATO skeptics, however, tend toward an analysis of NATO that ignores the continuity underpinning NATO's immediate post–Cold War and post–September 11 transformations. Rather than proving NATO's irrelevance—as some critics contend—September 11 actually served to reinforce the logic underpinning the 1990 decision to enhance NATO's political dimension and the new institutions and initiatives that ultimately sprang from it. As September 11 so clearly demonstrated, NATO territory will not be secure if instability reins along the Alliance's periphery. This is the same conclusion that led the Allies in the early 1990s to reach out to their neighbors in Central and Eastern Europe as Soviet power in the region collapsed. Engaging these former adversaries represented an essentially political means by which NATO could assist in the construction of a new European security order—one ultimately built on a foundation of liberal democratic values.

CHAPTER 3

The New NATO: A Vehicle for Democracy Promotion

In practice, NATO's commitment to projecting stability beyond its borders means promoting outside of NATO territory the liberal democratic norms and practices on which that stability is to be grounded. The values-based security order to which the Allies ultimately aspire, therefore, will ultimately hinge on whether NATO actually has the capacity to promote these norms and practices effectively—both within Europe and beyond it. On this question, the existing literature reflects a wide range of opinion, although much of it is ultimately skeptical of NATO's ability to serve as a vehicle for democracy promotion. As Michael Mandelbaum put it in 1995, "NATO is not only not the most effective instrument for promoting democracy, it is not in *essence* an organization for doing so. Rather, it is a military alliance, an association of some sovereign states directed against others."[1]

Proponents of the realist school of international relations theory, in particular, concluded during the 1990s that NATO had exercised little, if any, influence on the democratization process in Central and Eastern Europe. Their critiques generally followed one of three lines of argument. The first maintains that democratization in Central and Eastern Europe has been largely a function of factors other than NATO enlargement and would have occurred even in its absence. A second argument suggests that NATO had little to do with the regional reconciliation and cooperation that occurred in the region. Plenty of other incentives existed, such critics argue, for the states of Central and Eastern Europe to reconcile border and minority issues. Third, some NATO skeptics have suggested that, because democracy was clearly secondary to strategic considerations in shaping both enlargement decisions and member behavior during NATO's Cold War years, there are good reasons to doubt NATO's capacity for democracy promotion in the post–Cold War world.[2]

This chapter takes a decidedly more optimistic view. Indeed, the skeptics have largely ignored the complex processes by which NATO, partly through its interactions with other European institutions, helped to generate norms for the whole of Europe, which in turn influenced how the states of Central and Eastern Europe perceived their own interests and, consequently, their behavior at home and abroad. Indeed, the record of reform in Central and Eastern Europe over the past decade and a half supports the notion that NATO's identity as an alliance that has constructed the political and military means to defend the democratic values its members hold in common constitutes an important part of its appeal and, therefore, a source of its capacity to influence the behavior of prospective members.

Examining NATO's capacity for democracy promotion purely through the lens of NATO enlargement, as many critics have, also takes too narrow a view of NATO's role in the democratization process. Indeed, NATO's efforts to extend democratic values and practices eastward long preceded the decision to enlarge the Alliance. As noted in Chapter 1, NATO, as early as 1990, sought to encourage the growth of democracy through its outreach to former adversaries, leading ultimately to the formation of new institutions and partnerships. While the influence of these initiatives might have been slight initially, a more comprehensive and long-term assessment suggests that the Allies have effectively utilized new institutions and partnerships to facilitate democracy promotion activities by both NATO and non-NATO members alike. Moreover, NATO's latest partnership initiatives, including the Istanbul Cooperation Initiative and enhanced relationships with the Mediterranean Dialogue and Central Asian and Caucasus states reflect a belief on the part of the Allies that NATO has at least a limited role to play in encouraging the growth of liberal democratic values beyond Europe.

The Enlargement Process

Admittedly, it was the decision to admit new members that drew the most attention to NATO's democracy promotion efforts in the 1990s. As former NATO Secretary General Robertson put it, enlargement constitutes the "most concrete way" by which NATO has sought to "nourish a common culture of democracy and respect for human rights."[3] As noted earlier, the notion that opening NATO's door to new members would ultimately serve to extend NATO's values eastward was also at the core of the case for enlargement made by the Clinton administration. That argument was subsequently tested during two rounds of NATO enlargement. The first began in Madrid in 1997 and culminated in the accession of Poland, Hungary, and the Czech Republic in 1999. A second round of invitations was then issued at Prague in late 2002, leading to the accession of Bulgaria, Romania, Slovakia, Slovenia, Latvia, Lithuania, and Estonia in 2004.

NATO skeptics, however, have challenged the notion that prospective NATO membership serves as a significant lure or "carrot" by which NATO can encourage democratic reforms beyond its borders. Dan Reiter, for example, examined the experience of the three states invited to join NATO during its first post–Cold War round of enlargement and concluded that, in these cases, NATO did not speed the democratization process "because their societies and their elites were committed to democracy anyway." All three states had established competitive electoral systems and held free elections in 1990, long before the "NATO carrot was dangled before them." Hence, "NATO membership was not necessary for democratization."[4] This argument, however, does not accurately reflect the claims made by the vast majority of enlargement proponents. Even the Clinton administration, whose rhetoric regarding NATO's democracy promotion potential might have been somewhat overblown at times, never suggested that NATO enlargement was *necessary* for democratization or even that it constituted a primary incentive for democratization.

Additionally, many of the skeptic's assessments appear to have been based on rather simplistic conceptions of democracy. Free elections and a firm commitment by political elites to democratization are certainly important first steps in the democratization process, but they do not constitute the consolidation of *liberal* democracy, as opposed to simple electoral or majoritarian democracy, as NATO's new mission required. Indeed, scholars of democratization commonly cite the following as essential elements of liberal democracy: respect for individual rights, including minority rights; the rule of law; civil society; civilian and democratic control of the military; and the embedding of democratic values in the local culture.[5] In states with a long legacy of communist rule and little prior experience with democracy, achieving all of these elements has been, at best, a lengthy and difficult process.[6] Even in those Central and Eastern European states understood to have made considerable progress toward liberal democracy during the 1990s, significant problems remained a full decade following the collapse of communism, especially with respect to individual and minority rights.[7] A study published by the Congressional Research Service in 2000, for example, expressed concerns about the treatment of minorities throughout the region, including the Baltic states where language and citizenship laws were alleged to violate the rights of ethnic Russian minorities.[8] Reports of discrimination against the Roma throughout Europe were also common.

The process of consolidating democratic civilian control over the militaries of Central and Eastern Europe constitutes yet another area in which scholars have observed slow and uneven reform. For example, in a 1996 study of the region's civil-military relations, Jeffrey Simon observed that, while Slovakia was at that time the only member of the original Visegrád group (Poland, Hungary, and Czechoslovakia)[9] that had made no progress toward achieving "effective" democratic control over its armed forces, Poland, Hungary, and the Czech Republic all had "significant work to do" to make elected civilian control over the military "effective" and "ensure the reform process is irreversible."[10] A related difficulty plaguing the region stemmed from the lack of effective parliamentary oversight on defense matters. Given the absence of such oversight during the communist period, civilian parliamentary representatives with knowledge of defense issues were in short supply.[11]

The fragility of the region's democracies was also evidenced by decidedly undemocratic trends in Slovakia following Prime Minister Vladimír Mečiar's rise to power in 1993. Indeed, nearly ten years later, concern arose that Mečiar, whose party had lost its hold on power in 1998, might actually be returned to his former position during parliamentary elections in September 2002. Macedonia—a state lauded for much of the post–Cold War period as a model multiethnic democracy—also witnessed armed, ethnic-based conflict following the war in Kosovo, which ultimately required the deployment of NATO forces. The latter case, in particular, served to highlight the complexity associated with the democratization process, which depended on difficult social and cultural adjustments and reforms as well as free elections and a commitment to democracy by political elites.

The Lure of Enlargement

As for NATO's role in facilitating such change, the record suggests that, while the Alliance might not have served as the impetus for the region's democratization, it did have an impact on both the direction of domestic reform in prospective member states and the way in which these states interacted with each other. Although NATO has never established strict political criteria for membership, an internal study on enlargement (*Study on NATO Enlargement*) released in September 1995 concluded that NATO could contribute to enhanced security and stability in the Euro-Atlantic area by "encouraging and supporting democratic reforms," fostering in new members "patterns and habits of cooperation and consultation and consensus building," and "promoting good neighborly relations." The study, which was distributed to prospective members, stressed that new members would be expected to conform to the basic principles of the Washington Treaty—democracy, individual liberty, and the rule of law— and demonstrate a firm commitment to the principles and objectives of the Partnership for Peace Framework Document, which also commits its members to democratic principles and the peaceful resolution of disputes.[12] Additionally, prospective member states received notice that they would be expected to subscribe to the Organization for Security and Cooperation in Europe (OSCE) norms and principles, including the resolution of ethnic and external territorial disputes by peaceful means; the promotion of "stability and well-being by economic liberty, social justice and environmental responsibility," and the subordination of the military to civilian control. Following the study's release, NATO officials emphasized repeatedly that the willingness and ability of states to meet NATO's political as well as military standards would be a critical factor in decisions about who would be invited to join the Alliance.

Arguing that enlargement must be guided by the principles upon which the stabilization of Western Europe had depended—collective defense, democracy, consensus, and cooperative security—U.S. Secretary of Defense William Perry in 1995 also put forward several guidelines for enlargement, which ultimately became known as the Perry principles. First, new members were expected to demonstrate the capacity and the will to defend NATO. Second, new members were expected to "uphold democracy and free enterprise, protect freedom and human rights inside their borders, and respect sovereignty outside their borders" in addition to placing their military forces under civilian control. Finally, Perry argued that NATO would need to continue to operate on a consensus basis and that new members would be expected to achieve interoperability with NATO.[13]

While not formal membership criteria, the above expectations appear to have been taken seriously by NATO aspirants during both the 1997 and 2002 enlargement rounds. Much of the domestic political and economic reform that transpired in the region during this period undoubtedly would have occurred even in the absence of NATO enlargement, as some critics have suggested. And, yet, Central and Eastern European leaders have asserted repeatedly a link between the evolution of their foreign and domestic policies and the prospect of NATO enlargement. For example, during a series of three public hearings conducted in April 1997 by the U.S. Commission on Security and Cooperation in Europe to assess the progress of prospective NATO members in meeting their obligations under the Helsinki Final Act and OSCE agreements, invited representatives from ten aspirant states stressed that the prospect of NATO membership had served as an important incentive for both domestic reforms and improved relations with neighbors.[14] As the Bulgarian Ambassador-at-Large for NATO Accession put it, "The very prospect of joining the Euro-Atlantic institutions has been an essential driving force for the implementation of reforms in Bulgaria and one of the main incentives for Bulgaria's constructive foreign policy over the last 7 years."[15] A year later, the *New York Times* observed of Poland, Hungary, and the Czech Republic that, while they had "a way to go in meeting Western standards of democratic rule and stable market economies, no issue has dominated [their] internal political behavior...as much as the aspiration to belong to the Western security alliance."[16]

NATO's role was particularly important in shaping and consolidating, not merely civilian, but *democratic*, political control over the region's militaries—a complex problem given the fact that parliamentary control "over the actual execution of defence policies" was "weak or non-existent."[17] The problem was particularly acute in Poland where until 1997, the military was highly politicized and did not cooperate effectively with the civilian defense ministry.[18] The Polish Chief of Staff, General Tadeusz Wilecki, had resisted civilian authority, and President Lech Wałesa, who had appointed him, refused to order his dismissal. Finally, in 1997 Poland adopted a new constitution subordinating the Polish general staff to the Ministry of Defense—an absolute requirement for membership in NATO. Wilecki was then fired by incoming President Aleksander Kwasniewski, who was determined to bring Poland into the Alliance. As Rachel Epstein has argued, NATO's role in this reform was crucial. As she explains it, NATO's "decision to enlarge and the alliance's increasing engagement in the domestic political evolution of prospective members were crucial factors for empowering and legitimizing Polish reformers who ultimately chose to champion diffuse democratic civilian control."[19]

Moreover, while NATO's enlargement decisions—unlike those of the European Union (EU)—are ultimately political, the Allies invested considerable resources in assessing and providing aspirants with feedback regarding their progress in meeting the expectations of the 1995 *Study on NATO Enlargement*. NATO's determination not to admit states that had failed to meet these expectations was well-demonstrated by Slovakia's omission from the list of invitees issued at the Madrid Summit in 1997 due to widespread concerns about the authoritarian nature of Mečiar's government, even though Slovakia had originally been considered a top candidate. Again, in early 2002, the U.S. Ambassador to Slovakia, Ronald Weiser, warned that parliamentary elections scheduled for the fall would profoundly influence whether the country received an invitation to join the Alliance during the Prague Summit later that year. Noting that the Slovak government's values differed from those of the Alliance during NATO's first post–Cold War round of enlargement, Weiser declared that, if that scenario were to repeat itself, Slovakia would again be denied an invitation."[20]

The MAP

In 1999, following the accession of Poland, Hungary, and the Czech Republic to the Alliance, NATO sought to make the assessment process more structured and rigorous through the introduction of its Membership Action Plan (MAP), which drew heavily from lessons learned during the first round of enlargement. The MAP did not change the criteria for membership or establish a comprehensive set of legal commitments to which prospective members were required to subscribe, but it did require that each aspirant state draft and submit an Annual National Programme detailing its preparations for NATO membership in five key areas: political and economic, defense/military, resources (to meet member commitments), security (to protect NATO information), and legal (legal arrangements to govern cooperation with NATO).[21] NATO then agreed to provide each individual aspirant with feedback on its progress in meeting the goals established in its own national program.[22] Both scholars and NATO officials agree that, in many respects, the feedback received by MAP states with respect to their preparations for NATO has been much more critical than the feedback received by Poland, Hungary, and the Czech Republic.[23] According to diplomatic representatives from those states invited to join the Alliance at Prague in late 2002, MAP guidance had also become much more detailed through each annual cycle of the MAP. Those same diplomats have also consistently stressed that the MAP served to shape internal political debates over both domestic and foreign policy by providing leverage for the reformist elements of their societies.[24] One called it the "bible" for NATO membership and observed that the process had served as a "mirror" in front of his state's reform efforts.[25] On the other side, NATO diplomats and staff have also credited the MAP for what they characterize as significant progress by aspirant states in meeting NATO's expectations following the introduction of the process in 1999.[26]

It is also an indication of the seriousness with which NATO has approached the MAP process that Albania and Macedonia, both of them MAP and active PfP members, did not receive membership invitations at Prague. At that time, the Allies agreed that neither state had made sufficient progress in terms of domestic political reform to be considered seriously for membership. Concerns about possible regression on the part of the Prague invitees also led NATO to require that even the seven states that did receive membership invitations at Prague submit "timetables" detailing their plans for completion of expected reforms. Attached to letters from the invitees' foreign ministers, the timetables were understood to constitute a firm political commitment and thus a mechanism for maintaining NATO's leverage over the invitees for as long as possible.[27] Moreover, NATO elicited groans from some of the invitees by informing them at Prague that they would be expected to complete what would be their fourth cycle of MAP process and that new expectations might even be added after Prague.[28]

NATO also sought to build on the perceived success of the MAP at Prague with the introduction of the Individual Partner Action Plan (IPAP), an initiative designed to upgrade cooperation with partner states that had expressed a desire for closer cooperation with NATO but had not been deemed ready for participation in the MAP. Just as in the MAP, however, participants are expected to draft their own national plans detailing specific reforms they plan to undertake.[29] Then, following the presentation of the IPAP to NATO, the Alliance provides "focused, country-specific assistance and advice on reform objectives."[30] As with MAP, IPAPs have a political chapter, thereby affording NATO an opportunity to influence reform in the domestic political as well as defense sectors. Georgia became the first state to submit an IPAP followed by Armenia, Azerbaijan, Kazakhstan, and Moldova.

While the IPAP is not formally a "waiting room" for the MAP, NATO staff and diplomats did initially see it as an opportunity for NATO to assess how serious the Central Asian and Caucasus states were about making the kinds of reforms required of prospective NATO members. Indeed, given NATO's substantial commitment of resources to the MAP program, the Allies have been leery of admitting to the MAP, or even devoting additional resources to, states whose commitment to reform is questionable. However, as one member of NATO's international staff acknowledged shortly after the program's introduction, it was not yet clear whether the "carrot" offered—NATO's assistance in implementing political and military reforms—was sufficient to encourage actual change.[31]

As noted in the previous chapter, NATO and Ukraine also agreed to a new NATO-Ukraine Action Plan in 2002, designed to assist Ukraine in pursuing its goal of closer relations with NATO. In keeping with the spirit of the MAP, the plan outlined specific strategic objectives and principles toward which Ukraine has been working through the filing of Annual Target plans, which are consistent with the five reform areas identified in the MAP.[32] NATO has also sought to assist Ukraine's NATO aspirations and encourage further reforms through the launching of an "Intensified Dialogue" in April 2005. In short, NATO has actively leveraged the enlargement process as a means of promoting liberal democratic norms and practices throughout the whole of Europe. It has done so in part through the creation of a variety of new mechanisms, shaped by NATO's own experience since the mid-1990s and designed to maximize NATO's influence over domestic reform processes in both aspirant and nonaspirant states.

Regional Cooperation

Beginning in the mid-1990s, NATO also sought to leverage the lure of membership to encourage the resolution of long-standing ethnic and border disputes throughout Central and Eastern Europe. Indeed, the Allies alerted aspirant states through the *Study on NATO Enlargement* that resolving such issues would factor significantly in decisions regarding membership, and it appears that the message was well understood. Among the many agreements reached since the mid-1990s are treaties that Hungary signed, first with Romania in 1995 and, then, Slovakia in 1996, establishing mechanisms for dealing with large Hungarian minorities in both states.[33] Romania, as did Poland, also signed an agreement with Ukraine over border disputes and past recriminations.[34] For its part, the Czech Republic took a significant step toward improving relations with Germany in January 1997 when the two governments signed a much debated declaration acknowledging previous wrongs committed against each other—namely, Nazi crimes against Czechs and Czechoslovakia's expulsion of 2.5 million Sudeten Germans after World War II. At the time of the declaration, Germany pledged that it would work to facilitate the Czech Republic's entry into both the European Union and NATO.[35]

With an eye on NATO membership, aspirant states also launched a variety of regional cooperation mechanisms, including an interparliamentary assembly established by Lithuania and Poland to strengthen cultural relations and protect minority rights, and a forum known as the "Five Presidents," which brought together the leaders of Poland, Ukraine, Lithuania, Latvia, and Estonia to discuss regional security, economic cooperation, and cultural exchange issues."[36] Referencing these agreements in 1998, then U.S. Ambassador to Poland, Daniel Fried, suggested that "when Poland and Hungary became more confident of their NATO membership, they increased their outreach to their neighbors—Hungary to Romania, and Poland to Lithuania."[37]

Perhaps the best known association for regional cooperation is the Visegrád group, which materialized in February 1991 when the leaders of Poland, Hungary, and Czechoslovakia met in Visegrád, Hungary, to coordinate their efforts to join NATO and the European Union. Although cooperation lapsed somewhat after 1993, due partly to the breakup of Czechoslovakia, the Visegrád group revived itself in 1999 when its now four members (including Slovakia) met in Bratislava and proclaimed both a new beginning and a commitment to helping Slovakia join the Alliance.[38] Although the inception of the Visegrád group was self-initiated and not directly influenced by NATO decisions, the fact that its members sustained some degree of cooperation throughout the 1990s can be attributed to NATO's encouragement of such cooperation. In his analysis of the Czech Republic's security policies during this period, Stephen J. Blank observes that the country's "priority goal of gaining NATO membership" was the key factor prompting regional defense cooperation between Prague, Warsaw, and Budapest. Although the Czechs had previously shown little interest in cooperation with neighboring states, it mattered, in Blank's view, that NATO had advised aspirant states that they would not be accepted into the Alliance until they demonstrated an ability to work together on both economic and defense issues.[39]

The Clinton administration also made frequent reference to cooperative efforts throughout the region to support its case that the enlargement process was indeed generating stability and reform in Central and Eastern Europe. In order "to align themselves with NATO," Madeleine Albright observed in 1998, Central and East Europeans were "resolving problems that could have led to future Bosnias." "This," she said "is the productive paradox at NATO's heart: by extending solemn security guarantees, we actually reduce the chance that our troops will again be called to fight in Europe."[40] Former NATO Secretary General Javier Solana also observed that the message sent by NATO to prospective members was, "You have no chance of being in this club [unless] you make a real effort to solve minority problems."[41]

NATO skeptics, however, have maintained that the enlargement process was not necessary "as an incentive for European states to resolve their disputes with one another." Dan Reiter, for example, argues that "supposed successes" such as the treaty between Hungary and Romania in 1996 "should be weighed against Romania's failure to reach similar agreements with Moldova, Ukraine, and Russia."[42] In fact, Romania had addressed differences with both Moldova and Ukraine.[43] Perhaps more significantly, none of these three states (Russia, Moldova, and Ukraine) was, at the time, a formal applicant for NATO membership.[44] Indeed, in its 2000 report on the status of NATO applicants, the U.S. Congressional Research Service hypothesized that the signing of a border agreement between Russia and Estonia had been delayed because Russia did not wish to sign a treaty that it thought "might enhance Estonia's chances for NATO membership by removing what might be seen as a 'territorial dispute.'"[45]

Ronald Linden also asserts a direct link between the generally peaceful nature of Romanian-Hungarian relations during the 1990s and the process of NATO enlargement. The 1995 *Study on NATO Enlargement*, he notes, made clear to Hungary and Romania as well as other prospective NATO members that "simply reflecting Western norms would no longer be enough; action to put these into practice had to take place." It was at that point, he says, that both Hungary and Romania "realized that resorting to the 'old' ways of interethnic and interstate conflict would severely retard their chances of gaining entry into Western institutions." Linden also quotes Hungarian Prime Minister Gyula Horn who, himself, gave credit to the external pressures supplied by European institutions for regional dialogue and cooperation. "[We] have to put an end once and for all to the constant dissecting of imagined or real historical wrongs," Horn declared. "This Hungarian Government has recognized from the outset that the community of European states will under no circumstances admit into its ranks countries that squabble relentlessly among themselves."[46]

The willingness of Bulgaria, Romania, and other surrounding states to cooperate with NATO during the conflict in Kosovo, despite a lack of support among their respective publics, should also be construed as evidence of NATO's influence in the region. Indeed, Bulgaria's Prime Minister said, at the time, that support for the Alliance was "a question of Euro-Atlantic solidarity, and choosing European values."[47] Similarly, the Bulgarian Ambassador to the United States said of Bulgaria's supportive stance, "What we're trying to achieve now is not just a safe Bulgaria, a safe home ...Now we want a safe neighborhood."[48]

Indeed, Bulgaria's own NATO aspirations also led to further cooperation with Poland in October 2000 when the two defense ministries signed an agreement through which Poland offered to share information regarding its own preparations for NATO membership.[49] Subsequent months evidenced further cooperative efforts by NATO aspirants. In May 2001, for example, Romania and Macedonia signed a basic treaty designed to create a framework for bilateral cooperation to support both EU and NATO integration efforts.[50] That same month, Slovakia and the Czech Republic agreed to establish a Czech-Slovak military unit to operate within the Kosovo Force (KFOR) contingent in Kosovo.[51] Reflecting on these various agreements in the summer of 2001, NATO Secretary General Lord Robertson concluded that the prospect of NATO membership had indeed served as an important "incentive for aspirants to get their houses in order":

> Just look at Central and Eastern Europe today. NATO's decision to take in new members has sparked a wave of bilateral treaties, and supported the resolution of border disputes. It has also encouraged many to establish proper democratic control over their militaries. Why? Because all aspirants know that if they want to join NATO they need to do their homework. In short, NATO's willingness to open its doors has brought Europe closer together—in spirit and practice.[52]

A study later published by the RAND Corporation agreed that "from the perspective of improving regional security and advancing democracy in the former communist states in central and southern Europe, the NATO enlargement process has had the desired effect."[53]

Despite this record of reform, skeptics like Reiter remained unconvinced. Indeed, Reiter's own assessment of NATO's democracy promotion role draws its conclusions as much from the Cold War era as from the experience of the post–Cold War period. He notes, for example, that Turkey, Spain, Portugal, and Greece all experienced periods of undemocratic rule and manifested poor human rights records even following their accession to NATO between 1952 and 1981. He then concludes that, because NATO appeared to demonstrate little influence over the domestic politics of its members during the Cold War, there is little reason to

assume that NATO has the capacity to engage in effective democracy promotion today.[54]

The comparison, however, is of minimal relevance, largely because
NATO now operates in a fundamentally different environment than it
did during the Cold War, and decisions regarding new members follow
from a different set of criteria—one in which democratic values have
achieved a significantly higher profile. Alliance members are now
expected to "enhance overall security and stability in Europe," which
means, in practice, upholding the values underpinning the liberal security
order to which NATO has aspired since 1990.[55] The admission of Greece,
Turkey, and Spain to NATO during the Cold War was grounded largely
on strategic considerations. This is not to suggest that political factors
played no role, but it is clear that these states were not held to the same
standards that NATO's post–Cold War aspirants confront. Given the radically altered strategic environment in which NATO now operates, states
with questionable democratic credentials stand little chance of qualifying
as the security *producers* NATO demands today. In short, it makes little
sense to draw conclusions about NATO's current democracy promotion
potential based on a period during which the Alliance was preoccupied
chiefly with preventing a Soviet attack on Western Europe.

Yet another line of argument pursued by NATO skeptics suggests that it
was the EU rather than NATO that was best poised to leverage political
and economic reform in Central and Eastern Europe. Some have even
argued that the real value of an invitation to join NATO stemmed from
its utility as a reference for membership in the EU.[56] Ultimately it would
be impossible to sort out methodologically the precise impact of multiple
external forces on the processes of democratization and reconciliation in
Central and Eastern Europe. Institutions such as the EU and NATO as
well as the broader processes of globalization generated by global markets
and information technology have all clearly influenced the direction of
political, economic, and military reform throughout the region. As
Zdenek Kavan and Martin Palous noted regarding the post–Cold War
period in the Czech Republic, "the observed process is not just one transi-
tion, but the conjunction of transitions in the domestic, regional, and
international systems. The collapse of state socialism in Central and
Eastern Europe was accompanied by the collapse of the Soviet empire,
which has sparked further and broader processes occurring on a global
scale."[57] Indeed, the phenomenon of globalization, which is generally
understood to have narrowed appreciably the economic and political
choices available to states, has likely had a greater impact on the states
of Central and Eastern Europe than any one institution. At the same time,
however, both NATO and the EU clearly constitute part of this phenomenon of increasing political and economic integration. Indeed, the various

internal and external forces influencing the direction of reform in the region have been interactive and often by design mutually reinforcing.

On the question of whether the EU ultimately wields greater leverage than NATO, it is true that, because the EU has a formal acquis with explicit political and economic criteria for accession, its membership decisions are ultimately less political than those of NATO. Yet, as suggested above, NATO's own reform expectations, clearly articulated in the 1995 *Study on NATO Enlargement* as well as through the MAP process, have generally been consistent with those identified in the EU acquis. Moreover, as Linden observes, while the EU and NATO both made democratic institutions and processes a necessary condition for admission, only "NATO insisted that the East European states also pursue peaceful policies among each other, that they commit themselves to settling rather than replaying old conflicts and to setting up a system for settling present and future disputes."[58] Similarly, Zbigniew Brzezinski has argued that, ultimately, it has been NATO that has made reconciliation in Europe possible, both today and during the Cold War.[59] Referencing the numerous examples of regional cooperation witnessed in Central and Eastern Europe since the mid-1990s, he writes,

> [T]he ongoing reconciliation between Germany and Poland would not have been possible without the American presence in Germany and the related sense of security that Poland's prospective membership has fostered in Poland. The same is true of the Czech Republic and Germany, Hungary and Romania, Romania and Ukraine; and the desire to get into NATO is also having a similar influence on Slovenia's attitude toward Italy and Lithuania toward Poland.[60]

Indeed, the argument that membership in the EU rather than NATO constitutes the ultimate prize ignores the fact that, to the larger task of consolidating a liberal order in Europe, NATO contributes two crucial commodities that the EU cannot provide: military power in defense of shared values and a strong link to the United States, whose military strength continues to be regarded as vital to the defense of the values for which NATO stands. As Petr Lunak has observed, the paradox associated with the desire of Central and Eastern Europeans to join Western European institutions is that it has been "marked by a mistrust of purely European institutions"—a mistrust grounded, not only in the region's post–World War II experience, but also in the European Union's failure to prevent or stem the violence emanating from the former Yugoslavia in the early 1990s.[61] Indeed, Central and Eastern European leaders have repeatedly stressed the link between security and the consolidation of democracy in the region. NATO's appeal, Polish Foreign Minister Bronisław Geremek observed in 1997, stems from the fact that it "is an alliance which has put its immense military might in service of fundamental values and principles that we share. NATO can make Europe safe for democracy. No other organization can replace the Alliance in this role."[62] Václav Havel echoed these thoughts in slightly different terms. As he put it, "While the European Union focuses on political and economic integration, NATO constitutes an irreplaceable instrument for the collective defense of these values."[63]

What ultimately differentiates NATO from the EU is the presence of the United States, which Central and Eastern European leaders have long understood as essential to European security. In the words of former Polish President Aleksander Kwasniewski, "The two world wars proved to the peoples of Europe and America that without a U.S. presence in Europe, European security is unlikely to be achieved."[64] A Polish official, quoted by the *New York Times* just prior to Poland's accession to NATO, made the same point even more explicitly: "We want to be good Europeans. But more than anyone except perhaps the British, we understand how important it is to keep the Americans involved in Europe."[65] Indeed, the fact that Central and Eastern Europeans generally lined up on the side of the Bush administration during the transatlantic dispute over the Iraq war was itself a demonstration of the determination to sustain a U.S. presence in Europe.

The tendency of NATO skeptics to caricature NATO's democracy promotion efforts as little more than the carrot of security guarantees dangled in front of aspirants also neglects the role of NATO's new institutions and the many programs through which NATO members have provided practical democracy assistance to the states of Central and Eastern Europe since long before the decision to enlarge NATO was announced. In fact, as early as 1992, the North Atlantic Assembly, NATO's collective parliamentary arm, established the Rose-Roth Initiative—a series of seminar and training programs for parliament members and staff "designed to assist the development of parliamentary democracy" in Central and Eastern Europe. Civil-military relations, especially democratic control of the armed forces, has been a particularly popular theme for Rose-Roth activities.[66] Through its Partnership for Peace (PfP) and the Euro-Atlantic Partnership Council (EAPC), NATO has also sponsored a variety of conferences, workshops, and seminars for military officers and defense and foreign ministry officials, designed to assist the aspirants in carrying out political and defense-related reforms and, ultimately, meeting NATO's membership expectations.[67]

Individual NATO members have also provided a variety of educational opportunities for both aspirant and nonaspirant partner states. For example, the George C. Marshall European Center for Security Studies based in Garmisch, Germany, hosts courses annually for civil and military leaders from partner states aimed at assisting the democratization process in the region, including the establishment of democratic control of the military.[68]

These activities, which have not been limited to prospective members, led *Washington Post* reporter Dana Priest to suggest in 1998 that the Marshall Center had "become the intellectual center for the inconspicuous revolution taking place inside the militaries of Eastern Europe."[69]

Moreover, both PfP and the EAPC have provided a vehicle through which non-NATO, EU partners can help convey their knowledge and experience with democratic institutions to those partners whose democratic processes and institutions are far less well developed. For example, as a member of PfP, Switzerland has played a particularly active role in efforts intended to promote democratic control of the region's militaries, especially in Central Asia and the Caucasus states. These efforts include the establishment of the Geneva Centre for Democratic Control of Armed Forces, an institution designed to promote democratic reform of military force structures.[70] Within the PfP context, NATO also launched in 2004 a Partnership Action Plan on Defence–Institution Building intended to assist partner states in bringing defense institutions under firm civilian and democratic control—an objective that NATO has long characterized as "fundamental to stability in the Euro-Atlantic area and essential for security cooperation."[71]

Such initiatives allow military and civilian personnel from participating states considerable contact with their counterparts from well-developed democracies, thereby also providing them an opportunity to experience the culture and practices associated with liberal democracy. These encounters constitute part of what Igor Lukes termed the "pedagogical component" associated with NATO enlargement. "Administrators and soldiers who come into contact with the alliance," he suggested, would "gradually internalize the values reflected in its daily operations."[72] Alexandra Gheciu, in her work on NATO's efforts to promote liberal democratic norms, also observes that the Alliance utilized several types of sometimes overlapping "socialization practices" to influence the post–Cold War transformation of Central and Eastern Europe, including "teaching, persuasion, and role playing." What NATO ultimately sought, she argues, was not merely new institutions and practices, but "broader cultural change" or a new understanding of "appropriate norms of conduct in the domestic and international arenas for a modern liberal democracy."[73]

NATO as a "Norm Entrepreneur"

Indeed, in championing its own democratic values and practices as the linchpin of the peaceful and prosperous Euro-Atlantic community constructed after World War II and norms that should now govern the whole of Europe, NATO has been operating as what Martha Finnemore and Kathryn Sikkink have termed a "norm entrepreneur"—a state that attempts "to convince a critical mass of states (norm leaders) to embrace new norms."[74] By specifying political, economic, and military practices and arrangements that prospective members must adopt in order to be eligible for NATO membership, NATO has, in effect, articulated what proponents of a constructivist approach to international relations theory would characterize as "regulative" norms—norms that prescribe or identify what constitutes appropriate behavior within a given identity.[75] In fact, the RAND Corporation concluded in 2001 that NATO's enlargement strategy had served "to impose a behavioral regime on much of unintegrated Europe," including the establishment of "a set of behavioral incentives for new and prospective members' domestic and foreign policy."[76]

NATO's norms, however, are more than simply prescriptive; they are also instrumental to the Alliance's own identity. Indeed, NATO leaders have actively used the concept of identity as a means of influencing how the states of Central and Eastern Europe conceive their own interests and how they interact with others. Recognizing that many prospective members look to both NATO and EU membership as confirmation of their place in a particular civilization, NATO has consistently advised the aspirants that being identified as a member of the "West" requires first embracing and actively implementing its values. As Gheciu has convincingly argued, "NATO became involved in re-constituting Central and Eastern European polities through its efforts of promoting a liberal democratic set of classifications of reality, involving a particular, Western-defined boundary between acceptable and unacceptable modes of thinking and acting, elevating those classifications to the status of the 'official point of view.'"[77]

A Return to Europe

Indeed, the concept of identity has played an intriguing role in the enlargement process, reflected most visibly in the fact that Central and Eastern European leaders during the 1990s consistently characterized their desire to join NATO as a "return to Europe." Joining both NATO and the EU, they argued, symbolizes a return to a community from which they were alienated during the Cold War—a community to which they believed they rightfully belonged based on their history and culture.[78] Polish Foreign Minister Bronisław Geremek put it this way in late 1997:

> We have...spared no effort to return to the roots of our culture and statehood, to join the Euro-Atlantic family of democratic nations. We will not rest until Poland is safely anchored in Western, economic, political, and military structures. This is the essence of our aspirations to join NATO.[79]

Hungarian Foreign Minister János Martonyi echoed these thoughts upon Hungary's accession to NATO in March 1999. "Hungary has come home," he pronounced. "We are back in the family."[80] As John Gerard Ruggie has explained it, for NATO's "would-be members," NATO expansion was "less of an issue of security than of identity politics, an affirmation that they belong to the West."[81]

The notion of a "return to Europe," however, casts NATO's role in the region in a slightly different light than do portrayals of the Alliance as a vehicle for projecting democratic values eastward. The sentiments expressed by Central and Eastern European leaders suggest that NATO was not so much projecting its values eastward as it is that they were "moving westward," embracing opportunities denied to them during the Cold War. As Hungarian President Árpád Göncz put it,

> The rhetoric of NATO enlargement suggests that NATO is moving eastward at the instigation of the present 16 allies. Instead, what is happening is that the countries of Central and Eastern Europe are moving westward. Separated from West-European and Euro-Atlantic institutions for 40 years, these countries now have the freedom and opportunity to join institutions such as NATO, the European Union and the Western European Union.[82]

NATO Secretary General Lord Robertson, himself, utilized this sort of rhetoric in discussing Alliance efforts to persuade the Russians that they had no need to fear the expansion of NATO. While acknowledging that NATO "may not convince Russia fully," he also expressed optimism that "if a realistic attitude in Russia prevails, Moscow will see that NATO is not "moving East," but that Central and Eastern Europe—and Russia itself—are gradually moving West."[83]

If one accepts this perspective, NATO's ability to assist in the democratization and stabilization of Central and Eastern Europe, and perhaps even areas beyond Europe, derives as much from its pull as a guardian of democratic values as from the force of its military might. NATO, the initial enlargement experience suggests, does not so much project or impose its values as it pulls others to its core, in the process encouraging the necessarily indigenous reforms required of NATO members. The concept of a return to Europe also suggests that, contrary to realist assumptions, identity—presumably informed by history, culture, values, and ideas—has influenced how the governments of Central and Eastern Europe have defined their interests and, consequently, how they have behaved both domestically and in their interactions with others.

Perhaps one of the most interesting expressions of NATO as a unique political community and the desire to project that image to aspirants was the publication in 1997 of a collection of folk stories from NATO's then 16 member states entitled *The NATO Storybook*.[84] Presiding over the distribution of the book to schoolchildren in Prague in July 1997, a Major from the Czech Ministry of Defense explained the book's relevance by observing that it was "important to teach people that NATO is not just about armies. It's about a broader relationship between these countries."[85]

Although *The NATO Storybook* was not itself an official NATO publication, NATO leaders appear to have recognized NATO's identity as an important source of its influence with aspirant states, and they have unabashedly characterized the Alliance in terms of its values and, more broadly, Western civilization. In announcing his commitment to further enlargement in June 2001, for example, George W. Bush stressed that NATO is unique because its members share a common civilization and set of values. "Yalta," he declared, "did not ratify a natural divide: it divided a living civilization. The partition of Europe was not a fact of geography; it was an act of violence."[86] Recognizing the appeal of NATO's values even more explicitly, former NATO Commander Wesley Clark said of the Alliance in his farewell address in 2000, "Together we have demonstrated that there is nothing stronger than the power of ideas...ideas of freedom, law and justice and that democratic peoples united in a vision of a common imperative form an irresistible and magnetic force which is transforming the nature of Europe."[87] Similarly, former Secretary General Solana suggested that NATO functions as a "magnetic pole," enabling it "to shape the nature of security in Europe."[88]

Emphasizing the link between NATO, democratic values, and Western civilization, in fact, sent a critical signal to prospective NATO members: Being identified as a member of the "West" required first actively embracing and implementing its values. In making this connection, NATO was, in effect, exercising what Joseph Nye has labeled "soft power": "the ability to attract through cultural and ideological appeal."[89] As one member of NATO's international staff observed, NATO's ability to influence others derives in part from the fact that it has "something to show to others."[90] That something is a zone of peace and prosperity closely identified with liberal democratic values—a community of states that have *established* peace with one another.

Of course, it is also true that NATO has multiple identities. In many quarters, especially outside of Europe, the Alliance is still regarded as principally a military organization. Yet, as NATO's own mission has evolved, so too, it seems, has its identity in the eyes of its newest members. During the first phase of enlargement, many commentators argued that the aspirants wanted to join, not the "new NATO" but the "old NATO," which they equated with a firm security guarantee. This was perhaps particularly true of Poland, which for reasons of both history and geography still harbored fears of a military threat from Russia. NATO's transformation, however, has meant that the Alliance's focus has increasingly been directed outside NATO territory—a shift not lost on its newest members. Indeed, one Polish diplomat assigned to NATO observed that, contrary to Poland's expectations, the Allies did not focus on assisting its new members once they had acceded to the Alliance, but, instead, made it clear that the new members were expected to help those still outside the Alliance. Poland, it was assumed, would share the knowledge and experience gained through its reform and accession process with others, especially Ukraine.[91]

At the same time, it appears that new members' and partners' perceptions of their own security interests may be changing. By virtually all accounts, the Czech Republic performed miserably during NATO's first war in Kosovo, and its domestic public support for NATO actually declined during the war.[92] Since then, however, the Czechs have been active participants in NATO's various peacekeeping/stabilization missions, and, according to a survey conducted in late 2000 by a Prague-based firm and the RAND Corporation, public support for NATO improved substantially after the war. Seventy-four percent of those polled responded that the Czech Republic should help to defend other members and 49 percent agreed that the Czechs should participate in peacekeeping operations.[93] Indeed, the Czech Republic's 2001 national security strategy, which declared European security to be indivisible, identified participation in "peace operations" as a strategic interest.[94]

Conclusion

In assessing NATO's capacity for democracy promotion, the relevant issue is not whether the Alliance can create the impetus for democracy and respect for human rights in states where it would otherwise not exist. Clearly that impulse must be indigenous. The real issue is whether NATO, along with other external actors, can reinforce and assist in concrete and useful ways the difficult process of political and economic reform in fledgling democracies. This chapter concludes that NATO has assisted in this process, not simply by dangling the carrot of prospective membership in front of Central and Eastern Europeans, but also by actively aiding these states with the implementation of democratic principles and practices. Skeptics of NATO's potential for democracy promotion have also ignored the powerful effects of ideas and identity on state behavior and, specifically, the extent to which NATO's own identity as an alliance that has built the political and military means to defend the democratic values its members hold in common constitutes an important part of its appeal. Indeed, NATO has leveraged that appeal in promoting its values as norms that should govern the entire Euro-Atlantic community and, in the process, furthered a sense of collective identity that is closely identified with liberal democratic values.

As NATO increasingly looks to assist the growth of democracy beyond Europe, however, the challenges it will encounter will likely prove far more difficult than those faced in Central and Eastern Europe. Indeed, that experience raises important questions about the extent to which NATO can leverage its identity and values to "project stability" beyond Europe to areas not traditionally considered part of "the West," including Central Asia and the Middle East. As discussed in Chapter 6, however, this is precisely the task that NATO set for itself during its 2004 summit in Istanbul.

CHAPTER 4

September 11 and the Road to Prague

When George W. Bush assumed the presidency in early 2001, it was expected that enlargement would dominate the agenda for NATO's upcoming summit, scheduled to take place in Prague in late 2002. Indeed, as Poland, Hungary, and the Czech Republic acceded to the Alliance in the spring of 1999, NATO had emphasized that its door remained open to prospective members. The Allies had also initiated a Membership Action Plan (MAP) designed to assist the remaining aspirants with the political, economic, and military reforms necessary for membership.

The road to Prague, however, was marked by the terrorist attacks of September 11, prompting NATO for the first time ever to invoke Article 5 of the Washington Treaty and leading to some speculation that the anticipated enlargement might not go forward as planned. Yet, ultimately, September 11 did not derail NATO's plans to launch a second round of enlargement as some had feared. Rather the evidence suggests that the events of that day actually served to enhance prospects for a robust enlargement at Prague, in part because they influenced both the rationale driving the enlargement and the behavior of aspiring members.

The Warsaw Speech

In a speech delivered in Warsaw in June 2001, several months prior to the events of September 11, George W. Bush had put to rest the initial speculation as to whether his administration would support further enlargement of NATO. Returning to the phrase his father had used over a decade earlier in characterizing NATO's new mission, Bush told his audience that a Europe "whole and free" was "no longer a dream....It is the work that you and I are called on to complete."[1] Europe could not be "whole and free," however, without the new democracies of Central and Eastern Europe. Like Bill Clinton before him, Bush appeared to conceive of Europe and the space that could ultimately comprise NATO in terms of shared values rather than geography. "The future of every European nation must be determined by the progress of internal reform, not the interests of outside powers," he insisted. "Every European nation that struggles toward democracy and free markets and a strong civic culture must be welcomed into Europe's home." According to one former National Security Council staff member, although Bush offered no specific timeline for enlargement during the Warsaw speech, his language was designed to inspire those states enrolled in the MAP to continue with reforms by signaling that the Prague enlargement would not be minimal. Nor would it be the last.[2]

Much as his predecessor had, Bush also asserted that NATO could help to erase Cold War divisions. "The Iron Curtain is no more," he concluded. "Now we plan and build the house of freedom—whose doors are open to all of Europe's peoples and whose windows look out to global challenges beyond."[3] As Bush had characterized it, NATO's principal political mission remained the fulfillment of Europe whole and free. Visiting Brussels in the fall of 2002, Deputy National Security Adviser Stephen Hadley would also cast enlargement in a way that was fully consistent with the rationale embraced by the Clinton administration.[4] NATO, together with the European Union, he declared, "is a critical instrument through which Europe will become whole, free and at peace for the first time in its history, and Russia will find a comfortable place in Europe for the first time in generations."[5]

In short, the Bush administration's initial rationale for enlargement appeared to rest, just as the Clinton administration's had, on the notion that genuine peace could be constructed on the basis of shared democratic values. NATO's political rather than military dimension stood at the center of the enlargement case. As NATO Commander Joseph W. Ralston put it, " NATO's overarching objective of opening up the Alliance to new members is to enhance stability in Europe as a whole, more than to expand NATO's military influence or capabilities or to alter the nature of its basic defense posture."[6] NATO Secretary General Lord Robertson had made essentially this same point in June 2001: "NATO enlargement is not about accumulating military capabilities against 'the other side,'" he explained. "There is no 'other side' at the moment. The context of NATO enlargement today is about community building: about overcoming the divisions that still exist in Europe. It is about improving the security and stability of Europe as a whole."[7]

The Bush administration's public pronouncements regarding NATO also conveyed a strong sense that, historically and morally, enlargement was simply the right thing to do. Such sentiments were particularly evident in the language of the Warsaw speech. In planning NATO's enlargement, Bush insisted, "no nation should be used as a pawn in the agendas of others. We will not trade away the fate of free European peoples. No more Munichs. No more Yaltas."[8] Under Secretary of State for Political Affairs Marc Grossman also suggested that continued enlargement was the only course consistent with NATO's core values. In his words, "Not to embrace countries that have overcome years of communist dictatorship and have proven their ability and willingness to contribute to our common security, would be to abandon the very principles that have been NATO's source of strength and vitality."[9] As one official who served on the National Security Staff during both the Clinton and George W. Bush administrations observed, Article 10 of the NATO Treaty made it difficult to discern grounds on which the aspirants might justifiably be excluded, so long as they were willing and able "to contribute to the security of the North Atlantic area."[10] Indeed, Bush's Warsaw speech had also included a line that seemed to hint that the new administration was inclined to support a substantial enlargement. In making preparations for the 2002 Prague Summit, Bush told his audience, the NATO Allies should "not calculate how little we can get away with, but how much we can do to advance the cause of freedom."[11]

The speech served to allay earlier concerns that the Bush administration might be less committed than Bill Clinton to the enlargement process and perhaps even NATO itself. Early indications of a unilateralist bent to the Bush foreign policy coupled with candidate Bush's disparaging remarks about "nation-building" during the 2000 campaign had helped to fuel such speculation. National Security Adviser Condoleeza Rice had also aroused concern in Europe regarding the administration's commitment to NATO by telling the *New York Times* during the campaign that a Bush administration would not support U.S. involvement in NATO peacekeeping in the Balkans.[12] Consequently, Bush's ringing endorsement of enlargement in Warsaw came as a surprise to many observers in both the United States and Europe who had been looking for some indication as to the new administration's commitment to NATO, in general.

From the beginning, however, there were small indications that Bush would carry forward the process begun by his predecessor. Key members of his foreign policy team, including Rice, Hadley, and Secretary of State Colin Powell, were members of the U.S. Committee on NATO, a nonprofit organization formed in 1996 to support enlargement at a time when Senate ratification was in doubt.[13] Even more significant was Bush's appointment of Daniel Fried to his National Security Council staff as Director for European and Eurasian Affairs. As a member of Bill Clinton's National Security Council staff and then U.S. Ambassador to Poland from 1997 until 2000, Fried had been a strong proponent of NATO enlargement. Bush's decision to appoint him to a key position within his own administration might be construed as evidence that the President was, from the beginning, at least somewhat sympathetic to the enlargement process.[14] Not surprisingly, it was Fried who served as the principal author of Bush's Warsaw speech, which even some Defense and State Department officials privately characterized as "Clintonesque."[15]

The fact that many of the concerns that had featured prominently in the first enlargement debate had faded also bode well for a substantial enlargement at Prague. Concerns regarding both the cost of enlargement and the ability of NATO to function politically at 19 members appeared to have been overblown once Hungary, Poland, and the Czech Republic had actually acceded to the Alliance.[16] Moreover, a general consensus had emerged that NATO's open-door policy, together with EU enlargement, had indeed inspired prospective members to continue with democratic reforms and resolve potential conflicts with neighboring states.[17] Early predictions that enlargement would be disastrous for NATO-Russia relations also failed to materialize, although concerns about Russia would continue to play a role in the enlargement debate well into 2001.[18]

Still a substantial enlargement was far from assured. Some commentators speculated that NATO might admit just one or two new members, probably Slovenia and perhaps Slovakia, assuming that Vladimír Mečiar did not return to power. Fears of antagonizing Russia worked to the disadvantage of the Baltic states, while Romania and Bulgaria were often perceived as lagging behind the others in terms of their domestic political reforms. As noted earlier, the September 11 terrorist attacks in the United States, which occurred just months after Bush's Warsaw speech, also prompted speculation that enlargement would be slowed or perhaps removed from NATO's agenda altogether.

September 11 and the Logic of Enlargement

Within weeks, however, Secretary General Robertson was arguing that "September 11 had reinforced the logic of NATO enlargement." "We will not let the terrorist attacks of last month derail our agenda," he insisted. "We will indeed have to broaden and adapt this agenda. But we will not jettison the fundamentals. Because the core of what we do made sense on September 10, and continues to make sense after September 11."[19]

Nor did September 11 undermine the Bush administration's original case on behalf of enlargement. Speaking before the German Bundestag in May 2002, Bush used language that largely mirrored that of his Warsaw speech given almost a year earlier. "We must lay the foundation with a Europe that is whole and free and at peace for the first time in its history," he reiterated. "The dream of the centuries is close at hand."[20] That same month, following a meeting of the North Atlantic Council, Colin Powell stated that, while no final decisions would be made until the Prague

Summit, the Allies remained "hopeful" that there would be a "robust round of enlargement at Prague."[21]

In fact, September 11 appears to have enhanced prospects for such an enlargement. In its wake, Bush administration officials argued that "closer cooperation and integration between the United States and all the democracies of Europe" had only grown in importance.[22] As Under Secretary of Defense for Policy Douglas J. Feith put it, "A Europe united on the basis of democratic principles, the rule of law, respect for individual rights and the other tenets of the Alliance will be better able to resist and defeat terrorist threats and other threats. The U.S. government believes that an enlarged Alliance that conducts joint defense and operational planning, promotes interoperability, and encourages realistic training exercises will be a more effective partner in answering global security challenges."[23]

The events of September 11 also served to ease tensions with Russia stemming from NATO's 1999 war in Kosovo. Indeed, as Timothy Garton Ash has observed, rather than making a halt or slowdown of NATO enlargement the price of his participation in the "war on terrorism," Russian President Vladimir Putin "used that support as a launch pad for a strategic campaign to have Russia accepted as a full member of the West, and of Europe."[24] Putin even went so far as to suggest to Robertson that, if NATO were to become more of a political organization and involve Russia more closely in alliance deliberations, he would mute his opposition to enlargement.[25] This dialogue—supported by British Prime Minister Tony Blair, in particular—ultimately paved the way for agreement on the creation of a new NATO-Russia Council in May 2002. The new institution allowed Russia a seat at the table during NATO discussions of certain, specified issues, including terrorism and the proliferation of weapons of mass destruction. Although the Council grew out of a genuine desire for improved NATO-Russia cooperation, it was also, in the words of one NATO official, a means by which NATO could "sweeten the enlargement pill" for Putin.[26]

As Robertson observed during a December 2001 trip to Moscow, the events of September 11 were instrumental to this dramatic and unexpected turn in NATO-Russia relations. Noting the irony of the development, he even went so far as to suggest that "Osama bin Laden was the midwife of an incredible new rapprochement." "I don't think that in his wildest dreams this fanatical criminal would have thought that he would have ended forever the Cold War and brought NATO and Russia so closely together," Robertson remarked.[27] The new relationship also helped to overcome reservations held by some NATO members—especially Britain and Germany—regarding the possibility of extending invitations to the Baltic states at Prague.[28] Indeed, many of the Allies came to believe that it made sense to admit as many of the aspirants as possible while the Russians were in a cooperative mood. Doing otherwise risked stringing out the process and ensuring that enlargement would remain an issue in NATO-Russia relations for the foreseeable future.[29] In short, to the extent that the events of September 11 provided the impetus for a new NATO-Russia relationship, they also removed one of the primary deterrents to a substantial enlargement.

At the same time, however, the Bush administration displayed little interest in actually using NATO militarily, despite the Alliance's unprecedented invocation of Article 5 on September 12, 2001, and subsequent offers of assistance from Europe. As the United States prepared for a war in Afghanistan aimed at eliminating al Qaeda forces and the Taliban regime that had been harboring them, U.S. Deputy Secretary of State Paul Wolfowitz told NATO defense ministers in Brussels that the United States would look to "different coalitions in different parts of the world" and did not intend to rely on NATO structures.[30] U.S. Secretary of Defense Donald Rumsfeld had also stated shortly after September 11 that "the mission will determine the coalition" and "the coalition must not determine the mission."[31] Indeed, the lesson the Bush administration appears to have learned from the 1999 war in Kosovo—a war that highlighted the significant and growing military capabilities gap between the United States and Europe—was that NATO would be more of a decision-making nuisance than a source of true military assistance in the war in Afghanistan. Although NATO had adopted in 1999 a Defense Capabilities Initiative (DCI), designed to improve its military capabilities across the spectrum, and Robertson had repeatedly appealed to Europe to allocate more funds for defense, little progress had been made toward meeting the DCI's goals between 1999 and 2001.

Judging the Aspirants

Coupled with the decision to decline a role for NATO in Afghanistan, Bush's continued support for a substantial enlargement fueled speculation that he had already deemed NATO little more than a political organization like the Organization for Security and Co-operation in Europe and thus discounted concerns that the so-called "big-bang" approach to enlargement—issuing invitations to a substantial majority of the aspirants at once—would further dilute NATO's military capabilities.[32] Thomas L. Friedman, a strong opponent of NATO enlargement during the mid-1990s, expressed this view in a column in the *New York Times* shortly before the Prague Summit. He no longer had objections to enlargement, he wrote, because "as we already saw in the Afghan war, most NATO countries have fallen so far behind the U.S. in their defense spending and modernization, they really can't fight alongside of us anymore anyway. So what the heck, let's invite everybody in."[33]

Some observers, including former Clinton administration officials, also expressed concern that, what they perceived to be a determination by the Bush administration that NATO was no longer militarily relevant, had led to a lowering of the bar with respect to the political and military criteria by which the aspirants were judged. The administration, in their view, had failed to take full advantage of the leverage associated with the enlargement process to encourage continued reform.[34] NATO scholar Sean Kay agreed, putting it this way following the Prague Summit:

> The United States had a serious opportunity to use Prague as a major transformation summit, but in the end it failed to do so by not holding the invitees to serious measures of both established political, economic, and military criteria or demanding new criteria that fit into a more general concept of remolding NATO as a counter-terrorist institution.[35]

Such concerns stemmed in part from a widespread view that at least two of the three states issued invitations in 1997—namely, Hungary and the Czech Republic—had performed poorly upon their accession to NATO in 1999.[36] Unlike the Czech Republic, Hungary had conducted itself reasonably well during the Kosovo conflict—particularly given the sizable Hungarian population in northern Serbia—but still had not fulfilled earlier pledges to restructure its military forces. Indeed, during a courtesy call to Brussels prior to the Prague Summit, Robertson reportedly lectured Hungary's new Defense Minister, Ferenc Juhász, regarding Hungary's responsibilities as a member of NATO.[37] Another European security official went so far as to suggest that Hungary had "won the prize for most disappointing new member of NATO, and against some competition."[38] Such developments generated considerable concern that, once the new invitees were on board, NATO would lose much of its leverage over the reform process, given the absence of any mechanism for suspending or expelling from NATO states that fail to live up to its political and military standards.

Although Bush administration officials denied that the White House lowered the bar on standards or engaged in a "policy of benign neglect" toward NATO,[39] the context and process surrounding enlargement had changed fundamentally since 1997 when Poland, Hungary, and the Czech Republic received their invitations. The fact that the process of assessing the aspirants in 2002 differed from that employed in 1997 was to some extent a consequence of the MAP, which drew heavily on lessons learned during the accession processes for Hungary, Poland, and the Czech Republic. While the MAP did not alter the criteria against which the aspirants were judged or establish a formal acquis for NATO membership, it did serve to make the evaluation process more structured and rigorous. However, both observers and individuals directly involved in the enlargement process feared that NATO risked losing leverage over the aspirants if they were not rewarded for reforms achieved under the MAP. As explained by one NATO staff member who had worked closely with the aspirants, even if Slovakia, Bulgaria, and Romania were less prepared for membership than the other four aspirants, it would be extremely difficult to deny them invitations after "kissing and hugging them through three cycles of MAP."[40] Indeed, a Bulgarian diplomat argued at the time that the aspirants would no longer take the MAP seriously if their progress failed to be recognized.[41] James M. Goldgeier has also observed that, coupled with Robertson's June 2001 announcement that the "zero option" was off the table for Prague, the MAP "locked NATO into a process by which turning new members away in 2002 would cast severe doubts on the Alliance's credibility."[42] NATO's newfound cooperation with Russia had lessened the fear that enlargement would antagonize the Russians, but it also made it more difficult to exclude aspirants who had been working for three years to meet NATO's expectations under the MAP. The risk was that some aspirants might perceive that Russia was "getting in through the back door and getting more benefits" than partner countries without having met any of NATO's political and economic standards.[43]

Moreover, while it was generally agreed that Albania and Macedonia were simply not ready for membership, it was difficult to argue that any of the remaining aspirants were appreciably more or less qualified than the others. While Romania and, particularly, Bulgaria were perceived as lagging behind Slovakia, Slovenia, and the Baltic states in terms of their political and economic reform process, none of the eventual invitees stood apart from the others in terms of their qualifications to the degree that Hungary, Poland, and the Czech Republic had stood apart from the other prospective members in 1997. In the 2001–2002 rankings of Freedom House, a well-known human rights/democracy monitoring organization, Slovenia, Lithuania, Latvia, Estonia, and Slovakia scored a 1 + 1 or 1 + 2 for political freedoms + civil liberties (on a scale of 1 to 7, with "1" as the best possible score), putting them in line with present NATO members. Romania scored 2 + 2 and Bulgaria 1 + 2. The two other formal aspirants, Albania and Macedonia lagged farther behind, both at 3 + 3.[44]

Finally, as one Pentagon official observed, the Bush administration was operating in an environment in which it was somewhat easier to take democracy in Central and Eastern Europe for granted than had been the case during the Clinton administration, when the region's future seemed quite uncertain.[45] By 2001, the region appeared solidly oriented toward the West. Still, then U.S. Ambassador to NATO R. Nicholas Burns denied that the United States was "judging candidates on other issues like Iraq." "We are taking great care to make sure that the decision is based on such criteria as the applicants' military readiness, institutional strength and human rights record," he insisted.[46]

Yet, it was also clear that, from the Bush administration's perspective, September 11 had changed the entire context for thinking about enlargement. The United States ultimately pushed for invitations for seven of the then nine formal aspirants at Prague, but they were evaluated in terms of their ability to contribute, not to the pre-September 11 NATO, but rather to an Alliance whose future would now depend on its ability to address threats emanating from outside of Europe. Indeed, a meeting originally billed as an enlargement summit quickly came to be known as a "transformation summit" with an emphasis on the need for "new capabilities" and "new partners" as well as "new members."[47] Although enlargement remained on the agenda, the summit's principal focus shifted to the need to equip NATO militarily to respond to terrorism and weapons of mass destruction. Indeed, the Bush administration's decision to decline a role for NATO in Afghanistan rendered it virtually impossible for the Allies to ignore the capabilities problem at Prague.[48]

Perhaps, most significantly, however, the Bush administration was determined to use the Prague Summit to focus NATO's attention beyond Europe. In the wake of September 11, NATO would need to adopt a global rather than a regional focus. Burns explained the new agenda this way in a speech to the Konrad Adenauer Foundation in late May 2003:

> In the wake of the shocking events of September 11, 2001, the world changed and NATO had to change with it. We set out a year and a half ago to transform nearly everything about NATO so that it could help us meet the new and daunting threats of terrorism and weapons of mass destruction. At November's Prague Summit, President Bush and the NATO Leadership agreed on an ambitious, even revolutionary, reform agenda. We worked to pivot the new NATO from its prior inward focus on threats within Europe to a new outward spotlight on the recent challenges to peace in the arc of countries from South and Central Asia to the Middle East and North Africa.[49]

The New Membership Criteria

This reform agenda would also alter the lens through which the Prague aspirants were evaluated. As Jennifer Moroney, a defense consultant with DFI International observed at the time, the applications of the individual aspirants were, in practice, "measured against their willingness and ability to contribute to the War on Terrorism—requirements not explicitly found in the formal NATO Membership Action Plan (MAP)." A demonstrated appreciation for the transatlantic link, and to a more limited extent, geo-political factors also joined the formal MAP criteria in shaping the Bush administration's assessments of the aspirants. Consequently, the events of September 11 influenced not only the Bush administration's rationale for enlargement, but also the behavior of aspiring members.

Romania and Bulgaria, in particular (the two invitees generally regarded as lagging farthest behind in terms of democratic development) appeared to recognize early on that engaging in ally-like behavior would improve their prospects for NATO membership. Already active participants in NATO's peacekeeping efforts, both states now contributed a variety of capabilities to the war on terrorism, including backfilling troops serving in NATO's Stabilisation Force (SFOR) and Kosovo Force (KFOR) missions in the Balkans so that they could be deployed elsewhere.[50] Bulgaria also provided a nuclear, chemical, and biological weapons decontamination unit to the International Security Assistance Force (ISAF) in Afghanistan, as well as an airfield for refueling tankers.[51] For its part, Romania sent an elite group of about 400 troops known as the Red Scorpions to Afghanistan, many of whom served alongside U.S. soldiers from the Army's 82nd Airborne Division at Kandahar.[52] Additionally, the government signed an agreement with the United States in October 2001, permitting U.S. troops to transit through Romanian territory or be stationed there short-term.[53] It also made its airbases and Black Sea ports available for use in a possible war with Iraq and reportedly offered to help U.S. airplanes refuel and transport troops and equipment.[54] Finally, in an effort to curry favor with the United States, Romania agreed to a bilateral treaty, specifying that it would not turn U.S. citizens over to the International Criminal Court—a move that provoked strong criticism from the European Union, which Romania was also in line to join.[55]

Romania and Bulgaria were not the only aspirants to recognize and respond to new expectations. As Marc Grossman noted in testimony before the Senate Armed Services Committee in late February 2002, in addition to maintaining their peacekeeping responsibilities, many of the aspirants had offered the United States "overflight rights, transit and basing privileges, military and police forces, medical units and transport."[56] Latvia and Lithuania, for example, also backfilled SFOR and KFOR troops, and Lithuania sent its own forces to Afghanistan, as did Slovakia.[57] The Baltic states even sent troops to provide base security at a new allied air base at Manas in Kyrgyzstan.[58] Even subsequent to the Prague Summit, Romania, Bulgaria, Lithuania, and Estonia contributed forces to the U.S.–led coalition in Iraq.

These initiatives, as officials from both the Department of State and the Pentagon observed, reflected an understanding on the part of the aspirants that, in the wake of September 11, they would be "seen in a new optic."[59] Clearly acknowledging the new expectations, a Romanian army major leading a group of approximately 20 soldiers assigned to protect U.S. Army doctors in Afghanistan observed just before the Prague Summit that "Romania's road to NATO crosses through Kandahar." "We are no longer consumers of security," he asserted. We are now providers of security."[60] Indeed, the United States had stressed in the months before Prague that new members would be expected to "add value to the alliance" as well as demonstrate a "lasting and assured commitment to democracy."[61] "Adding value" meant taking an active role in responding to the new threats on which the Bush administration now sought to focus NATO's attention.

The fact that many of the aspirants did ultimately make contributions to the war in Afghanistan, with an expectation that their efforts to demonstrate solidarity with the United States would be rewarded, ultimately strengthened prospects for a substantial enlargement at Prague. According to one U.S. official closely associated with the enlargement process, the big-bang approach was far from certain in June 2001 when Bush spoke in Warsaw, but "September 11 changed the way we looked at enlargement." The war in Afghanistan had provided an opportunity for prospective members "to show that they were capable of acting like allies."[62] U.S. officials also acknowledged that even the Pentagon, which had previously shown little enthusiasm for NATO, much less the enlargement process, began to look seriously at the various kinds of contributions the aspirants might be able to make to the war on terrorism.[63] Indeed, the Bush administration had come to see the Prague invitees as providing a "platform from which to project power."[64]

While the aspirants fully expected that they would be rewarded for behaving as "defacto allies," U.S. officials simply expected such behavior.[65] As one Department of State official put it, had the aspirants not demonstrated the cooperation they did, it would have been the "kiss of death" for them. At the same time, however, both U.S. and NATO officials recognized possible costs associated with a minimal enlargement.[66] As NATO Commander General Joseph Ralston put it,

> We must consider the potential cost of not enlarging. The aspirant nations have put forth a strong effort in good faith toward becoming members, and have taken political positions in support of the Alliance in recent conflicts. Their elected officials have made membership an important part of their public agenda and sought to increase public support for NATO. From a military standpoint, the outstanding cooperation and support we have enjoyed in terms of troop contributions to ongoing operations and the use of infrastructure and transit rights could be jeopardized.[67]

To a more limited extent, geostrategic considerations also entered into the decisions about enlargement.[68] With its Black Sea ports and proximity to Turkey and the Gulf region, Romania provided a new staging ground for dealing with new threats farther east.[69] Just before the Prague Summit, Bush even pronounced that Romania would become "NATO's spearhead in Europe."[70] Romania later made its bases available to U.S. forces when the war in Iraq began in 2003.[71]

Additionally, the inclusion of Romania and Bulgaria in NATO served to create a continuum stretching from NATO to the Black Sea, the Caspian Sea and U.S. forces in Central Asia.[72] Their presence put the Alliance in a better position to reach out to Azerbaijan and Georgia, both of which were seeking closer cooperation with NATO. And bringing Slovenia on board, along with Romania and Bulgaria, offered NATO a foothold in the Balkans, a region still rife with ethnic tensions, organized crime, and the potential to serve as a haven for terrorists.[73] Plans for realigning U.S. forces in Europe to better facilitate a rapid response to the threats posed by terrorism and weapons of mass destruction also hinged on prospects for opening or expanding military bases farther to the east in such places as Bulgaria and Kyrgyzstan.[74]

These strategic advantages, suggested one Western diplomat based in Sofia, offset concerns about the slow pace of democratic reforms and corruption, which he suggested could "be fixed later."[75] Robert Hunter, U.S. Ambassador to NATO during the Clinton administration, put it even more directly, telling the *Washington Post,* "People are going to hold their noses and swallow hard on Romania and Bulgaria." Although the Clinton administration had not supported issuing invitations to Romania and Bulgaria in 1997, Hunter said that he too now supported their inclusion.[76]

New vs. "Old Europe"

The aspirants' enthusiastic support for the transatlantic link in the wake of September 11 also worked to their favor with the Bush administration. Both NATO's newest members and those ultimately invited to join the Alliance at Prague tended to be more supportive than some other Alliance members of American foreign policy and more appreciative of the role of U.S. military power in Europe. For them, NATO's proven value stemmed from the institutional link the Alliance provides to the United States, whose military power was perceived as still vital to the defense of the values for which NATO stands. NATO diplomats from the region, in fact, privately acknowledged that they remained skeptical regarding the prospects for a viable European Security and Defense Identity.[77]

Consequently, it was also the Central and East Europeans who demonstrated the greatest concern about what they perceived to be a loss of interest in NATO by the Bush administration. Former Polish Foreign Minister Bronisław Geremek, for example, told the European edition of the *Wall Street Journal* in November 2002, "I am convinced (from my visits to Washington) that NATO is becoming an institution of the past in the mind of American leaders. That is what we Europeans must combat."[78] As one Polish diplomat affirmed, the Bush administration recognized and turned these fears to its advantage.[79] Indeed, Central and Eastern Europeans felt compelled to make a show of their solidarity with the United States, partly as a means of maintaining U.S. interest in NATO and Europe, generally.[80]

Perhaps one of the most dramatic manifestations of the pro-American sentiment present in Central and Eastern Europe appeared shortly after the Prague Summit in the form of two statements involving Iraq—both of them sympathetic to U.S. policy. The first was an open letter published in the *Wall Street Journal* in late January 2003. Signed by the leaders of Hungary, Poland, and the Czech Republic as well as EU members Spain, Portugal, Italy, the United Kingdom, and Denmark, the letter stressed that the U.S. and Europe "must remain united in insisting that [Saddam Hussein's] regime be disarmed."[81] The other was a statement issued by the ten members of the "Vilnius Group" following U.S. Secretary of State Colin Powell's presentation to the UN Security Council on February 5, 2003.[82] "Our countries understand the dangers posed by tyranny and the special responsibility of democracies to defend our shared values," the statement declared. "The trans-Atlantic community, of which we are a part, must stand together to face the threat posed by the nexus of terrorism and dictators with weapons of mass destruction."[83] A series of pronouncements by French President Jacques Chirac and German Chancellor Gerhard Schroeder indicating that they were not yet prepared to support military intervention in Iraq had provided the impetus for the statements, and both were thus widely interpreted as a rebuke to Schroeder and Chirac for purporting to speak for the whole of Europe.[84] Notably, the *Wall Street Journal* letter also appeared just days after Rumsfeld generated some consternation in Europe with a remark made during a press briefing. When confronted with a question about European reluctance to support a war against Iraq, Rumsfeld had retorted,

> You're thinking of Europe as Germany and France. I don't. I think that's old Europe. If you look at the entire NATO Europe today, the center of gravity is shifting to the east and there are a lot of new members. And if you just take the list of all the members of NATO and all those that have been invited in recently—what is it? Twenty-six, something like that?...You look at vast numbers of other countries in Europe. They're not with France and Germany on this, they're with the United States.[85]

Indeed, Fried and others within the administration had reportedly argued that the Prague enlargement could serve to give the United States staunch new supporters within NATO.[86] Bush himself said in a speech that he delivered during the Prague Summit that one of the "advantages" of enlargement was that the "members recently added to NATO and those invited to join bring greater clarity to the purpose of our alliance, because they understand the lessons of the last century. Those with fresh memories of tyranny know the value of freedom."[87] As he put it in an interview with Radio Free Europe/Radio Liberty, the "love of freedom" the aspirants could contribute was "going to be really important—it'll add some vigor to the relationship in NATO."[88] Similarly, Rumsfeld remarked that both NATO's three newest members and the invitees brought a "spirit and enthusiasm" to NATO that were needed by the Alliance's other members.[89] From the administration's perspective, Latvia's President Vaira Vike-Freiberga demonstrated that spirit in a much-lauded address at the Prague Summit. As she put it,

> Our people have been tested in the fires of history. They have been tempered by suffering and injustice. They know the meaning and value of liberty. They know that it is worth every effort to support it, to maintain it, to stand for it and to fight for it. We make a solemn pledge and a commitment here today, on this historic and solemn occasion, that we will strive to do our utmost to contribute not just to the strength of the Alliance but also to do whatever needs to be done to create a world where justice and liberty are available to all.[90]

"Niche" Contributions

The fact that September 11 revealed how ill-equipped even NATO's long-time members were to address contemporary threats and to mobilize forces for "out-of-area" missions is also relevant to understanding the rationale underpinning the Prague enlargement. To exclude the aspirants on the basis of their generally poor military capabilities when some were at least marginally better equipped to address new threats than current members made little sense in the context of the Prague transformation. In fact, among both the Prague invitees and the three who had joined the Alliance in 1999, there were some who had developed so-called "niche" capabilities that would, according to one senior U.S. General, put them in a position to make significant contributions to the war on terrorism.[91] Among the most frequently cited examples of such capabilities was the Czech Republic's well-regarded chemical, biological, and nuclear defense capability. In fact, the Czechs had pledged to create a mobile anti-chemical and antibacteriological warfare unit within NATO and possibly serve as the headquarters for a NATO weapons of mass destruction defense center.[92]

Such capabilities acquired greater significance in the context of the agreement reached at Prague to develop a new, rapidly deployable NATO Response Force of approximately 20,000 soldiers drawn from throughout the Alliance, which NATO declared to be fully operational at its Riga Summit in late 2006. The force had originally been proposed by Hans Binnendijk and Richard Kugler at the National Defense University in Washington, D.C., as a means of addressing the growing capabilities gap between the United States and Europe, which was at the root of the Bush administration's rejection of a role for NATO in Afghanistan in the months after September 11. Binnendijk and Kugler recognized that subsequent calls for a division of labor in which the United States assumed responsibility for high-intensity warfare and the Europeans focused on peacekeeping would ultimately erode a sense of political solidarity among the Allies by assigning the bulk of the risk to the United States.[93] The NATO Response Force was intended to allow European forces to participate with U.S. forces in high-intensity conflict operations. Although NATO had previously resisted force specialization, it was understood at Prague that the new force would depend to some extent on "niche" contributions from member states. All NATO members, in fact, were expected to announce what capabilities they would make available for joint defense purposes. "The New NATO," Robertson explained just prior to the summit, "is going to be about countries who do different things, and do each of them well."[94] Although the new invitees still had considerable work ahead in the area of defense reform, the creation of the NATO Response Force offered at least an opportunity to contribute to the transformation of NATO's military capabilities also begun at Prague. As U.S. Ambassador to NATO R. Nicholas Burns put it, "Not every ally can do everything, but every ally, whether big or small, can contribute something."[95]

Moreover, the NATO Response Force was itself intended to serve as a means of transforming the capabilities of all participating states. "The advantage" of such a force, Rumsfeld explained in late 2003 "may ultimately prove to be not simply the existence of a NATO capability that has the ability to go do something useful in the world but also the fact that in developing it and working with it and exercising it and making it responsive, we will back those transformational aspects into their respective militaries of the NATO countries, just as we're trying to do in the United States."[96] It is also notable that, while the defense expenditures of some long-term Allies had actually fallen below the 2 percent of GDP expected of MAP members, some of the invitees had been spending above this level. It was marginally helpful, for example, that, as of August 2002, Bulgaria had been allocating 2.8 percent of its GDP to defense while Romania had been spending 2.4 percent of its GDP.[97]

In sum, the Bush administration appeared inclined toward a robust enlargement even before September 11, but the events of that day led the United States to view the enlargement question from a new perspective —one in which a global outlook and political solidarity assumed greater importance than might otherwise have been the case. As Radio Free Europe analyst Jeremy Bransten explained it,

> Bush presaged NATO's broad second wave of expansion in a Warsaw speech in June 2001, when he called for erasing the old dividing lines in Europe. But

the catalyst for going ahead with the plan can be found in the 11 September attacks against the United States, which prompted Washington to seek and reward committed allies.[98]

The U.S. Ambassador to NATO, R. Nicholas Burns, also observed that the key question after September 11 was no longer whether NATO could defend new members, but rather what value the invitees could bring to a new NATO. The "new, more modern argument for enlargement," Burns explained, "is it will give us seven new allies with whom to fight and keep the peace in Europe and beyond."[99]

None of the above should be read to suggest that the MAP criteria had become irrelevant or that the Bush administration had abandoned its original case for enlargement: namely, that stability could be constructed on the basis of shared democratic values. In fact, the decision to take in seven of the nine aspirants had reportedly been made by September 2002, but NATO put off making even informal announcements until just before the Prague Summit in order to keep maximum pressure on the aspirants to continue with reforms. As Thomas Szayna has noted, in the months preceding the Prague Summit, policy makers were "loath to make clear the 'who' and 'when' because the success of the process of enlargement depends on keeping an incentive system in place; and the incentive system would be less effective if the choices of 'who' and 'when' were known well in advance."[100] The Allies had even agreed that they would not open the subject for debate prior to their May 2002 meeting in Reykjavik so that there would be time, in the words of one NATO staff member, to "put the hammer on them [the aspirants]."[101] There is also little doubt that NATO would have again refused Slovakia an invitation if the fall 2002 elections had produced another government led by Vladimiír Mečiar, whose democratic credentials had been found severely wanting in 1997. As noted earlier, U.S. and other NATO member representatives repeatedly warned the Slovaks throughout 2002 that the results of the fall 2002 elections could determine whether Slovakia received an invitation at Prague to join NATO.[102] Ultimately, however, a consensus emerged among the Allies that all of the invitees—Slovakia included—had achieved significant reforms through the MAP process and were committed to addressing remaining difficulties, including NATO concerns about rampant corruption.[103] Moreover, it was made clear to the invitees that they would remain in the MAP program until their accession, which would remain contingent upon completion of the reforms detailed in the individual timetables that each was required to submit.

Importantly, the focus on military capabilities at Prague should not detract from the fact that the membership invitations issued in 2002 ultimately stemmed from political decisions based on primarily political rather than military factors. Although some of the invitees were in a position to provide modest geostrategic advantages to the Alliance, none was in a position to offer the United States truly valuable military capabilities. As the United States ultimately demonstrated in Iraq, what it sought most from future Allies was not military power, but rather political support.

The evidence also suggests that the commitment to a Europe whole and free made by former President Bush 1989 remained alive and well through the Prague Summit. As one U.S. Department of State official observed, the rationale for enlargement articulated in George W. Bush's Warsaw speech still made sense in a post–September 11 world. ''We can't assume that European history has stopped,'' he noted. This same official, however, also added that, while Europe whole and free remained an important goal, in the wake of September 11, it was ''no longer enough.''[104]

Indeed, while the tendency within NATO during the 1990s was toward thinking about security in largely political terms, the events of September 11 and a growing awareness of new threats stemming from outside Europe triggered a shift in the other direction—toward a greater emphasis on military capabilities and expanding NATO's reach. Bush may already have been more predisposed to thinking about security in military terms than his predecessor, but September 11 accelerated this shift, which served to influence not only the agenda for the Prague Summit, but also the yardstick against which the aspirants would be judged. If it was not sufficient that Europe be whole and free, the Prague Summit could no longer be simply about enlargement or extending the zone of peace and prosperity eastward. NATO's newest members would be expected to enhance security not only through their domestic policies and interactions with neighbors, but also by demonstrating a willingness to reach beyond Europe in both their political and security commitments.

Renewing NATO's Partnerships

Ultimately, the Prague agenda included not only new members, but also new capabilities and a renewed emphasis on partnership. In addition to endorsing the creation of a NATO Response Force, the Allies renewed through the Prague Capabilities Commitment (PCC) their commitment to addressing the capabilities commitments made, but not fulfilled in the 1999 DCI. Although the PCC actually served to reduce the overall number of commitments made by member states, it also identified priority categories in which improvements were required. These categories included strategic airlift; air-to-air refueling; defense against chemical, biological, and nuclear weapons; precision-guided weapons; deployable command-

and-control and communications capabilities; and deployable combat support.[105]

In anticipation of the Prague Summit, NATO had also moved to strengthen its partnerships through a Comprehensive Review of the Euro-Atlantic Partnership Council (EAPC) and Partnership for Peace (PfP). In part, the impetus for the review was a concern that once the seven invitees actually acceded to NATO in March 2004, the EAPC and PfP would become stratified. NATO had, in fact, recognized for some time that a second round of post–Cold War enlargement would likely have significant implications for the composition of the Partnership. NATO members would now outnumber Partners or nonmembers, and the remaining Partners would constitute a diverse lot, with widely dissimilar interests, objectives, and security needs. The most significant gap was understood to exist between the five European neutrals (Austria, Finland, Ireland, Sweden, and Switzerland) and the remaining Partners, all of which were significantly less advanced in terms of their political and economic development.[106] Of the latter group, only three (Albania, Macedonia, and Croatia) were formal NATO applicants. Given that preparing aspirants for membership had been a well-understood objective of PfP, the Allies recognized that a concerted effort would be required to maintain the relevancy of the Partnership. It would now need to serve not only the diverse interests of those Partners not seeking membership, but also the changing security needs of the Allies in a post–September 11 world.[107] Indeed, one NATO diplomat noted that, in addition to finding new ways to engage the Caucasus and Central Asian states, it was vital to keep the five non-NATO EU partners on board. Not only were they contributing to NATO's peacekeeping missions in the Balkans, but they also served as important "exporters of security" because they shared NATO's values.[108]

Determined to address these concerns and to make more complementary the relationship between PfP and the Euro-Atlantic Partnership Council, NATO endorsed at Prague a report calling for both Allies and Partners to "strive to ensure that EAPC discussions focus to a greater degree on shared NATO and Partner political priorities and key security concerns," which in the post–September 11 era inevitably included terrorism and weapons of mass destruction.[109] Heeding the report's call for "an issue-specific, result-oriented mechanism for practical cooperation involving Allies and interested Partners" on issues such as "border security, capabilities for joint action, civil emergency, management of resources or environmental issues," NATO also adopted at Prague its first "Partnership Action Plan." Designated the Partnership Action Plan against Terrorism (PAP-T), the initiative called for partners to intensify political consultations and information sharing, enhance preparedness for combating terrorism, impede support for terrorist groups, enhance capabilities to contribute to consequence management, and assist Partners' efforts against terrorism though PfP Trust funds and mentoring programs. These efforts were then to be consistent with the Allies' commitment "to the protection and promotion of fundamental freedoms and human rights, as well as the rule of law."[110]

September 11 also served to reinvigorate NATO's partnerships with Russia, Ukraine, and the Mediterranean Dialogue states. Indeed, NATO opened participation in the PAP-T and various PfP activities to its Mediterranean Dialogue partners as part of an effort to enhance both dialogue and cooperative activities with a region whose strategic significance to NATO had grown enormously. As noted earlier, Russia's own expressed desire for a more cooperative relationship with NATO ultimately led to an agreement in Rome on May 28, 2002, establishing the NATO-Russia Council, which now permits identified areas of mutual interest to NATO and Russia to be discussed with Russia in a "NATO at 20" format vs. the 19 + 1 format that characterized the previous NATO-Russia Permanent Joint Council. These areas include terrorism, crisis management, nonproliferation, arms control and confidence-building measures, theater missile defense, search and rescue at sea, military-to-military cooperation and defense reform, and civil emergencies.[111]

Additionally, improved relations with Russia made it possible for Ukraine to move closer to NATO. Indeed, Ukraine had publicly declared its desire to join NATO well before the Orange Revolution, which brought Viktor Yushchenko to power in the country's contested and tumultuous presidential election in late 2004. Although Ukraine had failed to make sufficient reforms under the regime of former President Leonid Kuchma to be considered eligible for the MAP process, NATO did agree in 2002 to a new NATO-Ukraine Action Plan, outlining specific objectives and principles to be met by Ukraine in its effort to move closer to the West.

As noted in earlier chapters, September 11 also moved NATO toward a resolution of the out-of-area debates by demonstrating that, in the twenty-first century, the greatest threats to NATO territory and values would likely stem from outside of Europe. NATO foreign ministers, in fact, agreed at a meeting in Helsinki in May 2002 that "NATO must be able to field forces that can move quickly to wherever they are needed, sustain operations over distance and time, and achieve their objectives...so that NATO can more effectively respond collectively to any threat of aggression against a member state."[112] The new security environment, Robertson subsequently observed, "does not afford us the luxury of fighting theoretical battles about what is 'in' and what is 'out-of-area.' We will have to look at threats functionally, not geographically. We will have to be able to act wherever our security and the safety of our people demand action."[113] At Prague, the Allies affirmed the Helsinki decision, stating in the final summit declaration that in order for NATO "to carry out the full range of its missions," it would need to "be able to field forces that can move quickly to wherever they are needed, upon decision by the North Atlantic Council, to sustain operations over distance and time, including in an environment where they might be faced with nuclear, biological, and chemical threats, and to achieve their objectives."[114] Months later, NATO undertook it first true out-of-area military operation when the Allies agreed on April 16, 2003, to take command responsibility for the ISAF in Afghanistan.

Conclusion

Although the ISAF mission was not enthusiastically embraced by all Allies, the events of September 11 had prompted an important shift, not in the nature of NATO's post–Cold War mission, but rather in its scope. Projecting stability could no longer be limited to Europe, given the global threats the Allies now faced, and such a mission would require both political and military means. Moreover, as evidenced by developments at the Prague Summit, the Bush administration now viewed the fulfillment of Europe whole and free as not only a prescription for internal stability within Europe. It also constituted a means of bolstering the Alliance's ability to address new external threats.

As the Allies moved beyond Prague, however, tensions over the war in Afghanistan and the Bush administration's determination to press ahead with a war in Iraq even in the absence of support from long-term NATO allies, including France and Germany, generated serious questions about whether the Allies truly shared a common conception of security that extended beyond Europe. Prague had affirmed that NATO remained committed to fulfilling its vision of a more democratic and unified Europe and perhaps even to improving the Alliance's military capabilities, but post-Prague developments would now raise troubling questions about Alliance solidarity and the strength of NATO's political dimension.

CHAPTER 5

"Bruised but Resolute"?: The Impact of Afghanistan and Iraq

Perhaps no event cast greater doubt on NATO's continued relevance than a decision taken by France, Germany, and Belgium in February 2003 to block Alliance preparations for the defense of Turkey. As it prepared for war in Iraq, the Bush administration had requested under Article 4 of the NATO Treaty that the Alliance make such preparations, given concerns that Turkey could conceivably be drawn into a wider war.[1] Although the crisis was eventually resolved by moving the decision to NATO's Defense Planning Committee where France does not have a vote, the event raised serious questions about the credibility of NATO's Article 5 security guarantee—the bedrock of all Alliance commitments. Prior to his departure from NATO in December 2003, former Secretary General Lord Robertson remarked that, while NATO "did defend Turkey after eleven days of dithering...it was all an unnecessary indulgence which must never be repeated."[2] The U.S. Ambassador to NATO, R. Nicholas Burns, went further, suggesting that the event constituted a "near death" experience for NATO.[3] Although Burns necessarily remained an optimist, characterizing NATO in a March 2003 *Wall Street Journal Europe* op/ed as "bruised but resolute," many commentators expressed considerable alarm over the deterioration in U.S.–European relations.[4] Former U.S. National Security Adviser Brent Scowcroft even went so far as to call the troubled state of transatlantic relations "the single most serious security threat in the world today."[5]

Perhaps most troubling were suggestions that the Alliance suffers not only from the loss of a single, commonly agreed-upon threat and outdated military capabilities, but also from a values or cultural gap that was eroding its foundation as a community of states committed to defending the values enshrined in the preamble to the original Washington Treaty: "democracy, individual liberty, and the rule of law."[6] At the heart of this debate are questions about the very essence of NATO. Has the Alliance become a mere talking shop or perhaps a regional peace-keeping organization, sustained by rules and procedures developed over many years aimed at achieving interoperability among NATO forces? Can the liberal democratic values so frequently invoked as NATO's foundation during the 1990s continue to sustain a sense of collective identity and common purpose among the Allies? Or will the dissolution of the Soviet threat ultimately prove fatal as many scholars continue to predict?

This chapter suggests that the most difficult and consequential issue is not whether NATO remains credible as a military alliance, although this is by no means an irrelevant concern. The critical issue is whether NATO continues to exist as a genuine political community, bound together by a common vision for the future, including a consensus on the meaning of security in the twenty-first century. Contrary to the skeptics' predictions, NATO's demise has never been inevitable. Indeed, the Allies have made remarkable progress since the early 1990s in transforming NATO to confront the challenges of the post–Cold War era, beginning with the effort to overcome Cold War divisions in Europe and extend liberal democratic values eastward. NATO's ability to survive in a post–September 11 world, however, will depend on a recognition by leaders on both sides of the Atlantic that NATO survived the Cold War, not simply because it retained secondary functions that were not specific to the Soviet threat. NATO survived because the United States led a concerted effort to enhance NATO's political dimension through the adoption of what was an essentially *political* rather than military mission. The desire to construct a Europe "whole and free" derived from a recognition that the zone of stability established in Western Europe during the Cold War years could not survive if the unfolding security vacuum and potential for instability along NATO's periphery were not addressed. Although the mission was indeed Euro-centric, it was, at the time, outward-looking in so far as the focus was on enlarging what former U.S. Ambassador to NATO Robert Hunter termed the European "civil space."[7]

Completing Europe whole and free remains an important project. In the wake of September 11, however, it no longer suffices as NATO's political mission. The events of that day revealed clearly that, in an increasingly globalized world, security can no longer be understood in purely regional terms. It is today, inescapably, a global enterprise. What NATO needs now is an enlarged political mission designed to address new threats posed, not simply by terrorism and weapons of mass destruction, but also by the political and economic conditions beyond the borders of Europe that fuel terrorist activity and potentially threaten the very civilization NATO was designed to preserve.

Invoking Article 5

NATO's unprecedented invocation of Article 5 on September 12, 2001— a decision taken without any encouragement from the United States— marked a moment of remarkable solidarity between the United States and its European allies. As it prepared for a subsequent war in Afghanistan, however, the Bush administration let it be known that it did not intend to rely on NATO, but would look to "different coalitions in different parts of the world."[8] Indeed, one Pentagon official, when asked about the role NATO would play, reportedly quipped, "NATO? Keep the myth alive."[9]

Much of Europe interpreted Washington's response as a slap in the face. As one newspaper columnist put it, "When the immediate expressions of solidarity after the attacks were met with a U.S. determination to pick its own allies, the result was a more fundamental disenchantment than many in Washington appreciate."[10] Former U.S. Department of State spokesman James P. Rubin similarly observed that the Bush administration's "'don't call us, we'll call you' message led many Europeans to conclude that NATO was no longer valued by the Americans."[11]

The development that ultimately led to what Ronald D. Asmus described as "a spectacular political trainwreck across the Atlantic," however, was the Bush administration's determination to go to war in Iraq even without the support of major European allies, including both France and Germany.[12] The resulting tensions became abundantly evident in the dustup that took place over NATO's defense preparations for Turkey. The U.S. Ambassador to NATO, R. Nicholas Burns, considered the development so potentially damaging to the credibility of NATO's collective defense clause that he personally reassured those states invited to join the Alliance at Prague of the United States' firm commitment to Article 5.[13] Diplomats from NATO's newest member states also considered the development very serious. One even acknowledged that it was cause for some "second thoughts about the alliance."[14] Burns was equally disturbed by the decision of France, Belgium, Germany, and Luxembourg to hold a mini-summit in April 2003 to discuss European defense cooperation, including the need for a European Defense and Security Union that could operate independently of NATO. Derisively termed the "bon-bon," or "chocolate-makers" summit, the meeting was widely interpreted as an effort to construct a counterweight to the United States and, ultimately, to undermine NATO. The United States and other Allies also understood a proposal for an independent European Union (EU) planning headquarters in the Brussels suburb of Tervuren as an effort to duplicate NATO structures.[15] Burns, in fact, called the plans "the most serious threat to the future of NATO."[16] Similarly, U.S. Secretary of State Colin

Powell told NATO foreign ministers that the United States could not accept independent EU structures that duplicate existing NATO capabilities."[17] As *The Economist* explained, the United States was "alarmed as much by the way the proposal came about as by its content: the four, all skeptics of the Iraq war, cooked it up...when tempers [over Iraq] were still running high."[18] Just as unsettling was the group's success in co-opting British Prime Minister Tony Blair, who met with French President Jacques Chirac in November 2003 and threw his support behind the creation of a common European defense force, although he reportedly opposed the Teruven headquarters and convinced Bush that the EU's defense plans would not undermine NATO.[19] By December 2003, the European Union had agreed to the creation of a small operations planning cell at the EU military staff headquarters to be used for EU missions independent of NATO.[20] NATO and the European Union also agreed, however, that the EU headquarters would contain a NATO military liaison component and that the EU would maintain a planning cell at Supreme Headquarters Allied Powers Europe—NATO's military headquarters—to be used for operations carried out with NATO or under the "Berlin Plus" rules agreed to by the EU and NATO in March 2003.[21]

From the perspective of some commentators, the new planning cell was not necessarily a direct challenge to NATO, but rather an "insurance policy" against declining U.S. interest in Europe—a fear exacerbated by suggestions that the Bush administration had come to view NATO as little more than a "toolbox" for its coalitions of the willing.[22] Indeed, while Blair insisted that he would "never put at risk NATO," he also observed in October 2003 that "there are going to be circumstances, we have them now in Macedonia, where America for one reason or another does not want to be involved."[23] Even so, the EU decisions raised legitimate questions about the extent to which European governments were committed to the transatlantic relationship and whether constructing a counterweight to the United States was indeed one of their goals.

A growing belief that the Allies now held divergent perceptions of the principal security threats they faced served only to heighten those suspicions. Indeed, as evidenced by intra-alliance tensions over Iraq, the Allies were divided over both the seriousness of the threat posed by Saddam Hussein and how to deal with it. As Michael Ignatieff explained it, "The U.S. saw the threat through the lens of the terrorist attacks of September 11, 2001 and decided that any risk, however low, of weapons development and transfer by the Hussein regime was unacceptable."[24] Timothy Garton Ash also took note of the impact of Iraq on threat perceptions, observing in mid-2003 that, during the Cold War it was Berlin that had "always felt itself to be more directly threatened than New York: now it's the other way around."[25] Ironically, it was September 11—a date that had for a short while generated remarkable solidarity among the

Allies—that many commentators now took to be the pivotal event in the deterioration of the transatlantic relationship. Indeed, Garton Ash and others have suggested that there are two 9/11's relevant to understanding the acrimony that characterized U.S.–European relations in 2003. For Americans that date is September 11, 2001; for Europeans who write the date before the month, the pivotal date is November 9, 1989, the date on which the Berlin Wall symbolically came down, paving the way for the reunification of Germany and the extension of the European Union project to the whole of Europe.[26] While the European Allies entered the twenty-first century focused on completing the new Europe—a project made possible by the events of 1989—the United States, jolted by the events of September 11, turned its attention away from Europe toward global threats.[27] As William Drozdiak, then executive director of the Transatlantic Center in Brussels, explained it in an op/ed piece in the *Washington Post* in September 2003,

> While Americans feel acutely vulnerable in the global war against terrorism and no longer enjoy the sense of protection once afforded by two oceans and a vast land mass, Europeans feel perhaps more secure than at any time in their history. For four centuries, every generation of young Germans and French prepared to wage war against each other. That prospect is now simply unthinkable with the waning of the Balkan wars and rapid integration of Russia with the West, Europeans generally believe they face no serious security threat—unless they are dragged into conflict elsewhere by the United States.[28]

One of the most pessimistic assessments of transatlantic relations came from American scholar Robert Kagan, who, in an oft-cited article published in *Policy Review* in June 2002, provocatively asserted that "on major strategic and international questions today, Americans are from Mars and Europeans are from Venus. They agree on little and understand one another less and less." Kagan further argued that this "transatlantic divide" was no "transitory" state of affairs. Rather, the factors underpinning it were "deep, long in development, and likely to endure."[29] Kagan, however, identified the source of the divide, not as the events of September 11, but rather the substantial gap in military power that had evolved between the United States and its allies.

Differences over the actual use of military power were also highlighted by the Bush Doctrine, which advocated what Bush administration officials termed "preemptive action," taken unilaterally if necessary to address the threat posed by the nexus of terrorism and weapons of mass destruction. The doctrine was at least partly responsible for the French scholar Dominique Moisi's assertion in late 2003 that Europe had come to regard the United States as a revolutionary rather than a status quo power—a label that had served to differentiate both the United States and Europe from the Soviet Union during the Cold War. "Today," Moisi argued, "it is the U.S. West that is revisionist, while Europe's West remains mired in introspection and is mistrustful of change."[30]

Looking at the divide from the other side of the Atlantic, Thomas Friedman expressed astonishment that Europeans could view "a dominant America" as "more threatening to global stability than Saddam's tyranny." "The more I hear this," he wrote, "the more I wonder whether we are witnessing something larger than a passing storm over Iraq. Are we witnessing the beginning of the end of 'the West' as we have known it—a coalition of U.S.-led, like-minded allies, bound by core shared values and strategic threats?"[31]

Indeed, much of the commentary published in late 2003 suggested that "the cultural basis of the transatlantic 'security community'" was "wearing thin" or questioned whether the West continued to exist as a relatively coherent cultural entity.[32] Arguments that a values gap was contributing to the deterioration of the transatlantic alliance frequently included references to long-standing and well-recognized cultural differences between the United States and Europe on issues such as religion, the death penalty, and gun ownership.[33] Others, however, suggested that the rift had less to do with divergent cultural attitudes and values than it did with particular personalities or "diplomatic ineptness on one or both sides of the Atlantic."[34] Indeed, at least one scholar questioned whether the United States and Europe truly faced a "value gap" or whether the true source of tension was a "Bush gap," defined as "unease among some European leaders and their populations, not with America, but with 'Americanism' as it is expressed and practiced" by the Bush administration.[35] Even former Spanish Prime Minister Jose Maria Aznar, arguably one of Bush's most sympathetic allies with respect to the war in Iraq, said of the President, "The combination of being a Republican, of being an emperor, a Texan and outspoken is a really bad mix. To be politically correct in Europe, people cannot digest the mix that is George Bush as I have described him. They are allergic to that." Although Aznar also suggested that Europeans are "too lackadaisical and in too much of a comfort zone or in denial" regarding the dangers of global terrorism and weapons of mass destruction, his remarks captured well a widespread view in Europe and even among some Americans that the Bush administration's conduct of foreign policy was arrogant and dismissive of the concerns of its European allies.[36]

Importantly though, differences over the Bush administration's Iraq policy existed, not just between the United States and Europe, but also within Europe itself. U.S. Secretary of Defense Donald Rumsfeld had sought to highlight those differences in the now infamous news conference in which he characterized France and Germany as "old Europe."[37] Within a week of those remarks Hungary, Poland, the Czech

Republic, Spain, Portugal, Italy, Britain, and Denmark issued their letter insisting on unity in calling for the disarmament of the Iraqi regime followed by the Vilnius Group's open letter just days later. Although the second letter was clearly influenced by the fact that its members were all NATO aspirants, who recognized that U.S. support was critical to their membership bids,[38] French President Jacques Chirac proved unable to hide his irritation over these so-called statements of "eight" and "ten." He declared the Central and Eastern European signatories "not very well behaved" and suggested that they had "missed an important opportunity to keep quiet." Chirac even went so far as to say that if Romania and Bulgaria had "wanted to diminish their chances of joining Europe, they could not have found a better way."[39]

At the same time, Bush was pursuing his own "divide and rule" strategy by exploiting tensions within Europe to the administration's advantage. "Among the most important geopolitical shifts of the past two years," Philip Stephens of the *Financial Times* wrote in May 2003, "has been the administration's judgment that its interest now lies in dividing rather than uniting Europe."[40] Indeed, diplomats representing those states invited to join the Alliance at Prague conceded that tensions between the United States and Western Europe had caused them to feel torn between the EU and NATO in ways that they had not foreseen and clearly did not appreciate. As one such diplomat observed, NATO and EU membership had originally been understood as one goal, premised on the coherence of the Western community.[41] A Polish government official put it this way: "We don't want to be called new Europe or the American Trojan horse. We don't want the West to be split."[42] Timothy Garton Ash also observed that, while his "old friends in the post-dissident political elites of Central and Eastern Europe" were "generally more pro-American than their French or German counterparts" and "grateful to the United States for its support in their struggle for freedom. . . . their message to Washington, on the one side, and to Paris and Berlin on the other" was "'Please don't ask us to choose between you!'"[43]

Indeed, both Bush and Chirac could be justly accused of using the NATO and EU enlargement processes to advance their own goals, in the process undermining the Europe whole and free these institutions were intended to support. Rather than serving as vehicles with which to promote European integration, NATO and the EU effectively became weapons in the escalating rift over U.S. policy in Iraq. This was particularly evident in the attempt by France, Germany, and Belgium to use NATO in the case of Turkey to thwart the Bush administration's Iraq policy. At the same time, the Bush administration's approach to dealing with Europe likely contributed to the push for a more independent European foreign and security policy. Indeed, Joshua Spero and Sean Kay suggested in August 2003 that "Bush's European strategy" had backfired to the detriment of "new Europe" and was now "unraveling the key stabilizing bridge between the East and West that the German-Polish reconciliation established during the early 1990s and NATO's enlargement codified in 1999."[44]

The United States even provoked some consternation among new allies in Central and Eastern Europe by proving slow to reward those who had solidly supported U.S. policy in the Middle East. For example, despite Poland's willingness to take command of one of the security sectors in Iraq in 2003 at the request of the Bush administration, the White House subsequently demonstrated little flexibility on the issue of visa requirements for Polish citizens traveling to the United States—a policy that was deeply unpopular in Poland. Additionally, the administration waited months before finally waiving sanctions automatically imposed on military assistance to six of the Prague invitees because of their refusal to sign agreements with the United States exempting U.S. citizens from the jurisdiction of the International Criminal Court. This occurred despite the fact that all had actively supported the United States in Iraq at some peril to their European Union bids.[45]

The Bush administration's tendency to favor some allies over others also contributed to a growing sense that the United States now viewed NATO as little more than a toolbox from which it could pull support for its various military ventures. As Josef Joffe put it as early as September 2002, the NATO "dedicated to the Three Musketeers' principle of 'all for one, and one for all' is being replaced by 'NATO II'....a collection of nation-states from which Washington draws coalition partners ad hoc."[46] A former U.S. Foreign Service officer even suggested that the United States' vision of NATO was no longer of an alliance that provided for European security, but rather one in which Europeans were required "to serve as auxiliaries in distant enterprises of questionable benefit to Europe."[47]

Not all, however, were convinced that NATO's undoing as a genuine alliance had to do with the policies of particular individuals or governments. *Ad hoc* coalitions are the wave of the future and "not specific to America," Francois Heisbourg argued, because threats have become more diverse and more "fluid" than was true during the Cold War. Heisbourg added that NATO was "particularly challenged" as an alliance because it "has ceased to be a war machine."[48]

NATO Goes "Out of Area"

Although NATO faces enormous challenges and there are good reasons to be concerned about its unraveling as both a political and a military entity, characterizations of the Alliance as a "relic" of the past do not square with the fact that NATO is today busier than at any time in its history. NATO maintains peacekeeping/stabilization forces in Kosovo and in Afghanistan, where the Allies initially took over responsibility for the International Security Assistance Force (ISAF) from Germany and the Netherlands on April 16, 2003, just two months after the crisis over Turkey. A little over a month later on May 21, 2003, NATO also agreed to provide logistical support to Poland in order that it might fulfill its command responsibilities in Iraq. As suggested earlier, these decisions were significant in that they affirmed NATO's newfound willingness to conduct military missions "out of area," meaning, in this case, outside of Europe. "Going out of area for the first time," Robertson remarked in late 2003, "is not the mark of an Alliance about to go out of business."[49]

Although France had initially resisted the ISAF decision, it constituted a precedent that will almost certainly not be reversed. In fact, Chirac, himself, told Jim Hoagland of the *Washington Post* in early 2004, "You have to be realistic in a changing world. We have updated our vision, which once held that NATO had geographic limits. The idea of a regional NATO no longer exists, as the alliance's involvement in Afghanistan demonstrates." Chirac even went so far as to suggest that France was "not against a role in Iraq for NATO if it comes to that."[50]

Since then, NATO has expanded its involvement in Afghanistan incrementally, agreeing in late 2003 to take its first steps outside of Kabul by assuming responsibility for Provincial Reconstruction Teams[51] in the northern and western regions of the country.[52] In December 2005, NATO agreed to deploy, beginning in May 2006, an additional 6,000 troops, thereby raising the total number of troops assigned to ISAF to 15,000 and giving the Alliance a security presence in approximately 75 percent of Afghanistan. The deployment also served to bring NATO forces for the first time into the less stable south where they are more likely to confront insurgents.[53] In October 2006, NATO again expanded its operations, this time assuming control of approximately 12,000 U.S. troops in the eastern part of the country and extending ISAF for the first time to the whole of Afghanistan. By late 2006, following additional troop contributions from participating states, ISAF numbered nearly 33,000 troops from 37 states.[54]

A World Without NATO?

NATO's military missions in Afghanistan, Iraq, and Darfur not only exemplify a vision of NATO's role that is far less Euro-centric than that which prevailed during the 1990s; they also beg the question of who would shoulder such responsibilities in NATO's absence.[55] As Hans Binnendijk and Richard Kugler noted in late 2003, the war in Afghanistan had required peacekeeping, stabilization, and reconstruction efforts aimed at preventing the Taliban from regaining power, and NATO had provided the framework for the necessary multilateral cooperation. "If NATO vanishes," they observed, "much of this cooperation would be lost, and terrorists would be given a new lease on life."[56] In a similar vein, Robertson attempted to explain NATO's decisions to go into Iraq and Afghanistan so soon after the debacle over Turkey by suggesting that Alliance members had "peered into the abyss of a world without the transatlantic alliance and recoiled."[57] Indeed, NATO's delinquent, but ultimately successful involvement in Bosnia, as well as its decision to intervene in Kosovo in the spring of 1999 served to highlight the paralysis of the United Nations, which even today has failed to achieve any consensus on intrastate conflicts or the issue of humanitarian intervention. Appeals by the UN for NATO to provide logistical support to African Union peacekeepers in Darfur and to contribute to an eventual UN peacekeeping mission there only bolster the point that, as a military institution, NATO remains in demand.

Despite the obvious and significant deficiencies in its current military capabilities, including considerable difficulties deploying adequate troops and equipment to Afghanistan, NATO does have well-established rules and procedures permitting the interoperability of its forces, and NATO members conduct joint training exercises, which regularly include Partnership for Peace forces. NATO's integrated military command also makes it particularly well suited to conducting the sort of multinational peacekeeping operations that have proven so necessary in the post–Cold War and post–September 11 worlds. As NATO Secretary General Jaap de Hoop Scheffer put it, "The reason that NATO is under pressure to do more is simple." "No other organisation can generate, deploy, command and sustain large, multinational military operations like NATO can. Very simply, NATO's capability makes it a unique resource for the Euro-Atlantic community."[58]

NATO's "integrated military structure and the practices of military co-operation it [has] fostered" are, in fact, frequently referenced by scholars attempting to explain NATO's longevity beyond the Cold War.[59] These capabilities were not specific to the Soviet threat and therefore permitted NATO to remain relevant even in its absence. Anthony Forster and William Wallace, for example, observed in *Survival* in late 2001 that "multinational forces under NATO command in Bosnia and Kosovo, using NATO procedures and doctrine" had "demonstrated levels of professionalism and effectiveness" that contrasted "sharply with UN forces in Sierra Leone and Rwanda.[60] Similarly the *Washington Post* observed in August 2003:

> The decision to shift the international force in Afghanistan from an ad hoc "coalition of the willing" to a full-fledged NATO command also reflects an important shift in American understanding. Recent tensions

notwithstanding, over the past half-century the alliance has worked out
methods to transfer commands smoothly and share responsibilities among
countries. More professional than the United Nations and with potentially
more soldiers to draw upon than the U.S. armed forces acting alone. NATO,
not a rotating set of random commanders, provides the right structure to
run multinational peacekeeping or military forces. In time, it might prove to
be the right force for Iraq as well.[61]

The German newspaper *Die Welt* proclaimed in mid-2003 that NATO was
the "only organization that is capable of meeting complex and simultane-
ous crises."

> It was NATO that created stability in the Balkans, which was devastated by
> civil wars. It was the alliance that paved the way for a gradual takeover of
> the stabilizing missions by the European Union. In the case of Afghanistan,
> NATO proved to be the only organization that is in a position to plan and
> carry out multinational operations over a longer period. It is the logical con-
> sequence that the alliance will take on this task also in Iraq.[62]

To date, NATO has demonstrated no inclination to assume responsibility
for a stabilization mission in Iraq, and continued inadequacies in terms
of both its military capabilities and the political will to use the Alliance
in a more robust fashion suggest that these testaments to its utility are
somewhat overblown.

Even so, as early as mid-2003, it appeared that even the Bush
administration now had some regrets over not having made greater use
of the Alliance in the months after September 11 and desired to heal the
rift with old Europe.[63] For example, in an article published in *Foreign
Affairs* in early 2004, Colin Powell acknowledged "differences with some
of our oldest and most valued NATO allies," but he also emphasized that
these were "differences among friends. "The transatlantic partnership,"
he observed "is based so firmly on common interests and values that neither feuding personalities nor occasional divergent perceptions can derail
it. We have new friends and old friends alike in Europe. They are all, in
the end, best friends."[64] Robertson also told reporters before departing
Brussels in December 2003 that he had witnessed, on the part of the
United States, a "big shift in attitudes, especially to organisations like
NATO."[65] Irritated by the refusal of some members to support an increase
in NATO's budget, Robertson also remarked that "it is not the U.S. who
does not want to pay more. The U.S. is now fully behind NATO."[66]
Another NATO diplomat agreed, observing that the Bush administration
had been "a bit self-obsessed" after September 11, but had now come
"to realise they cannot be so cavalier with their friends." He also added,
however, that the United States was "laying down the gauntlet, challenging the alliance to prove its worth."[67] Even the Pentagon, NATO diplomats suggest, came to realize that it couldn't afford to marginalize

NATO because it needed the Alliance's support in both Afghanistan and Iraq.[68] Indeed, Rumsfeld, not known to be a staunch NATO supporter, even during the Cold War years, observed during a NATO defense ministers' meeting and training exercise in October 2003 that the Alliance had made significant progress over the previous three years, citing as evidence NATO's first out-of-area missions and the creation of the NATO Response Force.[69]

The Bush administration, with strong congressional backing, also stepped up its efforts to involve NATO in Iraq.[70] During a visit to Brussels in December 2003, Powell indicated that the United States was "looking forward to consulting with our friends and allies for an enhanced NATO role in the participation of the Iraqi mission" and advised that the contingency planning for such a mission should begin.[71] He also suggested that NATO might follow the precedent set in Afghanistan and take over the Polish mission in Iraq, a troop presence of approximately 9,500 soldiers from seventeen states.[72]

Although neither Robertson nor his successor, de Hoop Scheffer, would close the door on Iraq,[73] it had also become clear that, for most Allies, the priority was Afghanistan, where some feared NATO might already be overextended.[74] Robertson was particularly frustrated, prior to his departure from NATO, over the Alliance's failure to get adequate troops or helicopters on the ground in Afghanistan.[75] Failure there, he warned in early December 2003, "would not just be a disaster for the Afghan people and a severe blow to the international fight against terrorism. It would also undermine NATO's credibility, not just in Afghanistan but in each and every area of Alliance business."[76]

"Capabilities, Capabilities, Capabilities"

Indeed, throughout his final year as secretary general, Robertson continued to voice what he termed his "clarion call" of "capabilities, capabilities, capabilities," focusing in particular on NATO's lack of deployable troops.[77] Of NATO's "1.4 million regular soldiers under arms in Europe and Canada and another one million or so reserves," he complained, "the vast majority are at present useless for the kind of missions we are now mounting."[78] NATO troops "need to be usable in circumstances where they would have to go very quickly to a troubled spot with the right equipment, and to be able to be supplied when they get there."[79] Robertson was particularly frustrated by the Allies' failure to produce adequate troops and equipment in Afghanistan. Indeed, he dismissed the need for an independent defense planning cell in Brussels in November 2003, declaring, "What I really want is more helicopters in Kabul."[80] He later added, "only when the Europeans have woken up to [the reality of too many unusable troops] and made more of their forces deployable will they be able to have anything like the same clout as the Americans."[81]

Broad gaps in military technology and power projection capabilities between the United States and Europe had, in fact, created an unequal distribution of labor, characterized by some as one in which the United States "does the cooking and Europe the washing up."[82] Arguably, this was true in the cases of both Kosovo and Afghanistan where the bulk of the fighting fell to the high-tech forces of the United States and Britain, leaving the Europeans to bear the brunt of the peacekeeping responsibilities. Those experiences led Timothy Garton Ash to counsel that "Europe needs to do more of the cooking; America, more of the washing up."[83]

As noted in the previous chapter, the NATO Response Force was itself grounded on a belief that such a division of responsibilities was not conducive to a genuine spirit of alliance among NATO members.[84] As has been well demonstrated in the cases of Afghanistan and Iraq, however, both the United States and Europe need also to improve their ability to conduct peacekeeping and postconflict stabilization missions.[85] Although some NATO critics have focused on NATO's missions in Bosnia, Kosovo, Macedonia, and Afghanistan as evidence that the Alliance has become little more than a peacekeeping organization, unable to conduct high-intensity warfare, it is worth noting that the capacity to do peacekeeping/stabilization missions is hardly peripheral to the security challenges facing NATO today. To suggest otherwise ignores the realities of a post–Cold War world in which the vast majority of conflicts have been intrastate in nature and in which failed states are increasingly recognized as magnets for terrorists and a host of other potential security threats. As Senator Richard Lugar observed in 2003,

> We have seen the consequences of allowing failed states such as Afghanistan and Somalia to fester. Successful "nation-building" must be an important objective for U.S. policymakers and their NATO partners. Iraq and Afghanistan must serve as models of how to make a sustained commitment to peace as part of the broader war on terror. Rehabilitating chaotic states is a complicated and uncertain business. At a minimum, it will require a broad range of military and peacekeeping skills, international legitimacy and more resources than the U.S. can comfortably muster alone. In short, this vital endeavor will require NATO if it is to have the best chance of success.[86]

Similarly former Swedish Prime Minister Carl Bildt wrote in the *Financial Times* in early 2004 that "the problems of fragile, failing or failed states have rightly attracted new attention in the post–September 11 world. The marriage between ancient hatreds and modern technologies makes indifference to chaos and disorder increasingly dangerous to us all." Bildt even went so far as to suggest that, while NATO's new rapid reaction force will be "certainly useful at times, forces for long-endurance stability operations will be even more in demand. That is where we really need a revolution in military affairs—the high technology enemies are mostly gone."[87]

Indeed, based on NATO's experience with assembling forces on an *ad hoc* basis in Bosnia, Kosovo, and Afghanistan, including considerable difficulties in meeting the requirements of the ISAF mission, Binnendijk and Kugler, the architects of the NATO Response Force (NRF), also proposed in September 2004 that the NRF be complemented by the creation of a NATO Stabilization and Reconstruction Force (SRF). In contrast to the NRF, a SRF would "consist of flexible and modular national forces... mostly ground forces, that could be assembled to generate the necessary mix of capabilities for S&R operations." As Binnendijk and Kugler envisioned it, however, such a force would not necessarily be separate from NATO combat forces, but, rather, capable of working closely with them "in situations where a mix of hostilities, war-termination, and peace establishment is taking place." The proposal also recognized the need to overcome deficiencies witnessed in NATO's stabilization operations in Bosnia, Kosovo, and Afghanistan in establishing the conditions necessary to support multiethnic, democratic societies, or "nation-building."[88] Indeed, ethnic tensions have remained high in both Bosnia and Kosovo, despite NATO's success in stabilizing these areas. Progress on the establishment of a stabilization and reconstruction force has been slow, however, partly due to U.S. concerns that it might serve to diminish European participation in the NATO Response Force. Additionally, some EU members have resisted a NATO stabilization and reconstruction force because they favor the construction of such a capability within the context of the European Security and Defense Policy and see a NATO force as a potential competitor. The absence of a strong, cooperative relationship between NATO and the EU also makes it difficult for the two institutions to engage in joint planning in this area.[89] U.S. support for such a capability appears to be growing, however. The Department of Defense in its 2006 Quadrennial Defense Review stated that it supported "efforts to create a NATO stabilization and reconstruction capability" and the issue was reportedly proposed by the United States as an agenda item for the Riga Summit in late 2006.[90]

A New Political Mission?

While there is no disputing the fact that NATO must continue to develop and enhance military capabilities suited to the threats of a post–September 11 world, the principal lesson stemming from the discord that erupted within the Alliance between 2001 and 2003 is this: If NATO is to be viable in the twenty-first century, it will require further political as well as military transformation. NATO may be only "bruised," as Burns suggested in early 2003, but it can be "resolute" only on behalf of a larger strategic vision that addresses the principal threats confronting the United States and Europe today. While many NATO skeptics have focused largely on the deficiencies in NATO's military capabilities, NATO's real problem is ultimately a political one. Indeed, no amount of military resources will save NATO if there is no agreement as to how, when, and where those capabilities should be used. Moreover, in the absence of such agreement, the Allies have little incentive to produce the necessary resources.

Ironically, despite NATO's almost exclusive focus on enhancing its political component during the 1990s, that dimension of the Alliance has been neglected in the post–September 11 period. As one long-time member of NATO's international staff observed in 2003, NATO's ventures outside of Europe had at that point been largely tactical moves, stemming from a recognition that these situations would benefit from NATO's capabilities.[91] It is not yet clear, however, that they reflect a larger, shared strategic vision such as the commitment to constructing Europe whole and free that NATO embraced in the early 1990s.[92] The absence of such a vision is troubling because NATO has never been an exclusively military alliance. As Strobe Talbott put it just before the Prague Summit, NATO's "military and political functions have always been intertwined...even at its inception NATO was about more than just banding together against a common enemy; it was also about creating, consolidating, and expanding a zone of safety within which common values and cooperative institutions could prosper."[93]

Indeed, the resources that NATO devoted to its mission of Europe whole and free—while largely political—demonstrated NATO's potential when armed with a clear strategic vision. Moreover, the new institutions, partnerships, and processes created in pursuit of Europe whole and free are highly relevant to the post–September 11 world. What is lacking, however, is the clarity of purpose that first generated these new initiatives during the 1990s.

What NATO needs now is an enlarged political mission that looks beyond Europe to those regions from which contemporary threats are most likely to emanate—threats that endanger not only NATO's territory, but also its values. This is not to suggest that the task of constructing Europe whole and free has been fulfilled. To the contrary, despite historic progress since the early 1990s, much work remains. Having reaffirmed that "NATO's door remains open," the Alliance continues to utilize its Membership Action Plan (MAP) to encourage and support liberal democratic reforms in Albania, Croatia, and Macedonia—all of which hope to be invited to join the Alliance in 2008, when NATO is expected to launch a third round of post–Cold War enlargement.[94] While not yet MAP members, Ukraine and Georgia could conceivably still become formal aspirants. As noted in Chapter 2, the Allies also remain committed to integrating the remaining Balkan states (Bosnia/Herzegovina, Serbia and Montenegro) into "Euro-Atlantic structures," assuming the commitment of those states to implementing further political, economic, and military reforms; regional cooperation; and "full cooperation with the International Criminal Tribunal for the former Yugoslavia" in bringing to justice all indicted war criminals.[95] Since turning its stabilization mission over to a European Union force beginning in late 2004, NATO has also maintained a military headquarters in Sarajevo, in part to assist Bosnia/Herzegovina with defense reform and other reforms necessary to join the Partnership for Peace.

As is discussed further in Chapter 6, NATO has also been exploring ways to foster further reform in Central Asia and the Caucasus states, several of which have shown interest in closer ties to NATO or possibly even full NATO membership.[96] As Ronald Asmus has observed, "in a post–September 11 world, the United States can no longer afford to treat these countries as a strategic backwater on Europe's periphery and must instead recognize their growing and critical role in the war on terrorism. . . . Locking in reform and a pro-Western orientation in these countries is the logical next phase in the Euro-Atlantic integration process."[97]

Continued outreach by NATO toward Russia will also remain an important component of expanding the European civil space. Although NATO-Russia relations improved significantly after September 11, recent indications of a lack of commitment on the part of the Putin government to liberal democratic principles and practices, coupled with its growing interference in the affairs of many of the former Soviet republics, raise troubling questions about whether Russia is on a path that is consistent with the liberal European security order the Allies have envisioned since the early 1990s.[98] In short, the vision of a Europe whole and free *and at peace* remains the Alliance's "greatest strategic objective."[99]

No longer, however, can Europe be whole and free *and* at peace with a strategy that focuses inward on Europe and ignores the many sources of instability simmering along NATO's new borders. Indeed, the absence of such a strategy has generated on both sides of the Atlantic a growing recognition that NATO's long-term future is indeed at risk. In May 2003, for example, a group of prominent academics and policy makers from both the United States and Europe issued a statement calling on Americans and Europeans to work together toward "a common agenda that would include the Israeli-Palestinian conflict, Iran, terrorism, and weapons of mass destruction."[100] The statement reflected a view widely shared on both sides of the Atlantic: NATO's future is likely to be decided in the Middle East.[101] As Ivo Daalder, Nicole Gnesotto, and Philip Gordon observe in a volume on U.S.–European strategy toward the Middle East, "no region in the world is remotely as relevant to some of the most important strategic issues of our time—from terrorism, weapons of mass destruction, and energy supplies to immigration, narcotic trafficking, and religious conflict or peace." "It would be an illusion," they argue, "to pretend that the transatlantic alliance can remain healthy if Americans and Europeans are feuding over the issues that matter most to their security."[102] NATO's new Comprehensive Political Guidance, endorsed during the Riga Summit in late 2006, also identifies as the principal threats facing the Alliance for the next 10 to 15 years terrorism and the spread of weapons of mass destruction, as well as "instability due to failed or failing states, regional crises and conflicts, and their causes and effects; the growing availability of sophisticated conventional weaponry; the misuse of emerging technologies; and the disruption of the flow of vital resources."[103]

Yet, as the Iraq war so clearly demonstrated, nowhere have the United States and Europe been more divided than they are over the principal region from which these threats emanate. That reality prompted Timothy Garton Ash to suggest in April 2003 that "the future of the West will be decided in the Middle East." If we care about the West," he asserted, "we need to work out together what to do about the Middle East. For where the threatening Soviet East once united us, the Middle East divides us."[104]

These divisions notwithstanding, NATO has become progressively more involved in the region. In addition to its ongoing military missions in Afghanistan and Iraq, the Alliance has since 1994 maintained a Mediterranean Dialogue which now comprises seven states from the region, as well as a counterterrorist, maritime operation in the Mediterranean known as Operation Active Endeavour, which was launched in late 2001. In 2004, the Allies also unveiled the Istanbul Cooperation Initiative, a new partnership initiative aimed at promoting dialogue and practical cooperation with the "Greater Middle East."

Yet, as the authors of an Atlantic Council policy paper published in September 2004 observed, "even though the strategic center of gravity for the transatlantic alliance has shifted to the Middle East region, the challenge the allies face there has not yet galvanized the kind of strategic dialogue and common response that the threat from Soviet communism forged in earlier decades."[105] In late 2005, the Madrid-based think tank FAES (Foundation for Analysis and Social Studies), headed by former Spanish Prime Minister Jose Maria Aznar, issued a report that went even further, asserting that "NATO no longer discusses important issues, having become just another bureaucratic mechanism that justifies itself by its own existence and by the services its offers its members."[106]

As multiple commentators have observed, however, addressing the key challenges arising from the Middle East will necessarily be as much a political task as it is a military one. As Ronald Asmus has framed the challenge,

> The West needs more than a military campaign plan. It needs an approach that addresses the root causes of these problems by changing the dynamics that produced such monstrous regimes and groups in the first place....Thus, the West must move beyond a strategy of trying to manage a crumbling status quo. Instead, it must actively try to help the region transform itself into a set of societies that can live in peace with one another and that no longer produce ideologies and terrorists who desire to kill in large numbers and who increasingly have access to the technology needed to do so.[107]

At the annual Munich Security Conference in late February 2004, German Foreign Minister Joschka Fischer also emphasized that any common strategy directed at the terrorist threat would necessarily have a strong political component. In his words,

> If we are to win the fight against jihadist terrorism, we will have to take a much broader and further-reaching approach on the Middle East. For behind the new terrorism lies a profound modernisation crisis in many parts of the Islamic Arab world. Our concerted efforts to foster peace and security are doomed to failure if we believe that only security issues matter. They certainly do, but security is a much broader concept in this fight against terrorism; social and cultural modernisation issues, as well as democracy, the rule of law, women's rights and good governance, are of almost even greater importance.[108]

Indeed, the state of NATO's political dimension was very much on the agenda during the 2004 Munich conference. There, U.S. Senator Richard Lugar advised that NATO's upcoming summit, scheduled for Istanbul in June 2004, represented an "opportunity to complete the process of reunifying the Alliance by coming to a political agreement on NATO's role in the Greater Middle East." Political transformation, he submitted, would allow the Allies to complete the work begun at Prague when "NATO launched its military mission for the 21st century."[109] Similarly Hans Binnendijk and Richard Kugler observed that, while NATO does still need new military capabilities as evidenced by the war in Afghanistan, "defense transformation is unlikely to succeed unless political transformation also occurs, and vice versa."[110] The need for a clear strategic vision, in fact, prompted Binnendijk and Kugler to propose the idea of a new Harmel Report in a National Defense University publication in late 2003. As they envisioned it, the report would be drafted by a team of independent European and American thinkers and would "address how the United States and Europe should work together to promote democracy and markets across the Middle East and elsewhere."[111]

German Defense Minister Peter Struck seconded their call, advising that the Allies must continue with dialogue aimed at "defining the political and strategic self-image and the changed role of the Transatlantic Alliance more clearly" and then "lay down the result in a new conceptual document as a foundation for the future of NATO." Like Binnendijk and Kugler, he suggested that such a report could "be commissioned at the Istanbul Summit" and "compiled by selected European and American experts. Its task would be to develop the appreciation of a renewed transatlantic partnership and to determine the role of the Alliance in a changed world." "A NATO which is limited to a 'toolbox' role," Struck warned, "will not be viable."[112] In short, by early 2004, the emerging consensus among NATO supporters was that NATO's continued viability now required a new strategic vision.[113]

The United States, however, was not inclined to support the drafting of a new Harmel Report. While such a report might have served to codify many of the changes that had transpired at NATO since 2001 or at least engaged the Allies in constructive dialogue regarding a new strategic vision, the Bush administration viewed the process as both a potential "marathon" and unnecessary. Rather, the administration had already determined where it wanted to take the Alliance.[114] "NATO's future," Burns pronounced several months prior to Istanbul, "is to look outward to the Greater Middle East to expand security in that arc of countries from South and Central Asia to the Middle East and North Africa—where the new challenges to global peace are rooted."[115] The goal, he further explained, was "long-term change in that vast region," which, "will, over time, whither the twisted roots of terrorism and give the seeds of democracy, civil society and prosperity the soil in which to take root."[116] In February 2004, the Bush administration circulated in Europe a set of ideas aimed at enlisting NATO in the effort to advance the cause of "freedom" in the Middle East. The proposals would set the stage for the Istanbul Summit, which ultimately focused on enhancing NATO's existing partnerships with the Mediterranean Dialogue, Central Asian and Caucasus states, and creating new partnerships with the states of the Greater Middle East.

Arguably, the mission that the Bush administration had proposed for NATO was in keeping with the appeal issued by Timothy Garton Ash in April 2003 that "a more united Europe and a less arrogant United States should work together with all the peoples of the Middle East to do for them what we did with and for the peoples of Middle Europe during the cold war." "This," he said, "can be our trans-Atlantic project for the next generation. Here's how we put the West together again."[117] Indeed, a more democratic, economically prosperous Middle East would not only serve the long-term interests of both the United States and Europe, it could also be construed as an extension of the principles and logic that drove NATO's first post–Cold War political mission: the construction of Europe whole and free. That commitment to projecting stability eastward, including the values on which it was to be grounded, represented a positive political mission around which the Allies could rally. It also kept the United States actively involved in the shaping of post–Cold War Europe. Might a new commitment to projecting stability even farther east and to NATO's south serve as a new rallying point, a common vision to bind the Allies together once again?

During a visit to Washington in January 2004, de Hoop Scheffer had suggested that, given its "successful models in the Mediterranean Dialogue and the Partnership for Peace," NATO did have potential to serve as a forum for discussion of "enhanced outreach to the Middle East."[118] Two weeks later, he posed the question: "If NATO can play its part in helping the countries of the Greater Middle East to reform, as part of a broader international effort, then how could we say no?" Indeed, the Secretary General observed that, "over its first forty years," NATO had "proved to be the most effective guarantor of the security of its members. Over the past fifteen years, the Alliance has demonstrated that it can export security as well."[119] As suggested in the following chapter, however, the Middle East, like Central Asia, poses challenges that NATO did not confront in Central and Eastern Europe. Moreover, given the nature of the threats confronting the Allies today—not all of them confined to the Middle East—it is not clear that such a mission provides the comprehensive strategic mission demanded by an increasingly globalized, post–September 11 world. NATO may have agreed to go out of area, but it is not yet clear how far or under what conditions.

CHAPTER **6**

The Istanbul Summit: A Bridge to the Middle East

Just prior to his departure from Brussels in March 2005, former U.S. Ambassador to NATO R. Nicholas Burns posed the question: "Should not NATO's central motivating purpose now be to help extend the flag of freedom, security and peace to peoples and countries farther south and east?"[1] The question expressed the Bush administration's hope that NATO would come to embrace a broader, less Euro-centric political mission, including a belief that NATO must expand its outreach to the states of the Caucasus, Central Asia, and the Middle East. Accordingly, the focus of NATO's 2004 summit in Istanbul, Turkey, was on enhancing NATO's existing partnerships and extending the partnership model to the Middle East. Indeed, the symbol that NATO utilized for the Istanbul Summit was a bridge—a metaphor the Secretary General put to good use in his remarks surrounding the meeting. Observing that Turkey's strong historical, cultural, and economic ties allowed it to serve as a vital bridge to help project security into the Caucasus and Central Asia, he declared that NATO would now "build bridges to the Mediterranean and the Middle East."[2]

Bridge building was, in fact, a key theme in 2004, and not only with respect to Central Asia and the Middle East. Given the acrimony that had characterized transatlantic relations in 2003, Jaap de Hoop Scheffer asserted that one of his principal priorities for 2004 would be "building bridges across the Atlantic Ocean."[3] The Allies faced "grave threats," he warned, against which they could only "defend in partnership" and "through NATO."[4]

Indeed, at Istanbul, the Bush administration sought to engage the Allies in an effort to project stability beyond the Euro-Atlantic area, beginning with the Central Asian and Caucasus states, but ultimately extending to the Middle East. As suggested earlier, the goal was to focus NATO's attention beyond Europe and to enlist its assets in a broader effort to democratize the Middle East. Although NATO had played an important role in the consolidation of liberal democracy in Central and Eastern Europe, the United States was now pushing an even more ambitious agenda with potentially significant consequences for the Alliance's future.

Indeed, three questions seem relevant here. First, does NATO currently have the capacity to act as a central forum for achieving consensus on a common strategy aimed at advancing liberal democratic principles and practices beyond Europe, including to the "Greater Middle East." Second, given that region's strategic importance to both the United States and Europe, what are the implications for NATO if the Allies fail to agree on a common political strategy for the region? Finally, to what extent does NATO have the capacity to promote liberal democratic values in geographic regions not historically considered to be part of the West?

The Istanbul Initiatives

NATO's decision to renew its emphasis on partnership at Istanbul included first an effort to strengthen the Euro-Atlantic Partnership [i.e., Euro-Atlantic Partnership Council (EAPC) and Partnership for Peace (PfP)] though a "special focus" on engagement with "Partners in the strategically important regions of the Caucasus and Central Asia."[5] Toward this end, the Allies agreed to send two liaison officers to the region—one to be assigned to the Caucasus and the other to Central Asia—and to designate a NATO special representative for the region. In the words of one commentator, the summit "represented a debut of sorts for the Caucasus and Central Asia, largely ignored by the alliance until now."[6] Although all of the Caucasus and Central Asian states minus Tajikistan had been members of NATO's PfP since 1994, none had been invited to participate in NATO's Membership Action Plan (MAP). Nor did any of these states enjoy the sort of privileged relationships with NATO that Russia and Ukraine had through the NATO-Russia Council and the NATO-Ukraine Commission.

Given the centrality of Central Asia in waging an effective military operation in Afghanistan, it was not surprising that the United States had pushed for greater attention to the region. The United States and its NATO Allies had benefitted tremendously from the post–September 11 cooperation of the Central Asian states, five of which border on Afghanistan and all of which provided support to Operation Enduring Freedom in various forms, including the use of military bases for U.S. and coalition forces, overflight rights, and refueling facilities.[7] Both the Caucasus and Central Asian states had also contributed troops to NATO's various stabilization missions, including both Afghanistan and Iraq.[8]

The United States responded by dramatically increasing economic and military assistance to the region, especially to Uzbekistan, which until mid-2005 served as a principal base for U.S. and coalition forces operating in Afghanistan.[9] In short, both the United States and NATO—following its assumption of responsibility for the International Security Assistance Force (ISAF)—found themselves dependent on close cooperative ties with the region's governments. Indeed, Colin Powell testified before the U.S. House of Representatives International Relations Committee in February 2002 that the United States would now "have a continuing interest and presence in Central Asia of a kind we could not have dreamed of before."[10]

To a significant degree, the cooperation that the United States and NATO enjoyed in the region after September 11, 2001, was made possible by political and military ties to the region forged during the 1990s through NATO's PfP.[11] That outreach had permitted the Allies the opportunity to conduct training exercises in the region and become familiar with local facilities. If "it wasn't for those contacts, for those engagements, for the links and, simply, the participation of various people on the political side, on the military side," a NATO spokesman explained, "it would have been very difficult to have these countries engaged in such a constructive manner in the collective effort in the fight against terrorism."[12] In testimony provided to Congress just before NATO's Istanbul Summit, U.S. Deputy Assistant Secretary for European and Eurasian Affairs Robert A. Bradtke agreed. In his words, "The war in Afghanistan proved the value of relations with the Caucasus and Central Asia. Ties forged with those countries through the Partnership for Peace (PfP) facilitated the establishment of a U.S. military presence in the region that has been one of the keys to success in Operation Enduring Freedom."[13] Given this experience and the need for ongoing cooperation with the governments of the region, the United States had considerable incentive at Istanbul to push for NATO to "intensify its efforts to engage" the Caucasus and Central Asian states.[14]

Notably, NATO's stake in Afghanistan increased significantly with a decision—also taken at Istanbul—to expand NATO's presence in the country.[15] As NATO's involvement in Afghanistan grew, so too did its interest in the Caucasus and Central Asia—a region that was once considered on the periphery of the Euro-Atlantic area. As NATO international staff member Robert Weaver explained, the fact that NATO was operating in Afghanistan, outside of its traditional defense perimeter, had necessitated more attention to the needs of the Central Asian states, which had permitted equipment needed by ISAF forces in Afghanistan to traverse their territory. "Relationships developed through the Partnership for Peace," he noted, had "laid the basis for the Allies to draw up bilateral agreements for the transit of material across these states and the basing of forces and supplies on their territory."[16] As a NATO Parliamentary Assembly Report published in May 2004 also observed, even though

NATO already had military ties to the region, the "war on terror" had provided an opportunity for greater NATO influence in the region, in part because "the physical presence of US and other international armed forces" in the region had an "important symbolic effect in emphasizing Central Asia's links to the Western world after a decade of obscurity and tenuous contacts."[17]

Growing U.S. and NATO interest in the Caucasus and Central Asia was not confined to NATO's needs in Afghanistan, however. Indeed, U.S. Secretary of Defense Donald Rumsfeld suggested in 2002 that there now existed a "broad arc of instability that stretches from the Middle East to Northeast Asia," encompassing "a volatile mix of rising and declining regional powers."[18] This new geostrategic environment would require that NATO enhance its ability to project force successfully to its east and south. While a secure, democratic, and economically prosperous Caucasus and Central Asia was, in itself, a desirable end, the Allies—especially the United States—had come to view the region as a "bridge" to the Middle East. As Ronald D. Asmus and Bruce P. Jackson have explained, the Caucasus or Black Sea region can be seen as "the epicenter" of the "grand strategic challenge of trying to project stability into a wider European space and beyond into the Greater Middle East." In their words,

> This is not just a matter of geography, territory, or Western access to military bases that might better enable us to prosecute the war on terrorism. We have a key interest in seeing the countries of the region successfully transform themselves into the kind of democratic and stable societies that can, in turn, serve as a platform for the spread of Western values further east and south. Azerbaijan's ability to transform itself into a successful Muslim democracy may be as important to our ability to win the war on terrorism as access to military bases on Azeri soil. What these countries become may be an important as where they are.[19]

NATO Goes South

As noted above, intra-alliance divisions over the Middle East have not prevented NATO from becoming involved in the region. In addition to its ongoing military missions in Afghanistan and Iraq, NATO has since late 2001 maintained a counterterrorist, maritime operation in the Mediterranean known as Operation Active Endeavour. Begun on October 26, 2001, as an Article 5 operation in the Eastern Mediterranean, Active Endeavor was intended to protect vital sea-lanes by monitoring maritime activity and providing escorts for merchant ships. NATO extended the operation to the Strait of Gibraltar in February 2003 and then to the entire Mediterranean in March 2003, when it also invited the participation of PfP and Mediterranean Dialogue partners as well as other selected states.

NATO's interest in the Middle East is not entirely a post–September 11 development, however. In fact, the Mediterranean Dialogue, which includes seven states in the region (Egypt, Israel, Morocco, Mauritania, Tunisia, Jordan, and Algeria), dates back to 1994.[20] Much like NATO's PfP and the EAPC, the Dialogue was originally envisioned as an outreach effort aimed at promoting mutual understanding with NATO's neighbors in the Mediterranean. Not surprisingly, the dialogue took on greater importance after September 11, and, beginning at their 2002 Prague Summit, the Allies embarked on an effort to enhance both its political and practical dimensions. Mediterranean Dialogue members were offered the opportunity to meet with NATO's North Atlantic Council, both bilaterally and multilaterally, and to participate in various PfP activities, including in the areas of civil-emergency planning, science and environmental activities, and crisis management.[21] NATO then decided at its 2004 Istanbul Summit to elevate the Mediterranean Dialogue to the level of a full NATO partnership. The aim was to strengthen practical cooperation with the region by "enhancing the existing political dialogue, building interoperability, encouraging defense reform, and working together in the fight against terrorism."[22] Alluding to the success of NATO's PfP, Secretary of Defense Rumsfeld had called for NATO to strengthen the Mediterranean Dialogue in the months preceding Istanbul. The Allies now had an opportunity to build on the positive changes NATO had inspired in the former Soviet bloc, he pronounced. The challenge would be "to think creatively about how we can harness the power of the Alliance and to contribute to similar democratic progress across the Middle East."[23]

The perceived success of the Mediterranean Dialogue, coupled with the post–September 11 strategic environment, also led at Istanbul to the launching of the Istanbul Cooperation Initiative (ICI)—a new program aimed at developing practical bilateral security cooperation between NATO and the states of the Greater Middle East. The ICI, which is viewed by NATO as complementary to the Mediterranean Dialogue, was initially directed toward, but not limited to, members of the Gulf Cooperation Council (GCC).[24] While it remains a work in progress, the Alliance has identified particular areas in which it seeks to offer, on a bilateral basis, tailored advice to participating states in a number of defined areas. These areas include defense reform, defense budgeting, defense planning and civil-military relations, military-to-military cooperation, information sharing and maritime cooperation, illegal trafficking, and preventing the proliferation of weapons of mass destruction. As of mid-2006, Bahrain, Qatar, Kuwait, and the United Arab Emirates had all joined the Initiative, while Saudi Arabia and Oman were still considering the offer.[25]

The "Freedom Agenda"

As suggested earlier, the new partnership initiatives introduced at Istanbul reflected the Bush administration's desire to enlist NATO assets in its so-called "freedom agenda," first articulated in a speech to the National Endowment for Democracy in November 2003.[26] There, Bush asserted that "sixty years of Western nations excusing and accommodating the lack of freedom in the Middle East" had done nothing "to make us safe because in the long run, stability cannot be purchased at the expense of liberty." The United States would therefore adopt "a new policy, a forward strategy of freedom in the Middle East." "As in Europe, as in Asia, as in every region of the world," the President declared, "the advance of freedom leads to peace."[27] Approximately three months later, the Bush administration circulated in Europe a set of ideas purportedly aimed at enlisting NATO in the effort to advance the cause of freedom in the Middle East. Those ideas, which ultimately took shape in the form of the Istanbul Cooperation Initiative and the decision to enhance the Mediterranean Dialogue, would, in the words of the *Wall Street Journal,* "form just one cog of a broader regional initiative," which the administration also sought to advance in summits with the European Union and the Group of Eight industrialized nations (G-8) that same month.[28] Making an impact on the region, R. Nicholas Burns had asserted just prior to NATO's Istanbul meeting, would require "bringing together the combined resources and experiences of the region with those of Europe, North America, and others of the international community."[29]

The Bush administration's broader agenda centered around its Greater Middle East Initiative (GMEI).[30] Put forward initially as a set of guidelines for promoting political and economic reform in the Greater Middle East in cooperation with the G-8, the proposal was later revised in consultations with both Arab and European governments.[31] Meeting then at Sea Island, Georgia (USA), on June 9, 2004, the G-8 formally adopted the Broader Middle East and North Africa Initiative. Billed as a multilateral development and reform plan aimed at fostering political, economic, and social reforms in the broader Middle East and North Africa, the initiative actually involved the adoption of two documents: a G-8 Plan of Support for Reform and the Partnership for Progress and a Common Future with the Region of the Broader Middle East and North Africa. Through the former, the G-8 agreed to a series of efforts aimed at promoting microfinance, improving literacy, enhancing support for business and entrepreneurship, and establishing a Democracy Assistance Dialogue, which would serve to bring together governments, civil society groups, and other organizations from the G-8 countries, the European Union (EU), and others to promote and strengthen democratic institutions.[32] Through the Partnership for Progress and a Common Future, the G-8 also agreed to establish a Forum for the Future. Characterized by the Bush administration as "an international venue to support the reform voice in the region," the forum aimed at bringing foreign, economic, and other ministers from the G-8 and the region together with business and civil society leaders to discuss political and economic reform. Its initial meeting was held in Morocco in December 2004.[33]

The Istanbul Cooperation Initiative was intended to complement this broader reform agenda and "other elements of support for indigenous reform in the Greater Middle East by engaging interested countries in the region to foster security and stability."[34] Based in part on NATO's experience in post–Cold War Europe, Burns suggested, the Alliance could "play a very important role" in establishing an atmosphere of regional security and stability that would be conducive to the flourishing of political and economic reform efforts.[35]

Beyond Europe Whole and Free

The Bush administration's Istanbul agenda must also be understood as part of a long-term U.S. effort to broaden NATO's focus beyond Europe. The Allies have a "responsibility," U.S. Ambassador to NATO Victoria Nuland asserted in late 2005, to take NATO and "turn its power outwards; to lead the rest of the world in offering a better future, one that embraces the core values of economic opportunity, pluralism, and democratic governance."[36] Whether the Allies are ready to take on the global responsibilities the Bush administration has been pushing remains open to question, but there is little doubt that NATO has moved well beyond the Euro-centric focus of the 1990s, as first evidenced by NATO's decision to take command responsibility for the ISAF in Afghanistan. In the wake of September 11, it is now well understood that the principal threats to the North Atlantic area, including terrorism and weapons of mass destruction, will likely stem from outside of Europe—to NATO's east and to the south. NATO's evolving role in the Middle East, as Jaap de Hoop Scheffer has explained it, is therefore a function of the "interplay between Middle Eastern and transatlantic security." The Secretary General further suggested that "cautious openings toward freedom and democracy" in parts of the region, and a recognition on the part of the Allies of the need to "be proactive in dealing with challenges to our shared security and common values" constitute further incentive for NATO's engagement with the region. NATO, he insists, is no longer a "static, Euro-centric organization."[37]

Importantly, NATO's outreach to the Middle East constitutes a shift, not in the nature of NATO's post–Cold War mission, but rather in the scope of its vision. Indeed, the emphasis at Istanbul on strengthening existing partnerships and building new ones stemmed ultimately from a recognition that, just as NATO had projected stability to its east during the 1990s, it must now seek to project stability well beyond the Euro-Atlantic area. Even in the complex, post–September 11 world, de Hoop Scheffer insisted in the months preceding Istanbul, the Allies can "still very much shape events, and not be their victims."[38] "Hunkering down and staying quiet will not preserve our security...our freedoms and our ways of life," he later warned. "We must reach out, to build stability, security and prosperity where it is needed."[39] Just prior to his departure from NATO in March 2005, Burns similarly asserted that Russia, Ukraine, the countries of the Caucasus and Central Asia, and the states of the Middle East would all "be critical to Europe's future security." "Building bridges to them," he pronounced, "should be among the highest priorities."[40]

An Evolving Policy of Partnership

To a significant extent, NATO's outreach to the Middle East as well as Central Asia and the Caucasus builds on the essentially political tools that it developed during the 1990s in pursuit of Europe "whole and free." Among these tools is the Partnership for Peace, which despite its early reputation as a poor substitute for enlargement, has generally been deemed a tremendous success, both in terms of encouraging political and military reforms in Central and Eastern Europe and in opening NATO's various peacekeeping/stabilization missions to participation by non-NATO members. As characterized by one member of NATO's international staff, the Alliance's partnerships have helped "to create a true Euro-Atlantic security culture—a strong determination to work together in tackling critical security challenges within and beyond the Euro-Atlantic community of nations."[41] This perception of success, coupled with a belief that new challenges share some commonalities with those that confronted NATO during the 1990s, is key to a full understanding of the Alliance's post–September 11 efforts to revitalize partnerships with the Central Asian and Caucasus states and expand the concept to the south. As Jeffrey Simon has noted, "the original strategic rationale for the PfP, enhancing stability among, and practical cooperation with the countries along NATO's periphery, has become even more compelling in the context of NATO's further enlargement, the war on terrorism, growing Western interest in Southwest and Central Asia, and the rise of authoritarian and neoimperialist sentiments in Russia."[42] Similarly, de Hoop Scheffer observed in a speech devoted to NATO's role in the Gulf region that as "an organization that has been dealing with multinational security cooperation for more than half a century, NATO has a wealth of experience to offer." Over the course of a decade, he added, NATO had "developed the necessary political and military links with non-NATO countries to make our cooperation very effective," thereby putting the Alliance in a "far better position to make a tangible contribution to…Gulf security."[43]

At the same time, the new partnership initiatives reflect a recognition that NATO's various partnership efforts must be further expanded or adapted in ways that will better serve the interests and needs of both Allies and Partners in a post–September 11 world. As noted in Chapter 4, NATO sought to reinvigorate the partnership concept through a Comprehensive Review of the Euro-Atlantic Partnership Council and Partnership for Peace just prior to its 2002 Prague Summit, leading ultimately to the adoption at Prague of NATO's first "Partnership Action Plan"—the Partnership Action Plan Against Terrorism (PAP-T). Although its focus was later narrowed somewhat, the PAP-T initially committed EAPC members to cooperate in combating terrorism in a variety of areas, including political consultations and information sharing, civil-emergency planning, force planning, air defense and airspace management, training exercises related to terrorism, border control, arms control, and nonproliferation.[44] At Istanbul in 2004, NATO launched a second PAP—this one focused principally on defense reform. Although targeted at Central Asia and the Caucasus, the Partnership Action Plan on Defence Institution Building (PAP-DIB) was open to all EAPC members and reflected NATO's conviction that bringing defense institutions under firm civilian and democratic control is "fundamental to stability in the Euro-Atlantic area and essential for international security co-operation." The Plan committed NATO members and Partners to dialogue, cooperation, and exchange of experience in a variety of areas, including the development of "effective and transparent" arrangements and procedures for achieving democratic control of defense activities, "promoting civilian participation in developing defence and security policy," and establishing "legislative and judicial oversight of the defence sector."[45] Both the PAP-T and the PAP-DIB also fit within a larger effort to enhance political dialogue and practical cooperation with Partners on a range of international and domestic issues, including terrorism, democratization, and Partner participation in NATO-led operations.[46]

To some degree, NATO's interest in partnership with the states of Central Asia, the Caucasus, and the Middle East might appear to be driven more by strategic realities than a genuine interest in democracy promotion. In fact, de Hoop Scheffer has repeatedly asserted that NATO is merely offering new partners opportunities for cooperation and does not seek to "impose" anything on them. Yet, at the same time, it is clear that the notion of "projecting stability," which the Secretary General has defined as "the precondition" for the Allies' security, continues to be inextricable from the promotion of liberal democratic values.[47] He drove home this point during an outreach trip to Central Asia in the fall of 2004, telling his listeners at several stops that NATO's liberal democratic values are "not only for the Allies but also our Partners. The more we share these fundamental values, the stronger our Partnership will be."[48] Implying that the same is true with regard to new partners in the Middle East, he announced at Istanbul that NATO is now "committed to defend[ing] and promot[ing] our common values and shared interests, in the Euro-Atlantic area and beyond." The Allies, Burns agreed, have "set forth to enlarge the democratic sphere of the trans-Atlantic community farther south and east than any of us would have ever imagined."

A New Era of Transatlantic Unity?

If projecting stability is to be understood in terms of democratic values, however, it will require broader cooperation between the United States and Europe—a reality that prompted the Bush administration to embark on an effort to improve transatlantic ties, beginning in early 2005. During a trip to Europe in February, U.S. Secretary of State Condoleeza Rice urged Europeans to join with the United States and "make the pursuit of global freedom our overarching organizing principle for the century."[49] Later that same month, while in Brussels for the NATO summit, Bush declared that it was time to "begin a new era of transatlantic unity" and called upon Europe to partner with the United States through NATO to advance the cause of liberal democracy, especially in the Middle East. The Allies cannot, Bush insisted, "live in peace and safety if the Middle East continues to produce ideologies of murder and terrorists who seek the deadliest of weapons."[50]

Absent from the rhetoric of administration officials was talk of "coalitions of the willing" or "Old Europe" vs "New Europe." In fact, in a speech to the American Enterprise Institute in late 2005, U.S. Assistant Secretary of State for European Affairs Daniel Fried acknowledged that, while "unilateral American action is, in theory, always an option....it is not the best option." The United States needed Europe as a partner, he asserted, because "together, America and Europe constitute a single democratic civilization with common values. Together, America and Europe constitute a quorum of democratic legitimacy."[51]

In a marked departure from its first term, the Bush administration also began in 2005 to profess repeatedly a commitment to European unity. "America supports a strong Europe," Bush asserted in Brussels, "because we need a strong partner in the hard work of advancing freedom in the world."[52] At the same time, however, the administration made it clear that it viewed NATO as the preferred forum for transatlantic discussion on important security issues. Former German Chancellor Gerhard

Schroeder had appeared, to the consternation of the Bush administration, to challenge NATO's role in this regard in early 2005 when he asserted that NATO "is no longer the primary venue where transatlantic partners discuss and coordinate strategies."[53] Not long after Schroeder made his remarks, Burns, who had assumed the position of U.S. Under Secretary of State for Political Affairs, pointedly disagreed, declaring that NATO remained the "most important TransAtlantic bridge."[54] Then U.S. Ambassador to NATO Victoria Nuland echoed this view, characterizing "expanding and deepening the level of political dialogue within the Alliance" as "just as important as developing the right military capabilities."[55]

A Role for NATO?

To some degree, the call for an enhanced political dialogue within NATO reflected a desire on the part of the Bush administration to use the Alliance more for both political and military purposes, especially in the Middle East.[56] Indeed, Burns noted in mid-2004 that, despite European complaints that the United States had lost interest in NATO, it was now the Americans who were "proposing the most ambitious multilateral missions for NATO—in Afghanistan, in Iraq, and in long-term outreach to the countries of the Greater Middle East." The question remains, however, as to whether NATO can indeed serve as a vehicle for the promotion of democracy in the Middle East. Although the Alliance played a significant role in the promotion of political and military reforms in Central and Eastern Europe, its experience with Central Asia suggests that promoting democratic reforms outside of Europe constitutes a more formidable challenge.

Indeed, extensive U.S. and NATO cooperation with the region has coincided with continued and, in some cases, heightened political repression. This has proved particularly true in Uzbekistan, where the government has engaged in serious human rights abuses, including torture, arbitrary arrest, and severe restrictions on freedom of speech and of the press. Although the United States was evicted from the Karshi-Khanabad (K-2) air base there in 2005 following a brutal crackdown on antigovernment demonstrators in Andijon in May,[57] the lack of democratization and continuing human rights abuse throughout the region has led some observers to charge the United States with pursuing a policy in the region that essentially "shores up" repressive, authoritarian regimes by providing them with economic and military assistance in exchange for their cooperation in the war on terror.[58] Writing in the pages of the *Financial Times* in April 2004, Quentin Peel noted that just one day prior to the release of the Department of State's annual human rights reports for

2003—which included a harsh assessment of Uzbekistan's human rights situation—U.S. Secretary of Defense Donald Rumsfeld was in the region praising the government for its participation in the war on terror and in Afghanistan. "Mr. Karimov could be forgiven for feeling confused," Peel wrote. "So could the people of Uzbekistan. They are getting very mixed messages from Washington."[59] A visit to the region by Vice President Dick Cheney in May 2006 also exposed the Bush administration to charges of hypocrisy. During a speech in Vilnius, Cheney strongly criticized Russia's democratic failures, but then traveled on to Azerbaijan and Kazakhstan, where he failed to denounce publicly the even more repressive regimes of those states.[60]

Although Kyrgyzstan's "Tulip Revolution" in March 2005 has generated some hope that a more democratic Central Asia is possible, trends in the region as a whole have been disturbing, particularly for an Alliance publicly committed to the promotion of liberal democratic values. Moreover, the challenges the Allies face in the region are not confined to egregious human rights practices and an absence of democratically elected governments. Other concerns include porous borders, regional rivalries, and the presence of at least one terrorist organization with ties to al Qaeda: the Islamic Movement of Uzbekistan.[61] Additionally, Central Asia's recent history is marked by regional competition rather than the cooperation that is a principal objective of PfP.[62] As Stephen Blank explains, during the Soviet era, these states were "parts of a centralized administration that often deliberately strove to keep them from being able to play complementary roles for each other."[63] In his own assessment of the region's prospects for democratic reform, Blank concludes, "Nowhere in this region will the requirements for and understanding of genuine democracy materialize anytime soon, either in elite or mass practice."[64]

Yet, as the effort to reinvigorate the Partnership with the Caucasus and Central Asia suggests, NATO has determined that the region is of sufficient geostrategic significance that it must, if possible, be integrated more closely with Western institutions. Indeed, NATO's success in Afghanistan will to some extent be dependent on continued cooperation with Central Asia. At the same time, Afghanistan's fate will also have significant implications for the security of Central Asia, in so far as armed insurgents from Afghanistan have taken advantage of relatively porous borders to infiltrate into Tajikistan, Kyrgyzstan, and Uzbekistan.[65] Furthermore, as numerous commentators have noted, NATO's disengagement from the region would serve only to consign it to the influence of Russia and possibly China, both of which see the Allies as competitors in the region.[66] Indeed, the Shanghai Cooperation Organization (SCO), formed in 2001 as an antiterrorism partnership between China, Russia, Kazakhstan, Uzbekistan, Kyrgyzstan, and Tajikistan, called on the United States in

2005 to close its military bases in Central Asia.[67] While China and Russia's concerns about a growing U.S. presence in the region are not surprising, greater Russian and Chinese influence in the region will most assuredly not enhance prospects for its democratization.

NATO's focus at Istanbul on enhancing the Alliance's outreach to Central Asia was also premised to some degree on a belief that NATO has at least the potential to encourage democratic reform in the region. Indeed, Georgia's Rose Revolution in 2003 followed by Ukraine's Orange Revolution in 2004 and the professed desire of both states to join NATO suggested that the lure of membership in the Euro-Atlantic community remained strong even in states once considered long shots for membership in either NATO or the European Union. Even for those states that do not aspire to NATO membership, NATO now has at its disposal a variety of tools designed to promote regional cooperation and stability, and, perhaps over time, gradual democratization. As suggested in Chapter 3, the EAPC and PfP have served as venues in which both NATO and non-NATO partners can share their democracy "know-how" with the region, especially in the area of democratic control over the armed forces. Indeed, NATO has sought to use the liaison positions agreed at Istanbul—one for the Caucasus and the other for Central Asia—to encourage defense reform, promote greater military cooperation and interoperability, and engage the region in a political dialogue on strategic issues. Among the tools available to those liaisons and to NATO members, generally, is the PAP-DIB, which was designed specifically to address the needs of Central Asia and the Caucasus. NATO has also identified as "primary instruments" for pursuing PAP-DIB objectives both the Individual Partner Action Plan (IPAP) and NATO's Planning and Review Process, which is the process by which PfP members identify and evaluate capabilities to be made available to PfP for multinational training and operations conducted with NATO forces.

The IPAP process—frequently described at NATO as a sort of "MAP-lite"—has also drawn interest from both the Caucasus and Central Asia. In fact, as of mid-2006, Georgia, Armenia, Azerbaijan, Kazakhstan, and Moldova had all submitted IPAPs. Although Uzbekistan had initially sought to take advantage of this opportunity for closer cooperation with NATO, the government later changed course by minimizing its own contact with the Alliance even before the crackdown on demonstrators at Andijon and the subsequent eviction of the United States from the K-2 air base in May 2005. NATO has sought to maintain some semblance of a relationship with Uzbekistan in the hope of avoiding the "empty seat" syndrome within PfP, but the Allies have also declined to assist the Uzbek government with defense reforms that might in any way contribute to an ongoing pattern of repression.[68]

The Conundrum

Indeed, NATO faces a conundrum with regard to Central Asia and, ultimately, the Middle East as well. How does partnership with either region, both of which are far from having implemented any far-reaching political reforms, serve to advance the values on which NATO's post–Cold War conception of security has been grounded? Can NATO engage with these regions without jeopardizing its own integrity as a values-based alliance? As an assessment of NATO's Partnerships issued by the NATO Parliamentary Assembly's subcommittee on Central and Eastern Europe observed in mid-2004, the Allies were "balancing serious concerns" regarding the human rights situation in Central Asia—particularly in Uzbekistan and Turkmenistan—"against important strategic interests that make ongoing engagement with these republics a key priority." The report further acknowledged that "hopes that closer engagement with the West would lead to an improvement in the human rights situation [had] not yet been fulfilled."[69] As a scholar attached to the NATO Defense College in Rome framed the question with respect to the Middle East, "How can these weakened regimes be prevented from exploiting their bilateral relationships with NATO to remain in power?[70] Indeed, an apparent concern that NATO's partnerships are not sufficiently grounded on a commitment to promoting democratic reforms, prompted the Foundation for Analysis and Social Studies (FAES), the Madrid-based think tank headed by former Spanish Prime Minister Jose Maria Aznar, to advocate in recommendations it issued for further NATO transformation in late 2005 the creation of a "Partnership for Freedom," modeled on PfP, but "aimed mainly at attracting the countries of North Africa and the Middle East." As envisioned by FAES, the new partnership would be open only to states that "demonstrate a clear desire for democratic reform."[71]

NATO's recognition of the tension inherent in its current partnerships is also evident in its expressed determination "to make the Euro-Atlantic Partnership Council and Partnership for Peace more effective value-based frameworks for enhancing international stability, extending interoperability and cooperation between Allies and partners, and promoting democratic values and reforms."[72] In attempting to use the partnership model as a vehicle for democracy promotion in Central Asia and the Middle East, however, NATO will inevitably encounter difficulties that it did not face in Central and Eastern Europe. First, NATO does not possess the degree of leverage with the governments of these regions that it enjoyed with the governments of Central and Eastern Europe, virtually all of which sought full NATO membership. Indeed, PfP, whose framework document expressly states that liberal democratic values are "fundamental to the partnership," came to be known as a proving ground for admission to the Alliance.[73] The ICI, on the other hand, has no explicit democratization objectives. Moreover, Bahrain, Kuwait, Qatar, and the United Arab Emirates—the four states that have joined ICI—already enjoy security and military cooperation agreements with the United States that are not contingent upon making democratic reforms.

The fact that Central and Eastern European leaders repeatedly suggested during the 1990s that their primary motivation for joining NATO had to do with its identity as a "Western" institution also raises legitimate questions about the relevance of NATO's experience in Central and Eastern Europe to the Middle East. Despite assertions by the Bush administration that the mission of democratizing the Middle East is similar to the one that the United States undertook in post–World War II Europe, the Middle East, unlike Europe, has virtually no past experience with democracy and shares no civilizational identity with the Allies.

Further complicating the picture is the reality that both the United States and NATO suffer from image problems in the region, albeit for different reasons. While public perceptions of the United States have suffered as a result of the war in Iraq, the Abu Ghraib scandal, and other allegations of prisoner mistreatment,[74] NATO's image problems have more to do with a lack of knowledge about the Alliance as well as Arab historical experience, including European colonialism.[75] In the Arab world, NATO is also recognized principally as a military alliance rather than a political entity.[76] There are also those in the region who believe that NATO's involvement there is little more than a substitute for a concerted effort to address the Israeli-Palestinian problem.[77]

A Strategy for the Middle East?

Given these challenges how does NATO assist in advancing democratic reforms beyond Europe? First it should be noted that any role on NATO's part must be part of a broader, multi-institutional effort to shape a global security order that is ultimately favorable to the liberal democratic ideals on which NATO was grounded. NATO's emphasis at Istanbul on building new partnerships and enhancing existing ones reflected an understanding that, given the global nature of today's threats, NATO has little choice but to reach beyond Europe and seek to influence internal developments in those areas from which key threats to the Allies now emanate. Indeed, as Chapter 2 suggests, NATO has since the end of the Cold War embraced a conception of security that rests on a belief that the internal order of states will ultimately shape their interactions with others.

In calling for a transatlantic strategy to promote democratic development in the Middle East, however, Ronald D. Asmus, Larry Diamond, Mark Leonard, and Michael McFaul have noted that the United States and Europe "do not currently have a functioning mechanism to develop and coordinate" a common approach to the region, although they acknowledge that an overhauled U.S.–EU relationship "could become a key forum." Indeed, they call on the West to "reorganize itself," including by adapting multilateral institutions and national security structures, so as to promote positive change rather than merely defend itself against threats stemming from the region.[78]

Whether the Allies will ultimately coalesce around a common strategic vision for the Middle East and even beyond remains to be seen, however. As noted in the preceding chapter, it is generally believed that the Allies continue to hold divergent views on the use of force and the best means of addressing the challenges stemming from the region.[79] While Europeans generally agree that the situation in Iraq will ultimately have implications for the region and even beyond it, they generally have not embraced the Bush administration's contention that Iraq is the central front in the war on terror. As Simon Serfaty has observed, "most, if not all, European allies feel less safe now than they were before the war in Iraq started, and many of them attribute their increased vulnerability to a misuse of U.S. military power and a related misunderstanding of the global conflict against terror."[80] Indeed, Europeans are still inclined to regard terrorism as principally a law enforcement issue rather than a military problem—a perspective that extends to NATO's role in fighting terrorism. As one group of scholars framed the debate, "While some U.S. policymakers see the Alliance as having a role in helping coordinate military training and doctrine relevant for fighting terrorism, many Europeans greet such suggestions with skepticism—not surprisingly given their doubts about a military response to terrorism generally."[81]

These divisions have also extended to the deployment of NATO forces in Afghanistan. Indeed, the Bush administration has been pressing since 2003 for NATO to assume command responsibility, not only for ISAF, but also for Operation Enduring Freedom—the U.S.–led counterterrorist operation in Afghanistan.[82] A new operational plan for Afghanistan approved in December 2005 provides for "enhanced coordination and deconfliction" between the two operations, but it also made clear that they would, at least in the short-term, continue to maintain separate mandates and missions.[83] Some Allies—among them France and Germany—had resisted the idea of placing the missions under a single command, fearing that a NATO combat operation would ultimately undermine what had been understood as a stabilization and security mission. Others, including Britain, insisted that, even if such a merger were to occur, the combat and stabilization functions would have to be kept separate.[84] Although NATO did assume responsibility for 12,000 U.S. forces in October 2006, thereby expanding its operations to all of Afghanistan,

approximately 8,000 U.S. forces engaged in air support and counterterrorism operations in the country remain outside the NATO command.

Moreover, NATO's December 2005 decision to expand its involvement
in the country was nearly thwarted by Dutch concern over the fact that
its forces, which constituted a sizable portion of the new deployment,
are likely to face hostile fire in the south.[85] News reports in November
2005 suggesting that the Central Intelligence Agency maintains secret
detention facilities in as many as eight European countries, coupled with
reports of prisoner abuse at U.S. detention facilities in Afghanistan, Iraq,
and at Guantanamo Bay, also prompted the Dutch government in late
2005 to ask for a memo of understanding with NATO and the government
of Afghanistan that the death penalty could not be applied to prisoners
taken by Dutch troops and that those prisoners would be treated in accordance with the Geneva conventions.[86]

Even with the additional forces, NATO has struggled to produce sufficient troops and equipment to fulfill the ISAF mission. Despite multiple
pleas from NATO Commander General James Jones in the summer and
fall of 2006 for further troop commitments from NATO members, only
90 percent of the mission's formal requirements had been filled as of
November 2006 when the Allies assembled for the Riga Summit. An additional problem stems from the fact that many participating states, including France, Germany, Italy, and Spain, have imposed restrictions on how
and where their forces can be deployed in the country, thereby raising
concerns about Alliance solidarity and burden sharing as U.S., British,
Canadian, and Dutch forces deployed in Afghanistan's more volatile
south and east continue to bear the brunt of the casualties. Although all
26 Allies agreed at Riga to lift these restrictions and come to each other's
aid anywhere in Afghanistan in the event of emergencies, the caveats
remain largely in place.[87]

These difficulties have only heightened the sense that NATO's ISAF
mission now constitutes a test of its political and military relevance in
the post–September 11 world—a reality that NATO itself has affirmed in
reiterating once again at Riga that Afghanistan remains "NATO's key priority."[88] Additionally, the fact that Afghanistan is well understood to be
NATO's chief priority has implications for its involvement elsewhere.[89]
Indeed, as former U.S. Ambassador to NATO Robert Hunter observes, resistance within the Alliance to deeper engagement in Iraq has derived in
part from the fear that NATO runs the risk of failure in Afghanistan if it
spreads its resources too thin.[90]

Divisions over how NATO's assets should be employed are not limited
to its military missions in Afghanistan and Iraq, however. Although
France acquiesced on Afghanistan in 2003, thereby making possible
NATO's first mission outside of Europe, it has in some respects continued

to resist the push for a more global NATO. This includes a lack of enthusiasm for the Istanbul Cooperation Initiative, driven in part by concern that NATO is becoming engaged in areas outside its "competence box."[91] France and others have also argued that the NATO Response Force should not be deployed in the absence of a genuine threat to the Allies own security, despite its initial deployment for humanitarian purposes in Pakistan following an earthquake in late 2005.[92]

On the subject of democracy promotion as well, the United States and Europe have not always seen eye to eye. Initially, at least, many of the Allies expressed considerable skepticism regarding the Bush administration's Greater Middle East Initiative, in part because the administration appeared to ignore the European Union's own long-standing efforts aimed at promoting political and economic reform in the region, including the Barcelona Process and European Neighborhood Policy. Concern also existed that the U.S. initiatives failed to recognize the need for local input and ownership of the reform process and therefore constituted an attempt to impose reform from abroad. "We support modernisation which comes as a result of consultations, cooperation between states," President Jacques Chirac remarked during a visit by Egyptian President Hosni Mubarak to Paris in March 2004. "On the other hand, we think that nothing can be imposed. In other words, modernisation yes, interference no."[93] Reflecting on such criticisms, an Atlantic Council policy paper published in September 2004 characterized the Greater Middle East Initiative as "an object lesson in the ills that have beset the transatlantic relationship in recent years. Conceived with little consultation with its intended partners, in Europe or the Middle East, and with even less regard for their existing programs and priorities, the GMEI stood little chance of adoption from the outset."[94] Indeed, the initial response of France and Germany was to circulate their own reform proposals calling for the EU to "define a distinct approach which complements that of the United States."[95]

Differences also emerged over the pace and consistency of reform efforts. On the one hand, Europeans expressed a clear preference for more gradual reforms.[96] At the same time, however, questions were raised about the integrity of the United States' commitment to its own reform agenda, given its friendly relations with Egypt, Saudi Arabia, and Pakistan. As *The Economist* put it in February 2005, "Mr. Bush's freedom talk is associated in European minds with a readiness to reach for the gun in a world drawn too simply in cowboy blacks and whites. It raises obvious questions of consistency: why so hard on Syria and Iran (which have just formed a "common front" to resist America), so soft on Egypt, Saudi Arabia, and Pakistan?"[97] Not surprisingly, Europeans also expressed concern that the Bush proposals constituted an effort to avoid dealing with the Israeli-Palestinian conflict. "Our big difference with the Americans," one EU source was quoted as saying, "is that we say there must be equal effort for wider reform in the region and for the Israeli-Palestinian conflict, while the Americans say we must not let the peace process hold back reform."[98]

Yet another point of contention has to do with the NATO-EU relationship. Secretary General de Hoop Scheffer has repeatedly stressed that the construction of a "pragmatic, strategic partnership with the EU" will be vital if NATO is to engage successfully with the Middle East, a view affirmed by NATO foreign ministers in December 2005.[99] Yet, as de Hoop Scheffer also concedes, a closer NATO-EU relationship has proved difficult thus far, and that reality is unlikely to change, at least for the foreseeable future.[100] The French, in particular, have resisted expanding the scope of NATO-EU cooperation, preferring to channel their counterterrorism activities through the European Union.[101] French Defense Minister Michele Alliot-Marie has also downplayed the significance of NATO's role, urging that the Alliance not venture into "areas where the competence of other organizations is more obvious."[102]

Despite the Bush administration's professed interest in using NATO as a central forum for transatlantic dialogue on important security issues, many Europeans also remain skeptical that the United States is ready to treat NATO as an alliance among equal partners.[103] Such views are colored in part by the U.S. response to European offers of support in the weeks and months after September 11, when as Simon Serfaty has put it, the Bush administration "seemed more intent on informing its European allies about decisions it had already made than consulting them before making these decisions."[104] From the skeptics' perspective, the United States still regards NATO as little more than a "toolbox," from which to draw coalitions of the willing or particular NATO assets. "For Washington," William Pfaff wrote in the *International Herald Tribune* in early 2006, "NATO now exists as a stock of individual foreign military units of varying specialties, expected to contribute to the support of U.S. operations undertaken, it is argued, in the common interest."[105]

Despite these differences, there does appear to exist on both sides of the Atlantic a growing recognition that the United States and Europe will need each other if they are to address successfully the challenges stemming from the Middle East and elsewhere.[106] Indeed, German Chancellor Angela Merkel's profession of interest in forging a closer relationship with the United States in early 2006 signaled that at least one member of Old Europe was determined to put past differences aside in the interest of the transatlantic community.[107] Tensions between the United States and France also gave way in early 2006 to close cooperation on both Iran's nuclear weapons program and the removal of Syrian troops from Lebanon.[108] And, in late 2005, NATO foreign ministers meeting in Brussels formally endorsed the goal of "enhanced political dialogue" within NATO, describing the Alliance as "the essential forum for transatlantic consultations on the security challenges we face at the beginning of the 21st century."[109] Discussions, in fact, were held at the Brussels meeting on a wide range of issues, including the Israeli-Palestinian peace process, Syria, Lebanon, and Iran.[110]

The annual Munich Security Conference held in February 2006 also reflected a growing interest in restoring NATO as a principal forum for discussion of transatlantic security issues, provided—from the European perspective—that the Alliance is actually used to debate and achieve consensus on these issues.[111] Urging the Allies to have an open discussion regarding NATO's role, German Chancellor Merkel suggested that there was a choice to be made. "Do we want to give NATO a kind of primacy in transatlantic cooperation, meaning an attempt first being made by NATO to carry out the necessary political consultations and decide on the required measures?" she asked. "Or do we want to relegate NATO to a secondary task?....In my view we should decide that NATO has that primacy, and that other courses should not be explored until the Alliance fails to arrive at an agreement."[112] German Defense Minister Franz-Josef Jung added that "if the Alliance wants to preserve its position as the first instance for consultation on security issues, it must become more political again, in other words, it must be used as a political instrument for shaping the security environment." "The shock of the transatlantic misunderstandings in 2002 and 2003," he concluded, "would produce some benefit if we realized that we must adopt a new culture of dialogue and dispute."[113]

Additionally, the conference evidenced broad agreement on the principal security threats confronting the Allies today. That list includes global terrorism, the proliferation of weapons of mass destruction, weak and failing states, organized crime, and energy security, virtually all of which were identified by the European Union in its first "national security strategy," released in late 2003. Much like the national security strategy issued by the Bush administration in 2002, it recognized as "the most frightening scenario...one in which terrorist groups acquire weapons of mass destruction." It also acknowledged that "in such cases deterrence would fail."[114]

Moreover, tensions over Afghanistan and Iraq have not prevented the United States and the European Union from establishing a closer relationship, built largely on the need for more intense cooperation after September 11 in such areas as law enforcement, intelligence sharing, protection of ports, and the eradication of terrorist financing. In fact, the United States and the European Union released a joint declaration on combating terrorism during their 2004 summit in Washington.[115] The United States and the European Union have also worked successfully together to support democracy in Ukraine, Georgia, and Kyrgyzstan, and, despite a rather shaky beginning, the Broader Middle East and North

Africa initiative has borne some fruit. Indeed, the Sea Island G-8 Summit was, itself, interpreted as evidence of a determination on both sides of the Atlantic to "leave the extreme disagreements of the previous year behind" and a "corresponding willingness" on the part of the Bush administration "to accept important modifications to its initiative in order to reach that consensus." Some Europeans also responded to the initiative by conceding that the Bush administration's emphasis on democratization had prompted them to reconsider the political dimension of the European Union's own reform initiatives.[116]

The United States and Europe also worked closely together in 2006 on the problem of Iran's nuclear weapons program and the difficulties posed by the Hamas victory in Palestinian Authority elections in February 2006. Indeed, the EU's foreign policy chief and former NATO Secretary General Javier Solana told the *Financial Times* just prior to the annual U.S.–EU summit in June 2006 that the United States and Europe were "working together in just about every important dossier," including Somalia, Sudan, Kosovo, and the Israeli-Palestinian problem. Affirming that U.S.–European relations had improved considerably since 2004, Solana also noted, "We talk less about ourselves and more about the type of things we can do together to create a better world."[117]

Indeed, the Hamas victory in February, together with the demonstrations and burning of European diplomatic missions in the Middle East following the republication in early 2006 of Danish cartoons depicting Mohammed, also served to highlight the fact that, for all their differences, the United States and Europe do share the same broad goals and fundamental values. British Defense Secretary John Reid was only one of many to make this point at the 2006 Munich Security Conference. "Together we form a community of values," he stressed. "Together, we are the greatest force for prosperity and stability in our world." Not insignificantly, he added that "the core of this relationship is NATO."[118] Although Reid also strongly emphasized in his speech that NATO would need to change to meet new security threats, that challenge should not detract from the fact that NATO continues to stand as a representation of the "West." That there is such an entity has been the subject of some dispute since the Cold War ended,[119] but as *The Economist* put it in early 2005, "The values that hold America and Europe together are still stronger than the differences pulling them apart—and stronger still than whatever bonds Europe or America seem likely to form elsewhere."[120] Suggesting that, from its earliest days, NATO's common interests have reflected "common values," Germany's Ambassador to the United States, Wolfgang Ischinger, agrees. "Not only during the Cold War but also in the post–Cold War era did the Western community fight for its principles and values on numerous occasions, from the Persian Gulf War to the war in Kosovo," he observed in 2005. "Why, if one may ask, should this community of values end now?

There is no evidence to support this claim—but much to support the view that 9/11 has, in fact, reinforced the shared belief in common Western values."[121]

Indeed, polling data from the German Marshall Fund on transatlantic trends in 2005 found that "significant popular support exists on both sides of the Atlantic for the United States and Europe to work together to face global problems." The data also suggested that majorities of both Americans and Europeans supported democracy promotion. In fact, Europeans supported such a policy by a greater margin than did Americans (74 percent to 51 percent). Majorities on both sides of the Atlantic also favored "soft power" options for promoting democracies—including monitoring elections and supporting nongovernmental organizations such as trade unions, human rights associations, and religions groups— while only 39 percent of Americans and 32 percent of Europeans supported the use of military force for this purpose. In fact, the report concluded that "democracy promotion may offer the greatest potential for transatlantic cooperation."[122]

Additionally an analysis published in early 2006 by Stratfor, a private intelligence consulting firm, suggested that the sometimes violent demonstrations over the Danish cartoons, coupled with the Paris riots in November 2005 and "deteriorating relationships between Muslims in Europe and the dominant populations," had made it "increasingly difficult for Europeans to distinguish between their own relationship with the Islamic world and the American relationship with the Islamic world." The report concluded that "a sense of shared fate" had emerged, "driving the Americans and Europeans closer together."[123] Similarly, Roger Cohen, writing for the *International Herald Tribune* observed in early 2006 that "terrorism in Europe and the emergence of Europe as a central theater of the fight between the West and fanatical Islam had prodded France, and Europe with it, toward a closer identification with American policies in fighting terrorism."[124]

Whether such developments will assist in facilitating a new transatlantic strategic consensus remains to be seen, but the fact that liberal democratic values are not only held in common by Americans and Europeans, but also underpin a shared vision of international peace and security, at least sets the stage for long-term cooperation on the Middle East and other vital issues, even if tactical differences persist. As Ivo Daalder, Nicole Gnesotto, and Philip Gordon observe, the challenge the Middle East poses to the West "is obviously not the same as that from the Soviet Union during the Cold War. But it is not entirely different either." Like the Soviet threat, they suggest, it "is a long-term multigenerational task that will require commitment, resources, unity, and resolve."[125]

Building on the Experience of the 1990s

Like the vision of Europe whole and free, however, the realization of a more democratic Middle East is not a project for NATO alone. The Allies will need, individually and collectively, to partner with other institutions, including the European Union and the G-8 to advance that vision. There is no need, as de Hoop Scheffer has acknowledged, for NATO to attempt to duplicate the efforts of other institutions, including the European Union, which has aimed to promote political and economic reform in the region since the early 1990s through its Barcelona Process and European Neighborhood Policy.[126] Rather, the Secretary General and other NATO leaders have repeatedly asserted that the principles of cooperation and complementarity will need to shape the Alliance's policies toward the Middle East.[127]

Importantly, however, while there is much that the European Union can do to foster democratic change that NATO cannot; there are also areas in which NATO enjoys advantages over the European Union, such as disaster relief, defense reform, and democratic control of the armed forces.[128] As discussed in Chapter 3, NATO acquired considerable experience in the latter two areas in Central and Eastern Europe during the 1990s. Such cooperation, as noted earlier in this chapter has also been a focus of NATO's engagement in Central Asia and the Caucasus.

Moreover, it is also generally accepted that, just as the reform process in Central and Eastern Europe required a security dimension, so too will any effort to democratize Central Asia and the Middle East.[129] As Stephen Blank has argued with respect to Central Asia, "the requirement for beginning a liberalization process that will end in something recognizable as democracy, in part or in whole, probably must be sparked by a *deus ex machina,* or external actor or actors who reinforce and strengthen domestic trends within those societies." The security guarantees provided by the presence of U.S. and NATO forces in Afghanistan and Central Asia, Blank suggests, have the potential to "provide a respite for terrorism and opportunities for building security that could also contribute to the general pacification and democratization of the entire area."[130] Asmus, Leonard, McFaul, and others also argue that NATO has a role to play in creating an external security environment conducive to democratic change in the Middle East, by providing the peacekeeping capabilities necessary to stabilize and reconstruct Iraq and Afghanistan and by promoting more democratic practices in the region through a "new version of the Partnership for Peace program." In a play on former NATO Secretary General Lord Ismay's famous line, they propose that "NATO's new role would be to keep the Americans and Europeans together, the aggressors out and the terrorists down."[131]

Indeed, despite continued gloomy predictions regarding NATO's future, the Alliance is remarkably well positioned to contribute to democratic change outside of Europe. NATO today has at its disposal a host of essentially political tools developed in pursuit of Europe whole and free, which it can now utilize and build upon in an effort to project stability farther south and east. While NATO's newest partnership initiative, the Istanbul Cooperation Initiative, does not have the explicit democratization focus of PfP, it does have the potential to build on NATO's experience elsewhere in encouraging the reform of regional security institutions and practices in ways that are ultimately conducive to democratization. As a policy paper released by the Atlantic Council observed, "through the Partnership for Peace and the Membership Action Plan, NATO has evolved ways of promoting and fostering such policies and institutions in countries in which they do not have deep roots. The great promise of the Istanbul Cooperation Initiative is that it would offer to apply these same approaches in those countries of the Broader Middle East."[132]

Although NATO officials acknowledge that PfP developed in a European context, and therefore cannot simply be transposed to the Middle East, they also observe that PfP "embrace[s] several areas of quite unique NATO expertise," which could prove valuable in the region, including "cooperation on border security, joint training and disaster preparedness."[133] In fact, implementation of the Istanbul Cooperation Initiative has drawn heavily on NATO's experience with the Mediterranean Dialogue (MD), which is itself adapted from PfP.

As noted earlier, NATO's Mediterranean Dialogue—now more than ten years old—has become a full NATO partnership and encompasses growing practical cooperation as well as both multilateral and bilateral political dialogue.[134] Since the Istanbul Summit, the Allies have held 26 + 7 foreign and defense ministers' meetings with the Mediterranean Dialogue Partners as well as regular, twice-a-year chief-of-staff meetings. The North Atlantic Council also met with all seven Partners together for the first time in Morocco in April 2006.[135]

Practical cooperation with MD states has also been enhanced through the introduction at Istanbul in 2004 of a new Individual Cooperation Programme (ICP), modeled to some degree on the Individual Partnership Program that PfP members established with NATO. The ICP was designed to permit MD Partners to frame their cooperation with NATO in a more strategic manner by establishing a specific program of activities with NATO, including mid- to long-term goals, rather than simply selecting individual activities from the annual Mediterranean Work Programme, which for 2006 included approximately 300 different activities available to Partners in 26 different areas of cooperation, including interoperability, military-to-military contacts, modernization of the armed forces, public diplomacy, terrorism, and weapons of mass destruction and armaments issues. Although the spectrum of particular interests among the MD partners varies, as of mid-2006, four of the Mediterranean Dialogue partners, including Israel, were in the process of establishing ICPs with NATO. Israel became the first partner to finalize its ICP in October 2006.

Since Istanbul, NATO has also begun to introduce defense reform in the framework of the Mediterranean Dialogue, although it remains a relatively undeveloped area of cooperation and participation in the PAP-DIB has not yet been opened to MD Partners. MD states have, however, been invited to participate in select PAP-T activities.[136] Notably several Mediterranean Dialogue states have also participated in NATO's various stabilization missions, namely, Morocco in Bosnia and Kosovo, while both Egypt and Jordan contributed to the NATO mission in Bosnia.

As noted earlier, NATO has stressed that it seeks not to impose an agenda on its partners, but rather to offer its expertise and opportunities for practical cooperation with NATO. Indeed, NATO has identified the following as key principles underpinning the Istanbul Cooperation Initiative: practical cooperation, complementarity, and joint ownership. The fact that the partnerships offered are bilateral also permits members to serve their own particular security interests by developing individual work programs with NATO that might involve dialogue or practical cooperation with the Allies in a wide range of areas, including counterterrorism, counter-WMD, civil emergency planning, training and education, participation in NATO exercises, defense reform, and military interoperability.[137] Drawing extensively on the annual Mediterranean Dialogue Work Programme, NATO has now established a Menu of Practical Activities for ICI in 12 areas of cooperation mostly in the military field.[138] Given that ICI remains a work in progress, it could potentially evolve in a number of directions.[139] One possibility might be the establishment of institutional links between NATO and the GCC, an idea in which some ICI states have expressed interest. To date, however, NATO has made no decisions in this regard.[140]

Additionally, Operation Active Endeavour not only continues, it is drawing increased interest and participation from throughout NATO's network of partners, including Russia and three Mediterranean Dialogue states: Algeria, Israel, and Morocco.[141] As of late 2006, NATO had also completed another expansion of ISAF and had developed in close consultation with the Afghan government an Afghan Cooperation program, which drew upon "selected Partnership for Peace instruments" to assist Afghan authorities with defense reform, defense institution building, and the military aspects of security sector reform.[142]

Despite negative perceptions of the Alliance in the Middle East, there are also advantages to putting a NATO face on the West's engagement there, assuming that it means a more visible role for Europe, particularly in the Gulf. Indeed, given the experience of the Iraq war, the United States might not be the ideal candidate for advancing a message about the need for political and military reform. As one professor from the United Arab Emirates University put it, it is NATO, not the United States, that is needed to address the regional security dilemma, which, he suggested, had only been exacerbated by the war in Iraq.[143] NATO has also sought to address its own image problems through a public diplomacy strategy targeted at local opinion leaders and comprising a variety of activities including conferences, seminars, and workshops.[144] For example, NATO hosted a seminar on the Mediterranean Dialogue at the NATO Defense College in Rome in May 2004 followed by another on the Istanbul Cooperation Initiative in March 2005, which brought NATO representatives together with ICI member state representatives, academics, and parliamentarians.

Conclusion

NATO's first steps in the Middle East might appear modest, and, indeed they are. They are not, however, without significance. As one researcher at the NATO Defense College in Rome summed up the Alliance's involvement in the region,

> To date, all NATO's activities in the wider Mediterranean region have been modest and above all, cautious. The Alliance has sought to handle regional sensitivities with care and not to put the progress that has been achieved at risk. At the same time, however, NATO has been building the regional expertise and investing in the necessary relationships that may, in time, enable the Alliance to become a more influential actor.[145]

In fact, NATO has been laying the foundation for its outreach to Central Asia and the Middle East since the early 1990s when the Allies agreed that their mission was no longer to defend an existing order but, rather, to construct a new one, grounded on democratic values and encompassing areas outside of NATO's traditional sphere of collective defense. As Jaap de Hoop Scheffer observed in the months prior to Istanbul, NATO has "built mechanisms for engaging countries as diverse as Ireland, Albania, Russia, Georgia, or Turkmenistan" and is working with them in "areas ranging from defence reform to combating terrorism," as well as in peacekeeping missions in Bosnia, Kosovo, and Afghanistan. "This, he asserted, "is a co-operative momentum unprecedented in Europe's history—a 'security culture' that now reaches far beyond NATO member states."[146]

Ultimately, however, NATO's partnerships, new institutions, and military capabilities must all be put in the service of a larger political purpose. NATO will not survive if it becomes little more than a toolbox for individual Allies or even the United Nations, which has no standing military capability of its own. Although the Alliance's newest partnership initiatives as well as its military missions outside of Europe represent positive first steps in adjusting to a strategic environment in which security can no longer be understood in regional terms, it is not yet clear that they are guided by a comprehensive, strategic vision that encompasses those issues that are of greatest importance to both the United States and Europe, including Iran, Iraq, and the Israeli-Palestinian conflict. As Daalder, Gnesotto, and Gordon have observed, while transatlantic cooperation aimed at transforming the Middle East "might provide some glue to hold the transatlantic partners together," the region's transformation cannot be achieved "if the more immediate and dangerous crises that have bedeviled the region are not addressed and resolved."[147] Indeed, if NATO is to function as a genuine alliance in what de Hoop Scheffer has termed a "world of globalised insecurity," its activities will ultimately need to be grounded on a shared strategic vision that extends well beyond the Middle East.

NATO is no longer the Euro-centric alliance of the 1990s. The Istanbul Summit affirmed NATO's recognition that its continued relevance will hinge to some extent on its willingness to accept the challenge of projecting stability well beyond the Euro-Atlantic area. However, the Allies have yet to resolve the larger question of just how global NATO should be. Indeed, while the mission of Europe whole and free was an ambitious one, it was also limited in so far as it was confined to a particular geographic space. Given the nature of the threats confronting the Allies today, however, NATO no longer enjoys the luxury of thinking about security in purely regional terms. The Allies must now articulate a new political mission in a more global context—a task that will invariably prove more challenging than the one NATO faced in the early 1990s. Although the Bush administration has resisted calls for a new Harmel Report, such an exercise might now be required, even if it risks provoking further discord among the Allies. It would at least invite the sort of focused dialogue regarding NATO's core purposes that has largely been absent in the post–September 11 period.

Conclusion

NATO's long-term future is far from certain, but this is no more the case today than it was in 1990 when the Alliance began a concerted effort to enhance its political dimension with the goal of projecting stability to the east. As former U.S. Ambassador to NATO Robert Hunter has observed, the United States, at that time, "led in nurturing the proposition that the Atlantic Alliance had an integrity that did not depend entirely on the Cold War from which it was born."[1] NATO's new mission was, in fact, deeply rooted in its Cold War experience with the pacification of Western Europe. Over the course of the 1990s, NATO would build on this experience by developing a variety of new mechanisms, including new institutions, new partnerships, and a process for enlarging the Alliance itself—all aimed at facilitating the creation of the liberal European security order that George H. W. Bush originally characterized as Europe whole and free.

NATO's skeptics legitimately cite among the sources of their pessimism both the continued capabilities gap and intra-alliance divisions over how to define and respond to the principal threats confronting the Alliance today. At the same time, however, they have failed to appreciate the relevance of the essentially political tools created in pursuit of Europe whole and free (e.g., new institutions, partnerships, and enlargement) to the post–September 11 world and the extent to which NATO is actively using these tools to project stability beyond Europe, including to the Caucasus, Central Asia, and the Middle East. In short, an Alliance that began its post–Cold War life devoted almost exclusively to constructing Europe whole and free is now reaching out to new partners well beyond the borders of Europe, while carrying out military missions in Kosovo, Afghanistan, Iraq, and the Darfur region of Sudan.

While NATO's less Euro-centric focus is generally welcomed by NATO supporters, the emphasis on new partners and stabilization missions outside of Europe has also prompted some to question whether NATO is sufficiently devoted to its traditional Article 5 or collective defense mission. For example, in late 2005, the Foundation for Analysis and Social Studies (FAES)—the Madrid-based think tank headed by Jose Maria Aznar—went so far as to suggest that NATO was "no longer a collective defense organization," having become instead "an organization designed to ensure regional security, either as an armed wing at the disposal of the

UN or as a defender of the principles of peaceful coexistence and respect for human rights."[2] FAES did not suggest that NATO should abandon such missions, but it did recommend that the Alliance develop a homeland security dimension aimed at confronting new threats to NATO territory, including those posed by weapons of mass destruction and cyberterrorism.[3] A concern that NATO's more global missions and partnerships must be balanced by a reminder that the Alliance must be able to make good on its Article 5 commitment also prompted a group of scholars at the National Defense University in Washington to issue a paper on homeland defense in May 2006 in which they appealed for NATO to introduce a homeland defense initiative at the Riga Summit accompanied by "parallel proposals" aimed at "strengthening partnerships with nonmembers and further improving NATO's military forces and capabilities for new-era missions." According to the authors, the "initiative would offer NATO both a 21st century approach to Article 5 and new meaning and credibility in the eyes of NATO publics who are concerned about threats to their homelands."[4]

Indeed, Article 5 has long been the bedrock of the NATO Alliance. It is worth reiterating, however, that, at least conceptually, NATO's post–Cold War evolution in no way reflects an abandonment of the collective defense clause. Rather, that evolution has been grounded on the assumption that NATO territory will not be secure so long as instability exists along its periphery or even far beyond NATO's borders. This was the lesson that inspired the mission of Europe whole and free and the evolution of a more proactive approach to security.

That said, the fact that this analysis has focused principally on the evolution of NATO's political rather than military dimension should not be read as an effort to diminish the importance of NATO's military component. Rather, the analysis presumes that the health of each component is inextricably linked to that of the other. Indeed, the Allies should take from their nearly 15 years of post–Cold War experience two key lessons. The first is that NATO will not be sustainable as a military alliance in the absence of relevant and competent military capabilities to which all members contribute. As Secretary General Lord Robertson stated repeatedly during his tenure at NATO, those capabilities constitute part of the "political glue" that holds the Alliance together. British Defence Secretary John Reid also stressed at the 2006 Munich security conference that Europe must be willing to share more of the burden, in terms of both ensuring that members' own forces are relevant to contemporary threats and having "the will and resolution to deploy forces."[5]

At the same time, however, the Allies must recognize that military capabilities alone cannot sustain an alliance that was predicated on a commitment to European integration and shared values. During the 1990s, NATO devoted considerable attention to enhancing the Alliance's political component, but, in the process, neglected its military capabilities. The Allies must now take care that they do not risk committing the reverse error: focusing on military transformation without a corresponding and sustained effort to shore up the Alliance's political dimension.

Indeed, it is not yet clear that NATO's missions outside of Europe are underpinned by the same clarity of purpose or common strategic vision reflected in the commitment to Europe whole and free. That vision not only inspired the creation of new institutions, new partnerships, and new programs; it also provided a context for the out-of-area military missions that NATO ultimately assumed in both Bosnia and Kosovo. Contrary to realist claims that NATO undertook those missions in opposition to its interests, the Allies concluded, albeit belatedly, that the construction of a new European security order—as they envisioned it—could not be fulfilled if ethnic cleansing in Bosnia and Kosovo was allowed to proceed unchecked.

Moreover, while NATO is no longer the Euro-centric alliance of the 1990s, the Allies have yet to achieve a consensus as to just how global the new NATO should be. That division has the potential to become even more pronounced. In fact, the Bush administration appears determined to push NATO in an increasingly global direction as evidenced by its agenda for the 2006 Riga Summit. Several aspects of that agenda were not new. Increased burden sharing in terms of both capabilities and funding for the Alliance remains a key U.S. concern,[6] as does continued development of the capacity "to plan and deploy...forces more rapidly."[7] Indeed, the Bush administration has urged that NATO not only do more to combat terrorist attacks, but also take on greater responsibility for combating drug trafficking and providing humanitarian assistance, as it did in 2005 in the United States following Hurricane Katrina and again in Pakistan where the NATO Response Force was deployed following an earthquake in late 2005. Additionally, the administration has urged NATO to build on its training expertise by establishing a NATO training mission that would focus initially on the Middle East, but could be extended to other regions at some later date.[8] Although the Allies did agree at Riga to establish a Training Cooperation Initiative for members of the Mediterranean Dialogue and Istanbul Cooperative Initiative, other aspects of the Bush agenda proved more controversial.

In particular, the Bush administration failed to achieve a consensus around its proposed Global Partnerships Initiative. The proposal, circulated by the United States and Britain, would have established a more formal political framework for NATO's relationships with Australia, Japan, South Korea, Sweden, and Finland. According to U.S. Department of State officials, the United States sought partnerships with these states, identified as "the five countries that most prominently train with us, exercise with us in NATO and deploy in the Balkans and Afghanistan with us," as a means of facilitating joint military training as well as advancing political dialogue in areas of shared strategic interest. Although he has cautioned that NATO is not becoming a "global alliance" or "global policeman," Jaap de Hoop Scheffer has also lent support to the idea of "global partners," in so far as global threats now require closer dialogue with states outside of Europe that share NATO's values.[9] As he put it in the weeks before the Riga Summit, "in dealing with 'globalized insecurity' it matters less and less where a country sits on the map. What matters more is its mental map, its willingness to engage, together with others, to make a difference. That is the logic of NATO's global partnerships."[10]

At Riga, the Allies did affirm the "political and operational value" of NATO's partnerships and agreed to "increase the operational relevance of relations with non-NATO countries, including interested Contact Countries; and in particular to strengthen NATO's ability to work with those current and potential contributors to NATO operations and missions, who share our interests and values."[11] French-led opposition within the Alliance to the more formal consultative framework proposed by the United States and Britain, however, ultimately led to what one newspaper described as a "watered down" version of the original proposal.[12] Voicing long-standing French opposition to a more global NATO, French Defense Minister Michele Alliot-Marie asserted in October 2006 that while it would be desirable "to improve the practical modalities" of NATO's relationships with non-NATO states such as Australia and Japan, "the development of a global partnership" could potentially "dilute the natural solidarity between Europeans and North Americans in a vague ensemble." Alliot-Marie also suggested that such partnerships would "send a bad political message: that of a campaign launched by the West against those who don't share their ideas."[13] Similarly, François Heisbourg lamented in the *Financial Times* just prior to the Riga Summit that NATO was "not sticking to its core competencies," but rather "in a quest to carve a greater role for itself and demonstrate global relevance" was "running the risk of overreaching itself in strategic and political terms, with potentially dangerous consequences." Heisbourg questioned the "wisdom" of a partnership between NATO and "like-minded states in the Asia-Pacific region," suggesting that it might lead to "needless friction with a rising China."[14]

Fears that NATO risks overextending itself are by no means confined to the French, particularly given the challenges the Allies currently confront in Afghanistan. Indeed, as NATO began deploying additional forces in Afghanistan in mid-2006, the prevailing view was that the Alliance was already being tested as Taliban forces operating in the southern part of the country took advantage of the transfer of authority from U.S. forces to seize additional territory, leading to a significant deterioration in the security situation. As all Allies clearly recognize, a NATO failure in

Afghanistan would have nothing short of catastrophic implications for NATO's credibility.

Given its post–Cold War evolution thus far, however, it is not inconceivable that NATO might one day cease to be a purely "Western" alliance. Although the Bush administration has been careful to stress that it is not currently endorsing the creation of a global alliance,[15] support for opening NATO to non-European members has been growing. Former Spanish Prime Minister Jose Maria Aznar, for example, has proposed that NATO "invite such countries as Israel, Japan, and Australia to join the organization." Taking such a step would, according to the FAES report issued in 2005, allow NATO "to fully and openly assume its true form...that of a free association of democratic countries that are committed to promoting an open and liberal way of life."[16] Similarly, Ivo Daalder and James Goldgeier proposed in *Foreign Affairs* in the fall of 2006 that NATO should view a "global partnerships" initiative not as "a final objective," but rather as preparation for the transformation of NATO "from a transatlantic entity into a global one."[17] "Any like-minded country that subscribes to NATO's goals," they argue, "should be able to apply for membership in the alliance—just as central and eastern European countries have been doing since the collapse of communism."[18]

At the same time, however, it is clear that NATO's own identity is deeply rooted in the idea of the "West." From the beginning, NATO saw its core function as one of "safeguard[ing] the freedom, *common heritage and civilisation* of [its] peoples, founded on the principles of democracy, individual liberty and the rule of law." As noted earlier, one of the most ardent defenders of the notion that NATO is, in essence, an alliance of Western civilization has been former Czech President Václav Havel. Indeed, on the question of whether NATO should be open to a democratic Russia, Havel has expressed firm opposition on the grounds that historically and culturally, Russia is not a member of the West. Any attempt to integrate it into NATO, he has argued, would hurt the identity of the Alliance and turn it into "just another boundless institution, a new OSCE or a new U.N."[19] Not all would agree with Havel's assessment of Russia's civilizational identity, but there is little question that NATO has actively promoted itself as a manifestation of the West and the values underpinning that identity, especially within the context of enlargement.

Yet, as Timothy Garton Ash has argued in *Free World*, given that the values generally associated with the West have now taken hold in corners of the world far from North America and Europe, the notion of enlarging the West may no longer be conceptually useful. Rather, he suggests that it might be time to employ new terminology and aspire instead to the creation of a "free world."[20] None of this is to suggest that NATO must necessarily become a global as opposed to a regional alliance. It does, however, beg the question of whether NATO's sense of self is more fundamentally rooted in its historical, cultural, and geographical origins than it is in the values for which the Alliance stands. Might the Allies someday conceive NATO as a growing federation of democracies, not confined to any particular geographic space, as Immanuel Kant appears to have envisioned in *Perpetual Peace*? Or is its identity and cohesiveness too grounded in its Euro-Atlantic origins?

The degree to which NATO evolves in a more global direction will also likely depend on whether NATO's identity as an alliance that has pacified Western Europe on the grounds of liberal democratic values resonates beyond Europe. As the Allies have well recognized, operating in a what Jaap de Hoop Scheffer has termed a "world of globalised insecurity" will require that they seek to project stability well beyond the borders of Europe and even Central Asia and the Middle East.[21] Whether there are limits to projecting stability in terms of shared liberal democratic values, however, remains an open question.

A more operational question is also relevant here. Given the fact that the United Nations maintains no standing army and the extent to which cleavages within the UN Security Council have prevented it from responding to regional conflicts since its inception, one might argue that NATO is in some respects already emerging as the more effective security provider. It was after all NATO that finally intervened to halt ethnic cleansing in the Balkans, just as it was NATO that assumed responsibility for the International Security Assistance Force in Afghanistan, deployed a training mission in Iraq, provided aid to earthquake victims in Pakistan, and to which the UN and the African Union have turned for peace-keeping assistance in Darfur.

Indeed, Ivo H. Daalder and James M. Lindsay suggested in 2004 that, while "efforts to improve the United Nations' capacity to respond to global security threats are laudable," they do not address the deeper problem, which is that the UN "treats it members as sovereign equals regardless of the character of their governments." On this issue, however, the Security Council has clearly been divided. While Russia and China remain committed to a traditional state-centric conception of sovereignty under which intervention is generally not permissible on human rights or humanitarian grounds, the NATO Allies have embraced a conception of security that is ultimately grounded on the rights of the individual and is therefore far less deferential to the Westphalian principle of nonintervention.

Given this division, Daalder and Lindsay proposed as a potential "alternative, and more legitimate, body for authorizing action," an "Alliance of Democratic States," which "would unite nations with entrenched democratic traditions, such as the United States and Canada; the European Union countries; Japan, South Korea, New Zealand and Australia; India and Israel; Botswana and Costa Rica." In addition to addressing the challenges posed by terrorism, weapons proliferation, infectious diseases, and global warming, such an alliance would "work vigorously to advance the values that its members see as fundamental to their security and well-being—democratic government, respect for human rights, a market-based economy." Indeed, Daalder and Lindsay suggest that "just as the prospect of joining NATO and the European Union remade the face of Europe, so too could the prospect of joining the Alliance of Democratic States help remake the world."[22] More recently, Daalder, together with James Goldgeier, has suggested that the enlarged NATO they have proposed would not necessarily undermine the United Nations, but rather "would become a more capable and legitimate adjunct to the UN by helping to implement and enforce its decisions." In cases such as Kosovo, in which the UN was unwilling to act, they argue, "a more global NATO, backed by the world's leading democracies, would enjoy greater legitimacy," which "should allay the fears of those committed to a strong international order."[23]

Whether or not NATO evolves to become a global "alliance of democratic states," there should be little doubt as to its role in defending and promoting the values its members hold dear. As NATO's newest members can perhaps best appreciate, the Alliance is far more than a bridge between the United States and Europe. It now stands as a manifestation of the success of a concerted effort to integrate Europe politically, as envisioned in Article 2 of the original NATO Treaty. Having constructed a community of states that have in Kantian-like fashion established peace with one another, NATO today enjoys an identity that goes well beyond the sum of its members. In the 1990s, that identity permitted the Allies to wield significant influence over those states that aspired to NATO membership, and it continues to generate tremendous appeal for those still seeking integration into Euro-Atlantic institutions. Ironically, perhaps, it may now be the Allies who are in need of NATO's pull. Indeed, NATO's mere presence should serve to highlight the consequences of allowing the transatlantic drift to continue and thereby offer an incentive for the development of coherent, long-term policies aimed at addressing the most pressing security challenges today. In formulating such policies, let us hope that the Allies will continue to take their cue from the liberal democratic values enshrined in the preamble to the original Washington Treaty. As George H. W. Bush avowed in 1989, for NATO, these values constitute "both an anchor and a course to navigate for the future."[24]

Notes

Introduction

1. The White House, Office of the Press Secretary, "Remarks by the President in Address to Faculty and Students of Warsaw University," Warsaw, Poland, June 15, 2001, http://www.whitehouse.gov/news/releases/2001/06/20010615-1.html (accessed June 2001).

2. Declaration on a Transformed North Atlantic Alliance (The London Declaration), July 6, 1990, http://www.nato.int/docu/basictxt/b900706a.htm (accessed January 1999).

3. Ibid.

4. Lord Robertson, Speech at NATO Parliamentary Assembly, Amsterdam, November 15, 1999.

5. Quoted in William Drozdiak, "Growing Pains at a New NATO," *International Herald Tribune,* July 11, 1997.

6. Lord Robertson, "NATO in the New Millenium," *NATO Review* 47, no. 4 (Winter 1999): 3.

7. Henry Kissinger, "Old Allies Face New Dilemmas," *Courier-Mail,* April 14, 2003.

8. See Charles Kupchan, "The Last Days of the Atlantic Alliance," *Financial Times,* November 18, 2002.

9. Robert Kagan, *Of Paradise and Power: America and Europe in the New World Order* (New York: Alfred A. Knopf, 2003), 3. For the *Policy Review* version of this essay, see Robert Kagan, "Power and Weakness," *Policy Review,* no. 113 (June 2002).

10. Lord Robertson, "NATO: A Vision for 2012," Speech at GMFUS Conference, Brussels, October 3, 2002, http://www.nato.int/docu/speech/2002/s021003a.htm.

11. Remarks by Ambassador R. Nicholas Burns, U.S. Ambassador to NATO, Royal Institute for International Affairs, Chatham House, London, May 27, 2004, at http://nato.usmission.gov/ambassador/2004/20040527_London.htm.

12. Jaap de Hoop Scheffer, Opening Remarks at the Meeting of the North Atlantic Council at the level of Heads of State and Government, Istanbul, June 28, 2004.

13. See, for example, Peter van Ham, "Security and Culture or, Why NATO Won't Last," *Security Dialogue* 2, no. 4 (2001): 394. Van Ham has argued that "cultural differences among allies will make cooperation in the security field more complicated, spoil the convivial atmosphere, and eventually undermine the notion of a united 'West' founded on shared interests as well as shared values."

Chapter 1

1. John J. Mearsheimer, "Back to the Future: Instability in Europe after the Cold War," *International Security* 15, no. 1 (Summer 1990): 52.

2. Owen Harries, "The Collapse of the West," *Foreign Affairs* 72, no. 4 (September/October 1993): 41.

3. Robert A. Levine, "NATO Is Irrelevant: A Bureacracy Whose Time Has Passed," *International Herald Tribune*, May 24, 2003.

4. Kupchan, "The Last Days of the Atlantic Alliance."

5. Richard E. Rupp, *NATO After 9/11: An Alliance in Continuing Decline* (New York: Palgrave Macmillan, 2006), 3.

6. John Duffield, "NATO's Function after the Cold War," *Political Science Quarterly* 109, no. 5 (Winter 1994/95): 767.

7. Rob de Wijk, "Towards a New Political Strategy for NATO," *NATO Review* 2 (Summer 1998): 15.

8. Robert McCalla, "NATO's Persistence," *International Organization* 50, no. 3 (Summer 1995): 445–75.

9. Ibid.

10. Robert O. Keohane, "Response to 'Back to the Future,'" in *The New Shape of World Politics: Contending Paradigms in International Relations* (New York: Foreign Affairs, 1997), 159–60.

11. See, for example, John M. Owen, "How Liberalism Produces Democratic Peace," *International Security* 19, no. 2 (Fall 1994): 87–125.

12. Michael W. Doyle, "Kant, Liberal Legacies, and Foreign Affairs, Part 2," *Philosophy & Public Affairs* 12, no. 4 (Fall 1983): 323–53.

13. Thomas Risse-Kappen, *Cooperation Among Democracies: The European Influence on U.S. Foreign Policy* (Princeton, NJ: Princeton University Press, 1995), 33. Risse's reference to "pluralistic security communities" stems from the work of Karl Deutsch, who in the 1950s defined a security community as one "in which there is real assurance that the members of that community will not fight each other physically, but will settle their disputes in some other way." Although Deutsch himself concluded in 1957 that NATO had not yet achieved the status of a security community, he noted that there was considerable support for tightening the Alliance in order that it might become "a pluralistic/security community." See Karl W. Deutsch, *Political Community and the North Atlantic Area: International Organization in Light of Historical Experience* (Princeton: Princeton University Press), 4–5, 9.

14. Thomas Risse-Kappen, "Collective Identity in a Democratic Community: The Case of NATO" in *The Culture of National Security,* ed. Peter Katzenstein (New York: Columbia University Press, 1996), 372–78.

15. Lord Robertson, "International Citizenship," speech by the Secretary General at the Roscoe Lecture, John Moore's University, Liverpool, September 6, 2001.

16. Madeleine K. Albright, statement before the Senate Foreign Relations Committee, Washington, D.C., October 7, 1997.

17. Quoted in Ian Thomas, *The Promise of Alliance: NATO and the Political Imagination* (Lanham, MD: Rowman & Littlefield, Publishers, Inc., 1997), 33.

18. Quoted in Sean Kay, *NATO and the Future of European Security* (Lanham, MD: Rowman & Littlefield, Publishers, Inc., 1998), 16.

19. Ibid., 31–32.

20. Václav Havel, "NATO's Quality of Life," *New York Times,* May 13, 1997. In a similar vein, Samuel Huntington characterized NATO in 1998 as a bulwark of "Western civilization." The perceived need to enlarge NATO at the end of the Cold War, he suggested, was at least partially responsible for the ensuing discussion over the nature of the West and a "renewed recognition that such a reality had existed." See Samuel Huntington, *The Clash of Civilizations and the Remaking of World Order* (New York: Simon & Schuster, 1998), 307.

21. Manfred Wörner, "The Atlantic Alliance and European Security in the 1990s, Address by the Secretary General to the Bremer Tabaks Collegium, May 17, 1990, at http://www.nato.int/docu/speech/1990/s900517a_e.htm (accessed May 2006).

22. Quoted in Jamie Shea, *NATO 2000: A Political Agenda for a Political Alliance,* Brassey's Atlantic Commentaries (London: Brassey's, 1990), 2.

23. Quoted in David S. Yost, *NATO Transformed: The Alliance's New Roles in International Security* (Washington, DC: U.S. Institute of Peace, 1998), 51.

24. See U.S. Policy toward NATO Enlargement, Hearing before the House Committee on International Relations, 104th Congress, 2nd session, June 20, 1996, 37.

25. Kay, *NATO and the Future of European Security,* 33.

26. The North Atlantic Treaty, Washington, D.C., April 4, 1949, http://www.nato.int/docu/basictxt/treaty.htm.

27. Yost, *NATO Transformed*, 35–36.

28. See "The Future Tasks of the Alliance" ("The Harmel Report"), Brussels, December 13–14, 1967, http://www.nato.int/docu/basictxt/b671213a.htm.

29. Text of the Report of the Committee of Three on Non-Military Cooperation in NATO," December 1956, http://www.nato.int/docu/basictxt/treaty.htm.

30. See Shea, *NATO 2000,* 60–61, 64–65.

31. The Alliance's Strategic Concept (1999), approved by the Heads of State and Government participating in the meeting of the North Atlantic Council, Washington, D.C., April 23–24, 1999, http://www.nato.int/docu/pr/1999/p99-065e.htm.

32. Javier Solana, "NATO in the 21st Century: An Agenda for the Washington Summit," *Congressional Digest* (April 1999): 104–6. Similarly, a 1998 U.S. Congressional Research Service report on NATO's evolving role asserted that NATO's "survival beyond the end of the Cold War suggests that its value foundation remains an important part of the glue that holds the Alliance together and attracts new members." See CRS Report for Congress, NATO's Evolving Role and Missions, March 13, 1998, http://www.senate.gov/~dpc/crs/reports/pdf/97-708.pdf (accessed January 1999).

33. George H.W. Bush, "Proposals for a Free and Peaceful Europe," Speech at Mainz, Federal Republic of Germany, May 31, 1989 (Current Policy no. 1179).

34. Declaration of the NATO Heads of State and Government participating in the meeting of the North Atlantic Council (the 40th anniversary of the Alliance), Brussels, May 29–30, 1989, at http://www.nato.int/docu/basictxt/b890529a.htm. During a meeting in Brussels in March 1988, the Allies had already asserted that "genuine peace" would require more than arms control; it would need to "be firmly based on full respect for fundamental rights."

35. See James Baker, "A New Europe: A New Atlanticism: Architecture for a New Era," December 12, 1989 (Current Policy no. 1233), 2.

36. Declaration of a Transformed North Atlantic Alliance (The London Declaration), July 6, 1990, http://www.nato.int/docu/basictxt/b900706a.htm. It was not until just before the London Summit that the Bush administration took it upon itself to produce a draft declaration to be issued during the meeting. The draft, written largely by the National Security Council staff in consultation with Department of State and Defense personnel, was shared directly with Allied leaders, bypassing the usual negotiation process involving the NATO bureaucracy. As adopted in London in July 1990, the declaration differed little from the United States' original proposal. Author interview with NATO international staff member, Brussels, December 2001. See also Robert L. Hutchings, *American Diplomacy and the End of the Cold War: An Insider's Account of U.S. Policy in Europe 1989–1992* (Washington, DC: The Woodrow Wilson Center Press, 1997), 135.

37. Former National Security Adviser Brent Scowcroft notes that then Soviet Foreign Minister Shevardnadze had repeatedly stressed to U.S. Secretary of State James Baker that the declaration issued at the 1990 London Summit would be critical to selling German sovereignty and NATO membership to the Soviets. See George Bush and Brent Scowcroft, *A World Transformed* (New York: Alfred A. Knopf, 1998), 264–68.

38. See Hutchings, *American Diplomacy and the End of the Cold War,* 144.

39. George H.W. Bush, "Security Strategy for the 1990s," Address at the U.S. Coast Guard Academy, May 24, 1989 (Current Policy no. 1178).

40. James A. Baker, III, *The Politics of Diplomacy: Revolution, War & Peace, 1989–1992* (New York: G.P. Putnam's Sons, 1995), 256–57.

41. Hutchings, *American Diplomacy and the End of the Cold War,* 157.

42. Bush and Scowcroft, *A World Transformed*, 268. At the time, Mitterand feared that any expansion of NATO's role would constitute a threat to the European Union project.

43. Wörner, "The Atlantic Alliance and European Security in the 1990s."

44. Declaration of a Transformed North Atlantic Alliance (The London Declaration).

45. Quoted in Hutchings, *American Diplomacy and the End of the Cold War,* 134.

46. Message From Turnberry, Ministerial Meeting of the North Atlantic Council, Turnberry, United Kingdom, June 7–8, 1990.

47. Hutchings, *American Diplomacy and the End of the Cold War,* 136.

48. Baker, *The Politics of Diplomacy*, 89.

49. Declaration of NATO Heads of State and Government participating in the meeting of the North Atlantic Council, Brussels, May 1989.

50. Quoted in Thomas, *The Promise of Alliance,* 145.

51. Hutchings, *American Diplomacy and the End of the Cold War,* 147–48.

52. Ibid., 144.

53. The initiative followed a visit to the region by then U.S. Secretary of Defense Richard Cheney in 1991.

54. Stephen J. Flanagan, "NATO and Central and Eastern Europe. From Liaison to Security Partnership," *The Washington Quarterly* (Spring 1992): 144.

55. Bush, "Proposals for a Free and Peaceful Europe," 2.

56. Declaration of NATO Heads of State and Government participating in the meeting of the North Atlantic Council, Brussels, May 1989.

57. Baker, "A New Europe: A New Atlanticism."

58. Partnership with the Countries of Central and Eastern Europe, Statement issued by the North Atlantic Council in Ministerial Session, Copenhagen, June 7, 1991.

59. Declaration on Peace and Cooperation issued by the Heads of State and Government participating in the meeting of the North Atlantic Council (including decisions leading to the creation of the North Atlantic Cooperation Council (NACC) ("The Rome Declaration"), Rome, November 8, 1991.

60. 1991 (Rome) Strategic Concept, http://www.nato/int/docu/basictxt/6911108a.htm (accessed January 1997).

61. Flanagan, "NATO and Central and Eastern Europe," 148.

62. Interview with U.S. Department of State official, May 2002.

63. Baker, *The Politics of Diplomacy*, 584.

64. Quoted in Yost, *NATO Transformed*, 101.

65. Hutchings, *American Diplomacy and the End of the Cold War*, 291. Hutchings claims that the "fatal blow" to the NACC came during its second meeting held in March 1992 following the disintegration of the Soviet Union. A decision at the meeting to invite all of the Newly Independent States to join the NACC, he says, served only to weaken it as a security institution, 292.

66. Hutchings, *American Diplomacy and the End of the Cold War*, 307.

67. Quoted in Jeffrey Gedmin, testimony before the Senate Foreign Relations Committee, March 24, 1999, http://www.aei.org/publication/pubID.16929,filter.all/pub_detail.asp.

68. The Alliance's Strategic Concept agreed by the Heads of State and Government participating in the meeting of the North Atlantic Council, Rome, November 8, 1991, http://www.nato.int/docu/basictxt/b911108a.htm.

69. Przemyslaw Grudzinski and Peter van Ham, *A Critical Approach to European Security: Identity and Institutions* (London and New York: Pinter, 1999).

70. Hutchings, *American Diplomacy and the End of the Cold War*, 283.

71. Author interview with Ambassador Przemyslaw Grudzinski, Washington, D.C., May 2002. See also Ronald D. Asmus, *Opening NATO's Door: How the Alliance Remade Itself for a New Era* (New York: Columbia University Press, 2002), 15–16.

72. Flanagan, "NATO and Central and Eastern Europe," 143.

73. The fact that the meeting took place at Visegrád was historically significant and symbolically important. Visegrád had been the site of an important meeting in 1335 between the Polish, Hungarian, and Czech kings, which was also designed to promote regional cooperation.

74. See Asmus, *Opening NATO's Door*, 17.

75. James M. Goldgeier, *Not Whether But When: The U.S. Decision to Enlarge NATO* (Washington, DC: Brookings Institution Press, 1999), 18.

76. Author interview, U.S. Department of State, May 2002.

77. Asmus, *Opening NATO's Door*, 17.

78. Author interview with senior U.S. Foreign Service officer, Washington, D.C., May 2002.

79. See, for example, Flanagan, "NATO and Central and Eastern Europe," 145. Flanagan notes that Central and East European governments believed that

"NATO governments were much more interested in allaying Soviet concerns than in helping them emerge from the legacy of Communist rule."

80. Flanagan, "NATO and Central and Eastern Europe," 141.

81. George Kennan, the original architect of U.S. containment strategy toward the Soviet Union during the Cold War, would ultimately label the decision to expand NATO the "most fateful error of American foreign policy in the entire post–cold war era" due to what he perceived as its potential to "inflame nationalistic, anti-Western and militaristic tendencies in Russian opinion." George Kennan, "NATO: A Fateful Error," *New York Times,* February 2, 1997.

82. For further discussion on the views of Clinton's principal foreign policy advisers, see Asmus, *Opening NATO's Door;* Stanley R. Sloan, *NATO, the European Union, and the Atlantic Community: The Transatlantic Bargain Reconsidered* (Rowman & Littlefield, 2003); and Goldgeier, *Not Whether But When.*

83. Hans Binnendijk, "NATO Can't Be Vague About Commitment to Eastern Europe," *International Herald Tribune,* November 8, 1991.

84. Asmus, *Opening NATO's Door,* 31.

85. Richard Lugar, "NATO: Out of Area or Out of Business. A Call for U.S. Leadership to Revive and Redefine the Alliance," Overseas Writers Club, Washington, D.C., June 24, 1993.

86. See Sloan, *NATO, the European Union, and the Atlantic Community,* 139; and Asmus, *Opening NATO's Door,* 30.

87. Ronald D. Asmus, Richard L. Kugler, F. Stephen Larrabee, "Building a New NATO," *Foreign Affairs* 72, no. 4 (September/October 1993): 28–49.

88. See, for example, Barry Bearak, "Havel Wants a NATO Open to Democracies," *The New York Times,* May 15, 1997.

89. Havel, "NATO's Quality of Life."

90. See Václav Havel, "A Call for Sacrifice," *Foreign Affairs* 73, no. 2 (March/April 1994) 3. At the CSCE summit in Budapest in December 1994, Havel observed, "Many countries that shook off their totalitarian regimes still feel insufficiently anchored in the community of democratic states. They are often disappointed by the reluctance with which that community had opened its arms to them. The demons we thought had been driven forever from the minds of people and nations are rousing themselves again." See Václav Havel, "A New European Order?" *The New York Review of Books,* March 2, 1995. Havel also warned in 1996 that the "spirit of Munich" was returning to Europe. See also "Havel's Reminder to the West," *The Economist* (March 30, 1996): 50.

91. "Postcommunist states" had appealed to the West not to close itself, Havel wrote, because they were "concerned about the destiny of the values and principles that communism denied, and in whose name [they] resisted communism and ultimately brought it down." See Havel, "A Call for Sacrifice," 4.

92. Quoted in Asmus, *Opening NATO's Door,* 24.

93. William Clinton, "Partnership for Peace, Building a New Security," Remarks to the North Atlantic Council, Brussels, January 10, 1994.

94. See Partnership for Peace Invitation, issued by the Heads of State and Government participating in the Meeting of the North Atlantic Council, Brussels, January 10–11, 1994.

95. On the ambiguity surrounding the time frame for enlargement, see Goldgeier, *Not Whether But When,* 57–58.

96. France and Italy had lobbied in favor of including Slovenia and Romania in the first round of enlargement. Britain, however, preferred a small enlargement, and the Clinton administration ultimately concluded that three would be a sufficient challenge in terms of winning the necessary Senate ratification. See, for example, Sloan, *NATO, the European Union, and the Atlantic Community,* 148.

97. Some critics also charged that Clinton's support for enlargement stemmed from domestic political considerations. *New York Times* columnist Thomas Friedman, for example, accused Clinton of politicizing the issue through "a cynical effort to attract votes from Polish, Czech and Hungarian Americans by promising their motherlands membership." See Thomas Friedman, "Bye-Bye NATO," *New York Times,* April 14, 1997.

98. See, for example, Sloan, *NATO, the European Union, and the Atlantic Community,* 147; and Asmus, *Opening NATO's Door,* xxv.

99. Clinton, Remarks to the North Atlantic Council, Brussels, January 10, 1994.

100. NATO Enlargement Fact Sheet. See also Madeleine Albright, "Enlarging NATO," *The Economist* (February 15, 1997): 22; and Strobe Talbott, Speech at the Atlantic Council, May 20, 1997.

101. Madeleine Albright, "NATO Expansion: Beginning the Process of Advice and Consent," Statement before the Senate Foreign Relations Committee, Department of State *Dispatch,* October 17, 1997, 31. See also "Excerpts from Speech: Binding Broader Europe," *New York Times,* January 10, 1994. Asmus also notes that, unlike many conservatives, Clinton did not see NATO enlargement as "part of a policy of neo-containment toward Russia. On the contrary, building a new cooperative relationship with a democratic Russia remained a leitmotif for him thoughout his tenure in the Oval Office." See Asmus, *Opening NATO's Door,* 26.

102. Albright, "NATO Expansion," 4.

103. U.S. Mission to NATO, Report to Congress on Enlargement of the North Atlantic Treaty Organization: Rationale, Benefits, Costs and Implications—Executive Summary, February 24, 1997.

104. Study on NATO Enlargement, Brussels, September 3, 1995, www.nato/int/docu/basictxt/enl-9501.htm (accessed January 1999).

105. Quoted in U.S. Commission on Security and Cooperation in Europe, *Report on Human Rights and the Process of NATO Enlargement,* June 1997, 7.

106. Sean Kay, "NATO Enlargement: Policy, Process, and Implications," in *America's New Allies: Poland, Hungary, and the Czech Republic in NATO,* ed. Andrew A. Michta (Seattle, WA and London: University of Washington Press, 1999), 170.

107. Strobe Talbott, "Why NATO Should Grow," *The New York Review of Books,* 42, no. 13 (August 10, 1995).

108. Strobe Talbott, Speech on NATO Enlargement at the Atlantic Council, May 20, 1997. In his 1994 speech in Brussels, Bill Clinton had, in fact, posed the following questions: "Why should we now draw a line through Europe just a little further east? Why should we now do something which could foreclose the best possible future for Europe? The best possible future would be a democratic Russia committed to the security of all of its European neighbors. The best possible future would be a democratic Ukraine, a democratic government in every one of the newly independent states of the former Soviet Union, all committed to market cooperation, to common security, and to democratic ideals." See Bill Clinton, Remarks to the North Atlantic Council, Brussels, January 10, 1994.

109. Madeleine Albright, "The NATO Summit," May 28, 1998, U.S. Department of State *Dispatch* (June 1998): 9.

110. Flanagan, "NATO and Central and Eastern Europe," 149.

111. Alexander Vershbow, "European and Atlantic Integration, Shared Values, Shared Destiny," Speech at the Conference on Euro-Atlantic Integration, Vilnius, September 3, 1998.

112. The PJC was replaced in 2002 with the NATO-Russia Council (NRC).

113. Richard G. Lugar, "NATO after 9/11: Crisis or Opportunity?" Speech before the Council on Foreign Relations, March 4, 2002.

114. Manfred Wörner, Speech by the Secretary General of NATO to the IISS, Brussels, September 10, 1993, http://www.nato.int/docu/speech/1993/s930910a.htm.

115. Sloan, *NATO, the European Union, and the Atlantic Community,* 96; and Lawrence S. Kaplan, *NATO United, NATO Divided: The Evolution of an Alliance* (Westport, CT: Praeger, 2004), 120.

116. Wörner, Speech by the Secretary General of NATO to the IISS, Brussels, September 10, 1993.

117. Sloan, *NATO, the European Union, and the Atlantic Community,* 97–98.

118. Wörner, Speech by the Secretary General of NATO to the IISS, Brussels, September 10, 1993.

119. See, for example, Warren Christopher, "NATO's True Mission," *New York Times,* October 21, 1997, A21. See also Craig R. Whitney, "NATO at 50: With Nations at Odds, Is It a Misalliance?," *New York Times,* February 5, 1999, A7.

120. Asmus, *Opening NATO's Door,* xxv.

121. Lugar, "NATO after 9/11."

122. Background briefing by NATO Secretary General Jaap de Hoop Scheffer on an upcoming ministerial meeting in Sofia, Bulgaria, NATO Headquarters, Brussels, April 25, 2006.

Chapter 2

1. The Clinton administration argued that NATO should play a role in addressing common interests outside of Europe, including such threats as the proliferation of weapons of mass destruction, terrorism, and the potential disruption of the flow of oil. The European allies objected strongly to what they saw as an effort by the United States to turn NATO into a global alliance. See, for example, Ronald D. Asmus, *Opening NATO's Door: How the Alliance Remade Itself for a New Era* (New York: Columbia University Press, 2002), 290–91. See also Warren Christopher, "NATO's True Mission," *New York Times,* October 21, 1997, A21; and Craig R. Whitney, "NATO at 50: With Nations at Odds, Is It a Misalliance?," *New York Times,* February 15, 1999, A7.

2. Lord Robertson, "NATO: A Vision for 2012," Speech at GMFUS Conference, Brussels, October 3, 2002, http://www.nato.int/docu/speech/2002/s021003a.htm.

3. At Prague, the Allies identified priority categories for improvements in defense capabilities through the Prague Capabilities Commitment. See Ahto Lobjakas, "NATO Members Commit Themselves—Again—to Modernization," Radio

Free Europe, Radio Liberty, November 2002, http://www.rferl.org/features/2002/11/21112002162242.asp (accessed January 2003).

4. Jaap de Hoop Scheffer, "Projecting Stability," Speech given at the conference "Defending Global Security: The New Politics of Transatlantic Defence Cooperation," Brussels, May 17, 2004.

5. Javier Solana, "An Alliance Fit for the 21st Century," *NATO Review* 47, no. 3 (Autumn 1999): 3.

6. Lord Robertson, "NATO in the New Millenium," *NATO Review* 47, no. 4 (Winter 1999): 3.

7. Michael Mandelbaum. "A Perfect Failure: NATO's War against Yugoslavia," *Foreign Affairs* 78, no. 5 (September/October 1999): 3–5. Mandelbaum suggests that, in Kosovo, NATO "aspired to establish a new doctrine governing military operations in the post–Cold War era," comprising two parts: "the use of force on behalf of universal values instead of the narrower national interest for which sovereign states have traditionally fought; and, and in defense of these values, military intervention in the internal affairs of sovereign rather than mere opposition to cross-border aggression."

8. See, for example, Thomas Risse-Kappen, *Cooperation among Democracies: The European Influence on U.S. Foreign Policy* (Princeton, NJ: Princeton University Press, 1995), 9.

9. George Bush, "Security Strategy for the 1990s," Address at the U.S. Coast Guard Academy, May 24, 1989 (Current Policy no. 1178).

10. U.S. Commission on Security and Cooperation in Europe, *Document of the Copenhagen Meeting of the Conference on the Human Dimension of the CSCE,* Washington, D.C., 1990, 102.

11. Thomas Buergenthal, "Copenhagen: A Democratic Manifesto," *World Affairs* 153, no. 1 (Summer 1990): 6–7.

12. During the 1990 NATO summit in London, the Allies had also called upon the CSCE to hold another summit at which members would issue a further endorsement of democratic principles and processes.

13. CSCE, Charter of Paris for a New Europe, November 19–21, 1990, at http://www.osce.org/documents/mcs/1990/11/4045_en.pdf (accessed November 2006).

14. Robert Hunter, "Enlargement: Part of a Strategy for Projecting Stability into Central Europe," *NATO Review* 43, no. 3 (May 1995): 3–8.

15. Timothy Garton Ash, "Europe's Endangered Liberal Order," *Foreign Affairs* 77, no. 2 (March/April 1998): 64.

16. Final Communique of the Ministerial Meeting of the North Atlantic Council (including the Oslo decision on NATO support for peacekeeping activities under the responsibility of the OSCE), Oslo, June 4, 1992, http://www.nato.int/docu/basictxt/b920604a.htm. Meeting in Petersberg, Germany, that same month, Western European Union (WEU) states agreed to deploy military units of WEU member states for "humanitarian and rescue tasks, peacekeeping tasks, tasks of combat forces in crisis management, including peacemaking" on the basis of a mandate from the CSCE or the UN Security Council.

17. Rob de Wijk, *NATO on the Brink of the New Millennium: The Battle for Consensus*, Brassey's Atlantic Commentaries (Brassey's, 1997), 55.

18. Final Communique of the Ministerial Meeting of the North Atlantic Council (including decisions on NATO support for peacekeeping operations under the responsibility of the UN Security Council), Brussels, December 17, 1992, http://www.nato.int/docu/basictxt/b921217a.htm.

19. The Alliance's Strategic Concept, April 23–24, 1999, available in *The Reader's Guide to the NATO Summit in Washington* (Brussels: NATO Office of Information and Press, 1999), 47–60.

20. Final Communique of the Ministerial Meeting of the North Atlantic Council, Oslo, June 4, 1992, http://www.nato.int/docu/comm/49-95/c920604a.htm.

21. The Washington Declaration, April 23–24, 1999, in *The Reader's Guide to the NATO Summit in Washington,* (Brussels: NATO Office of Information and Press, 1999), 11–12.

22. Steven Erlanger, "Pressure on NATO to Expand," *New York Times,* February 9, 1996.

23. See "Strengthening Transatlantic Security: A U.S. Strategy for the 21st Century." In Berlin in December 1989 U.S. Secretary of State Baker had also remarked that there was no single institution, including NATO, capable of achieving a Europe "whole and free." See Stephen J. Flanagan, "NATO and Central and Eastern Europe: From Liaison to Security Partnership," *The Washington Quarterly* (Spring 1992): 142. The OSCE's 1999 Istanbul Charter also recognized that "the risks and challenges we face today cannot be met by a single state or organization." See OSCE, The Charter for European Security (The Istanbul Charter), November 18–19, http://www.osce.org/documents/mcs/1999/11/4050_en.pdf (accessed November 2006).

24. The first five states constitute the Mediterranean Dialogue's original membership. Jordan joined in 1995 and Algeria in 2000.

25. Istanbul Summit Communique, Press Release (2004) 096, June 28, 2004, http://www.nato.int/docu/pr/2004/p04-096e.htm. See also Fact Sheet on Mediterranean Dialogue, Ministerial Meeting, December 8, 2004, http://www.nato.int/med-dial/2004/041208e.pdf.

26. "NATO Elevates Mediterranean Dialogue to a Genuine Partnership, Launches Istanbul Cooperation Initiative," NATO Update, June 29, 2004, http://www.nato.int/docu/update/2004/06-june/e0629d.htm.

27. The Alliance's (1999) Strategic Concept.

28. See the Washington Declaration, April 23–24, 1999, 11–12.

29. Partnership for Peace: Framework Document, January 10–11, 1994, http://www.nato/int/docu/basictxt/b940110b.htm (accessed January 1997).

30. Quoted in David S. Yost, *NATO Transformed: The Alliance's New Roles in International Security* (Washington, DC: United States Institute of Peace Press, 1998), 177.

31. The NATO-Russia Permanent Joint Council created in 1997 has since been replaced by the NATO-Russia Council, established in May 2002.

32. Author interview, NATO Headquarters, Brussels, December 2001.

33. "NATO Launches 'Intensified Dialogue' with Ukraine," NATO Update, April 21, 2005, http://www.nato.int/docu/update/2005/04-april/e0421b.htm.

34. See Partnership Action Plan against Terrorism, Prague, November 22, 2002, http://www.nato.int/docu/basictxt/b021122e.htm.

35. Partnership Action Plan on Defence Institution Building (PAP-DIB), Brussels, June 7, 2004, http://www.nato.int/docu/basictxt/b040607e.htm.

36. The Washington Declaration, April 23–24, 1999.

37. For further information on CCMS, see http://www.nato.int/ccms.

38. John Gerard Ruggie, *Winning the Peace: America and World Order in the New Era* (New York: Columbia University Press, 1996), 85.

39. Karl W. Deutsch, *Political Community and the North Atlantic Area: International Organization in Light of Historical Experience* (Princeton: Princeton University Press), 191.

40. See 1991 (Rome) Strategic Concept, http://www.nato.int/docu/basictxt/b911108a.htm (accessed January 1999); and The Alliance's (1999) Strategic Concept.

41. OSCE, The Charter for European Security (The Istanbul Charter).

42. Václav Havel, "NATO's Quality of Life," *New York Times,* May 13, 1997.

43. See, for example, Barry Buzan, Morten Kelstrup, Pierre Lemaitre, Elzbieta Tromer, and Ole Waever, *The European Security Order Recast: Scenarios for the Post–Cold War Era* (London: Pinter Publishers, 1990), 3. See also Edward Newman, "Human Security and Constructivism," *International Studies Perspectives* 2, no. 3 (August 2001): 239. As Newman explains it, "'human security' seeks to place the individual—or people collectively—as the referent of security, rather than, although not necessarily in opposition to, institutions such as territory and state sovereignty."

44. Lloyd Axworthy, "NATO's New Security Vocation," *NATO Review* 47, no. 4 (Winter 1999): 9.

45. The Washington Declaration, April 23–24, 1999.

46. U.S. Department of Defense, *Strengthening Transatlantic Security: A U.S. Strategy for the 21st Century* (December 2000), 38.

47. Richard Cohen, "From Individual Security to International Stability," in Richard Cohen and Michael Mihalka, *Cooperative Security: New Horizons for International Order,* The Marshall Center Papers, no. 3, 7–8.

48. See, for example, Kofi Annan, Nobel Lecture, Oslo, December 10, 2001, http://www.nobel.se/peace/laureates/2001/annan-lecture.html. For a collection of research essays and extensive bibliography regarding the concepts of sovereignty and intervention and how they should be understood in an international security context, see *The Responsibility to Protect, Research, Bibliography, Background: Supplementary Volume to the Report of the International Commission on Intervention and State Sovereignty* (Ottawa, ON, Canada: International Development Research Centre, 2001).

49. Tony Blair, "Doctrine of the International Community," (The "Blair Doctrine"), Speech before the Chicago Economic Club, April 22, 1999, *Online Newshour,* http://www.pbs.org/newshour/international/jan-june99/blair_doctrine4-23.html.

50. Address by the Honourable Lloyd Axworthy, Minister of Foreign Affairs to the Permanent Council of the Organization for Security and Cooperation in Europe, Vienna, October 22, 1998.

51. Axworthy, "NATO's New Security Vocation," 11.

52. de Wijk, *NATO on the Brink of the New Millennium,* 54.

53. Boutros Boutros-Ghali, *An Agenda for Democratization* (New York: United Nations, 1996), 6.

54. Kofi Annan, Nobel Lecture, Oslo, December 10, 2001.

55. See Commission on Human Rights Resolution 1999/57, released by the Commission on Human Rights, United Nations, New York, April 27, 1999, http://www.state.gov/www/global/human_rights/democracy/9957_unresolu-tion. html; and "U.S. Applauds Decision by the United Nations Commission on Human Rights to Pass a Resolution on the Right to Democracy," Press Statement by James P. Rubin, Spokesman, April 25, 2000, http://secretary.state.gov/www/briefings/statements/2000/ps000525.html.

56. For one example of the growing willingness to label democracy as a human right, see Thomas Franck, "The Emerging Right to Democratic Governance," *American Journal of International Law* 86 (January 1992): 46–91. In this oft-cited article, Franck argued that democratic government was increasingly being recognized by the international community as the only form of legitimate government and a "requirement of international law."

57. Thomas Risse, in *The Third Force: The Rise of Transnational Civil Society,* ed. Ann M. Florini (Washington, DC: Carnegie Endowment for International Peace and New York: Japan Center for International Exchange, 2000), 178.

58. In his own memoirs, Carter observes that his administration was initially "inclined to define human rights too narrowly." It was not "merely a matter of reducing the incidence of summary executions or torture of political prisoners," he acknowledges. "It also included the promotion of democratic principles such as those expressed in our Bill of Rights." See Jimmy Carter, *Keeping Faith: Memoirs of a President* (New York: Bantam Books, 1982), 144.

59. Ronald Reagan, "Promoting Democracy and Peace," speech before the British Parliament, London, June 8, 1982.

60. Lord Robertson, "International Citizenship," speech in Skopje, Macedonia, September 2001, http://www.nato.int/docu/speech/2001/s010906a.htm (accessed May 2003).

61. Volker Rühe, "Shaping Euro-Atlantic Policies: A Grand Strategy for a New Era," *Survival* 35, no. 2 (Summer 1993): 134.

62. Cohen, "From Individual Security to International Stability," 8.

63. Quoted in Ove Bring, "Should NATO Take the Lead in Formulating a Doctrine on Humanitarian Intervention," *NATO Review* 47, no. 3 (Autumn 1999): 24–27.

64. *The Responsibility to Protect, Report of the International Commission on Intervention and State Sovereignty* (Ottawa, Canada: International Development Research Centre), December 2001. See also Gareth Evans and Mohamed Sahnoun, "The Responsibility to Protect," *Foreign Affairs* 81, no. 6 (November/December 2002). The 12-member commission, which was chaired by former Australian Foreign Minister Gareth Evans and Special Advisor to the UN Secretary General Mohamed Sahnoun of Algeria, compiled its report after a series of consultative meetings held with national officials, civil society representatives, NGOs, and academics in Ottawa, Geneva, London, Washington, D.C., Santiago, Cairo, New Delhi, Beijing, and St. Petersburg between January and July 2001.

65. Kofi Annan, "Two Concepts of Sovereignty," *The Economist* (September 18, 1999): 49–50.

66. Václav Havel, address to the Senate and the House of Commons of the Parliament of Canada in *Kosovo: Contending Voices on Balkan Interventions,* ed. William Joseph Buckley (Grand Rapids, MI: Wm. B. Eerdmans Publishing Co., 2000), 245.

67. See, for example, Michael J. Glennon, "The New Interventionism," *Foreign Affairs* 78, no. 3 (May/June 1999): 2–7.

68. Robert O. Keohane and Joseph S. Nye, in *Governance in a Globalizing World* (Washinton, DC: Brookings Institution Press, 2000): 25.

69. See, for example, *A World at Peace: Common Security in the Twenty-first Century* (Stockholm: Palme Commission on Disarmament and Security Issues, April 1989).

70. Stanley Hoffman, *World Disorders: Troubled Peace in the Post–Cold War Era* (Lanham, MD: Rowman & Littlefield, 1998), 156.

71. Neil Winn, "Europe: Old Institutions, New Challenges," in *International Security in a Global Age: Securing the Twenty-First Century,* ed. Clive Jones and Caroline Kennedy-Pipe (Portland, OR: Frank Cass Publishers, 2000), 92–93.

72. See, for example, Richard Falk "'Humanitarian Wars,' Realist Geopolitics and Genocidal Practices: 'Saving the Kosovars'" in *The Kosovo Tragedy: The Human Rights Dimensions,* ed. Ken Booth (Portland, OR: Frank Cass, 2001), 329. As Falk puts it, "the acknowledgment of moral guilt by leading governments in relation to these severe instances of ethnic strife in the early 1990s, especially in the setting of former Yugoslavia made it politically unacceptable to wait on the sidelines while a new tragedy unfolded in Kosovo. This consideration was strengthened by the extremely dirty hands of the West resulting from its earlier willingness to strike a Faustian bargain with Milosevic as a helpful means of finding a diplomatic solution to the Bosnian War at Dayton in 1995." See also Adam Roberts, "NATO's 'Humanitarian War,'" *Survival* 41, no. 3 (Autumn, 1999): 104.

73. See, for example, Nicholas J. Wheeler, "Reflections on the Legality and Legitimacy of NATO's Intervention in Kosovo" in *The Kosovo Tragedy,* 145.

74. Roberts, "NATO's 'Humanitarian War,'" 106–107.

75. Falk, "'Humanitarian Wars,' Realist Geopolitics and Genocidal Practices," 332.

76. Robertson offered both legal and moral justifications for NATO's action in Kosovo in his speech before the Institut de Relations Internationales et Strategiques in Paris in May 2000. See Lord Robertson, "Law, Morality, and the Use of Force," May 16, 2000, speech at the Institut de Relations Internationales et Strategiques, Paris, http://www.nato.int/docu/speech/2000/s000516a.htm (accessed May 2003).

77. Statement on Kosovo, issued by the heads of State and Government participating in the meeting of the North Atlantic Council, Washington, D.C., April 23–24, 1999.

78. Blair, "Doctrine of the International Community." Similarly, the Canadian Ambassador stated that "humanitarian considerations underpin our action. We cannot simply stand by while innocents are murdered, an entire population is displaced, villages are burned." Quoted in Wheeler, "Reflections on the Legality and Legitimacy of NATO's Intervention in Kosovo," 153.

79. Blair, "Doctrine of the International Community."

80. Richard Falk among many others has argued that the "viability of NATO depended upon quickly finding a new raison d'etre." Falk, "'Humanitarian Wars,' Realist Geopolitics and Genocidal Practices," 329.

81. Javier Solana, "Fresh Cause for Hope at the Opening of the New Century," in *Kosovo: Contending Voices on Balkan Interventions,* ed. William Joseph Buckley (Grand Rapids, MI: Wm. B. Eerdmans Publishing Co., 2000), 255. NATO Secretary General Lord Robertson later justified the intervention in similar terms. "This issue goes to the heart of our morality," he asserted. "If we had allowed this ethnic cleansing to go unanswered, we would have fatally undermined the basis of the Euro-Atlantic Community we are trying to build, as we enter the 21st century." See Lord Robertson, "Law, Morality, and the Use of Force."

82. William Jefferson Clinton, "A Just and Necessary War," *New York Times,* May 23, 1999.

83. Madeline Albright, "A New NATO for a New Century," remarks at the Brookings Institution, April 6, 1999, in U.S. Department of State *Dispatch* 10, no. 3 (April 1999): 7.

84. See Madeleine Albright, "U.S. and NATO Policy toward the Crisis in Kosovo," testimony before the Senate Foreign Relations Committee, April 20, 1999, in U.S. Department of State *Dispatch* 10, no. 4 (May 1999): 6.

85. Tony Blair, "Doctrine of the International Community." In addition to asking whether national interests were involved, Blair suggested that NATO should address four other questions in making determinations about whether to intervene: "First are we sure of our case? . . . . Second, have we exhausted all diplomatic options? . . . Third, on the basis of a practical assessment of the situation are there military operations we can sensibly and prudently undertake? Fourth, are we prepared for the long term?"

86. Author interviews, NATO Headquarters, Brussels, December 2001.

87. Roberts, "NATO's 'Humanitarian War,'" 120.

88. Javier Solana, "A Defining Moment for NATO: The Washington Summit Decisions and the Kosovo Crisis," *NATO Review* 47, no. 2 (Summer 1999): 8. During a press conference in Brussels on April 20, 1999, Solana had also asserted that NATO "actually defends" the values it proclaims. "This," he said, "is why we had a responsibility to act in Kosovo and that is why we have done so." See Javier Solana, Press Conference, Brussels, April 20, 1999, http://www.NATO.int.

89. Robertson, "Law, Morality, and the Use of Force."

90. Author interview with NATO international staff member, NATO Headquarters, Brussels, December 2001.

91. During a news conference in Montenegro, Robinson said, "If civilian lives are lost, that certainly hasn't achieved a humanitarian objective." "World Europe: Robinson Attacks NATO Campaign,"*BBC News Online Network,* May 9, 1999, http://news.bbc.co.uk.

92. "Civilian Deaths in the NATO Air Campaign," *Human Rights Watch Report* 12, no. 1, February 2000, http://www.hrw.org.

93. Zbigniew Brzezinski, "NATO Must Stop Russia's Power Play," *Wall Street Journal,* June 14, 1999, in *Kosovo: Contending Voices on Balkan Interventions,* 326–27. Brzezinski further stated, "Just consider how the public would feel if some policemen, reacting to thugs throwing children in a swift river, confined themselves to merely arresting the thugs, on the grounds that any attempt at rescue might risk

a policeman's life. Gloating over the ultimate 'score' of 5,000 Serbs killed to zero Americans simply reinforces the global perception of a troubling moral standard." Similarly, Neil Winn observed that this reluctance to risk casualties certainly invited "the question of whether the Alliance was willing to 'elevate' human rights only at a limited cost to its members." See Winn, "Europe: Old Institutions, New Challenges," 93.

94. Carl Cavanaugh Hodge, "Casual War: NATO's Intervention in Kosovo," *Ethics & International Relations* 14 (2000): 39–54.

95. Riga Summit Declaration, issued by the Heads of State and Government participating in the meeting of the North Atlantic Council in Riga, PR/CP (2006) 150, November 29, 2006.

96. Author e-mail interview with R. Nicholas Burns, U.S. Ambassador to NATO, January 31, 2005.

Chapter 3

1. Michael Mandelbaum, "Preserving the New Peace: The Case Against NATO Expansion," *Foreign Affairs* 74, no. 3 (May/June 1995): 10.

2. In addition to Mandelbaum, see, for example, Dan Reiter, "Why NATO Enlargement Does Not Spread Democracy," *International Security* 25, no. 4 (2001): 41; Christopher Layne, "Why Die for Gdansk? NATO Enlargement and American Security Interests" in *NATO Enlargement: Illusion and Realities*, ed. Ted Galen Carpenter and Barbara Conry (Washington, DC: CATO Institute, 1998), 58; and Karl Heinz-Kamp, "The Folly of Rapid NATO Expansion," *Foreign Policy* no. 98 (Spring 1995): 123.

3. Lord Robertson, "International Citizenship," speech by the Secretary General at the Roscoe Lecture Series, John Moore University, Liverpool, September 6, 2001, http://www.nato.int/docu/speech/2001/5010906a.htm.

4. Reiter, "Why NATO Enlargement Does Not Spread Democracy," 59–60.

5. See, for example, Larry Diamond, *Developing Democracy: Toward Consolidation* (Baltimore: Johns Hopkins University Press, 1999).

6. See, for example, the work of Thomas Carothers, including: *Aiding Democracy Abroad: The Learning Curve* (Washington, DC. Carnegie Endowment for International Peace, 1999).

7. See, for example, Mary Kaldor and Ivan Vejvoda, eds., *Democratization in Central and Eastern Europe* (London: Pinter, 1999), 9. Kaldor and Vejvoda cite the lack of a rights-based culture in Central and Eastern Europe as one obstacle to democratization. As they put it, "The legacy of social guarantees under communism has left an inclination to view human rights as equated not with individual, civic and political rights, but largely with economic and social rights..." This lack of experience with individual rights, in their view, has led to discrimination against minorities.

8. Steven Woehrel, Julie Kim, and Carl Ek, *NATO Applicant States: A Status Report,* Congressional Research Service Report to Congress, February 7, 2000. The report was requested by Senator William Roth and "contains brief assessments of the NATO applicants' qualifications, compared to those of Poland, The Czech Republic and Hungary."

9. The Visegrád states consist of Hungary, Poland, Slovakia, and the Czech Republic. The group acquired its name from the town of Visegrád, Hungary, the site where the presidents of Hungary, Poland, and Czechoslovakia first met in February 1991.

10. Jeffrey Simon, *NATO Enlargement and Central Europe: A Study in Civil-Military Relations* (Washington, DC: National Defense University Press, 1996), 313. See Jane Perlez, "With Promises, Promises, NATO Moves the East," *New York Times*, April 26, 1998, A16. See also *Meeting the Challenges of Post–Cold War World: NATO Enlargement and U.S.–Russia Relations. A Report to the Committee on Foreign Relations*, submitted by Joseph R. Biden Jr. in *The Debate on NATO Enlargement*, hearings before the Committee on Foreign Relations, 105th Congress, 1st session, October/November 1997, 353.

11. For a discussion of the need to educate civilian officials on defense matters, see Charlie Rose, "Democratic Control of the Armed Forces: A Parliamentary Role in Partnership for Peace," *NATO Review* 42, no. 5 (October 1995): 15–19. See also Woehrel, Kim, and Ek, *NATO Applicant States*.

12. The *Study on NATO Enlargement* (September 1995) is available at http://www.nato.int.

13. William J. Perry, "The Enduring Dynamic Relationship That Is NATO," remarks to the Wehrkunde, Munich Conference on Security Policy, February 5, 1995 *Defense Viewpoint* 10, no. 9 (1995), http://www.defenselink.mil/speeches/1995/s19950205-perry.html.

14. Representatives from Bulgaria, the Czech Republic, Estonia, Hungary, Latvia, Lithuania, Poland, Romania, Slovakia, and Slovenia participated in the 1997 hearing. U.S. Commission on Security and Cooperation in Europe, *Report on Human Rights and the Process of NATO Enlargement*, June 1997.

15. U.S. Commission on Security and Cooperation in Europe, *Report on Human Rights and the Process of NATO Enlargement*.

16. Perlez, "With Promises, Promises, NATO Moves the East," A16.

17. Anton Bebler, "The Evolution of Civil-Military Relations in Central and Eastern Europe, *NATO Review* 42, no. 4 (August 1994): 28–32.

18. See Simon, *NATO Enlargement and Central Europe*, 299.

19. Rachel Epstein, "When Legacies Meet Policies: NATO and the Refashioning of Polish Military Tradition," *East European Politics and Societies* 20, no. 2 (May 2006): 257.

20. RFE/RL *Newsline* 6, no. 3, pt. II (January 7, 2002).

21. Membership Action Plan (MAP) Press Release NAC-S(99)66, April 24, 1999, http://www.nato.int/docu/pr/1999/p99-066e.htm.

22. Feedback takes place in part during annual 19 + 1 meetings of the North Atlantic Council. See Factsheet on NATO's Membership Action Plan, April 20, 2000. See also Membership Action Plan, Press Release NAC-S(99), April 24, 1999, http://www.nato.int.

23. See, for example, Jirí Sedivý, "The Puzzle of NATO Enlargement," *Contemporary Security Policy* 22, no. 2 (August 2001) 3; and author interviews, NATO Headquarters, Brussels, December 2001.

24. Author interviews, NATO Headquarters, Brussels, December 2001.

25. Author interview with aspirant state representative, NATO Headquarters, Brussels, December 2001.

26. See, for example, the testimony of representatives from Bulgaria, the Czech Republic, Estonia, Hungary, Latvia, Lithuania, Poland, Romania, Slovakia, and Slovenia during a 1997 hearing before the U.S. Commission on Security and Co-operation in Europe. See U.S. Commission on Security and Cooperation in Europe, *Report on Human Rights and the Process of NATO Enlargement.*

27. Author interviews, NATO Headquarters, Brussels, May 2003. The Prague Summit Declaration also states that progress on the timetables would ''be expected before and after accession.'' See Prague Summit Declaration, Press Communique PR/CP (2002)127, issued by the Heads of State and Government participating in the meeting of the North Atlantic Council in Prague, November 21, 2002.

28. Author interviews, NATO Headquarters, Brussels, May 2003.

29. IPAPs are two-year rather than annual plans, as is the case with MAP.

30. Author interviews, NATO Headquarters, Brussels, May 2003.

31. Ibid.

32. Ibid.

33. Hungary and Romania also supported each other's inclusion in the first phase of enlargement and have established a joint peacekeeping battalion.

34. For discussion of the significance of these various examples of regional rapprochement, see Elizabeth Pond, *The Rebirth of Europe* (Washington, DC: Brookings Institution Press, 1999), 14, and, especially, 74–77.

35. Craig R. Whitney, ''Germans and Czechs Try to Heal Hatreds of the Nazi Era,'' *New York Times*, January 22, 1997.

36. Pond, *The Rebirth of Europe*, 76–77. See also *The Debate on NATO Enlargement*, hearings before the Committee on Foreign Relations, 105th Congress, 1st session, October/November 1997, 300. During his visit to Warsaw in June 2001, President George W. Bush thanked Poland for ''acting as a bridge to the new democracies of Europe and a champion of the interests and security of [its] neighbors such as the Baltic states, Ukraine, and Slovakia.'' See ''Remarks by the President in Address to Faculty and Students of Warsaw University,'' June 15, 2001.

37. Perlez, ''With Promises, Promises, NATO Moves the East,'' A16.

38. See RFE/RL *Newsline*, January 6, 1999; and ''Visegrád Countries Call for Rapid Entry of Slovakia into NATO,'' *Central Europe Online*, January 20, 2001, http://www.centraleurope.com. See U.S. Department of Defense, Strengthening Transatlantic Security: A U.S. Strategy for the 21st Century (December 2000), 38.

39. Stephen J. Blank, *Prague, NATO and European Security* (Carlisle, PA: U.S. Army War College, Strategic Studies Institute, April 17, 1996), 4–5.

40. Madeleine Albright, ''NATO Enlargement: Advancing America's Strategic Interests,'' statement before the Senate Foreign Relations Committee, February 2, 1998, in Department of State *Dispatch* 9, no. 2 (March 1998): 14.

41. Quoted in Pond, *The Rebirth of Europe*, 74.

42. Reiter, ''Why NATO Enlargement Does Not Spread Democracy,'' 50.

43. Pond, *The Rebirth of Europe*, 74–76.

44. Progress in resolving regional disputes, however, is not confined to NATO applicant states. Poland has made considerable strides in improving its relations with Ukraine. In fact, both Poland and Romania have signed agreements with Ukraine resolving border disputes.

45. Woehrel, Kim, and Ek, *NATO Applicant States.*

46. Ronald H. Linden, "Putting on Their Sunday Best: Romania, Hungary, and the Puzzle of Peace," *International Studies Quarterly* 44, no. 1 (March 2000): 136.

47. John Tagliabue, "Bulgarians Bet Future on a Link to NATO," *New York Times*, May 2, 1999, A12. During a visit to Sofia in November 1999, Bill Clinton thanked Bulgaria for supporting the NATO campaign in Kosovo—in part by opening its airspace to NATO for bombing missions—and held out the possibility of NATO membership for Bulgaria in the future. See Marc Lacey, "A Grateful Clinton Offers Encouragement to Bulgaria," *New York Times*, November 23, 1999.

48. Francis X. Clines, "NATO's Next Applicants Preen, Jostle and Hope," *New York Times*, April 25, 1999.

49. "Polish, Bulgarian Defense Ministers Sign Agreement," *Central Europe Online*, October 13, 2000, http://www.centraleurope.com/news.php3?id=209208.

50. RFE/RL *Newsline* 5, no. 84, pt. II (May 2, 2001).

51. "Havel, Dzurinda Discuss NATO, Czech-Slovak KFOR Unit," *Czech News Agency*, May 29, 2001, lexisnexis.com.

52. Lord Robertson, "NATO's Challenges: Illusions and Realities," speech at the Chicago Council on Foreign Relations, June 19, 2001.

53. For further discussion regarding NATO's impact on political reform and regional cooperation in Central and Eastern Europe, see Thomas S. Szayna, *NATO Enlargement, 2000–2015: Determinants and Implication for Defense Planning and Shaping*, RAND Corporation, http://www.rand.org/publications/MR/MR1243. See especially 20–21.

54. For example, citing the Cold War case studies of Turkey, Spain, Portugal, and Greece, Reiter writes, "Overall, the cases provide almost no evidence that NATO membership significantly promoted democracy: The transgovernmental effects on civil-military relations were uneven, the stick of NATO ejection was never applied to members that reverted to autocracy, and in the instance of NATO entry there is no evidence of the NATO carrot spurring democratization." Reiter, "Why NATO Enlargement Does Not Promote Democracy," 56–57.

55. The Washington Declaration, April 23–24, 1999, in *The Reader's Guide to the NATO Summit in Washington*, (Brussels: NATO Office of Information and Press, 1999).

56. See, for example, Thomas S. Szayna, "The Czech Republic," in *America's New Allies: Poland, Hungary, and the Czech Republic in NATO*, ed. Andrew A. Michta (Seattle: University of Washington Press, 1999), 117.

57. Zdenek Kavan and Martin Palous, "Democracy in the Czech Republic," in Kaldor and Vejvoda, *Democratization in Central and Eastern Europe*, 78–79.

58. Linden, "Putting on Their Sunday Best," 126.

59. In the case of the Cold War, Brzezinski offers the examples of France's reconciliation with Germany, as well as France and Britain's ultimate acceptance of German reunification.

60. Zbigniew Brzezinski, "NATO: The Dilemmas of Expansion," *The National Interest*, no. 53 (Fall 1998): 13.

61. Petr Lunak, "Security for Eastern Europe: The European Option," *World Policy Journal* 11, no. 3 (Fall 1994): 128. See also Rachel Epstein, "NATO Enlargement and the Spread of Democracy: Evidence and Expectations," *Security Studies* 14, no. 1 (January–March 2005): 74. Epstein argues that, "for Poland, NATO had enormous symbolic value" in part because of the United States' "leading

role in the alliance and its strong public stand against both the Soviet Union and communism."

62. Bronisław Geremek, address on occasion of the accession protocols to the North Atlantic Treaty, December 16, 1997.

63. Václav Havel, "A Chance to Stop Exporting Wars and Violence," *Transitions* (December 1997): 17.

64. Aleksander Kwasniewski, "Isolationism Is an Anachronism," *Transitions* (December 1997): 23.

65. Steven Erlanger, "3 Fragments of Soviet Realm Joining NATO's Ranks," *New York Times,* March 12, 1999.

66. Simon Lunn, "NATO's Parliamentary Arm Helps Further the Aims of the Alliance" *NATO Review* 46, no. 4 (Winter 1998): 8–9.

67. Alexandra Gheciu notes that 63 courses/workshops on democratic control of the armed forces and defense structures were conducted within the context of the Partnership for Peace in 1997 alone. See also Alexandra Gheciu, *NATO in the "New Europe": The Politics of International Socialization after the Cold War* (Stanford, CA: Stanford University Press, 2005), 118–19.

68. U.S. Department of State Annual Report to Congress on PFP, July 29, 1997. See also Robert Kennedy, "Educating Leaders for the 21st Century—A Snapshot of the Marshall Center for Security Studies," *NATO Review* 46, no. 4 (Winter 1998): 28–29. For more information on the Marshall Center's activities, see the Marshall Center's Web site at http://www.marshallcenter.org.

69. Dana Priest, "U.S.–Run Center Helps Shape Future Leaders," *Washington Post*, December 14, 1998, A29.

70. Author interviews, NATO Headquarters, Brussels, December 2001.

71. Partnership Action Plan on Defence Institution Building (PAP-DIB), Brussels, June 7, 2004, http://www.nato.int/docu/basictxt/b040607e.htm.

72. Igor Lukes, "Central Europe Has Joined NATO: The Continuing Search for a More Perfect Habsburg Empire," *SAIS Review* 19, no. 2 (Summer–Fall 1999): 51.

73. Gheciu, *NATO in the "New Europe,"* 13, 110.

74. Martha Finnemore and Kathryn Sikkink, "International Norm Dynamics and Political Change," *International Organization* 52, no. 4 (Autumn 1998): 895.

75. Peter J. Katzenstein, "Introduction: Alternative Perspectives on National Security," in *The Culture of National Security* (New York: Columbia University Press, 1996), 5.

76. Szayna, *NATO Enlargement, 2000–2015,* 9, 15. This study also notes that NATO's current strategy for enlargement "represents a complete switch from the way NATO enlarged during the Cold War."

77. Gheciu, *NATO in the "New Europe,"* 13.

78. Central and East Europeans tend to view the Cold War period as one marked by an artificial separation from the West and subjugation by an alien power and culture. See, for example, Czech author Milan Kundera's well-known essay, "The Tragedy of Central Europe," in *From Stalinism to Pluralism: A Documentary History of Eastern Europe Since 1945,* ed. Gale Stokes, 2nd ed. (Oxford, England: Oxford University Press, 1996).

79. Address by Polish Foreign Minister Geremek on the occasion of the protocols to the North Atlantic Treaty on the accession of Poland, the Czech Republic, and Hungary, Brussels, December 16, 1997.

80. "Poland, Hungary, Czech Republic Formally Join NATO," *New York Times*, March 12, 1999.

81. John Gerard Ruggie, *Winning the Peace: America and World Order in the New Era* (New York: Columbia University Press, 1996), 85.

82. Árpád Göncz, "The Least Expensive Way to Guarantee Security,"*Transitions* (December 1997): 9.

83. Lord Robertson, "NATO Challenges."

84. The NATO Storybook was published by the Manfred Wörner Foundation. The compilation was largely the idea of the Secretary General's wife. Author interview with senior member of NATO's international staff, NATO Headquarters, Brussels, December 2001.

85. "And NATO Countries All Lived Happily Ever After," *The Prague Post*, July 2–8, 1997, A2.

86. "Text: Bush in Poland," *Washington Post*, June 15, 2000.

87. "NATO's Clark Hands Over Alliance Military Command," *Central Europe Online*, May 4, 2000, http://www.centraleurope.com.

88. Pond, *The Rebirth of Europe*, 82.

89. Joseph S. Nye, Jr., *Soft Power: The Means to Success in World Politics* (New York: PublicAffairs, 2004). Nye has explicitly recognized the "Western democratic and humanitarian values that NATO was charged with defending in 1949" as "significant sources of soft power." See Joseph S. Nye., Jr. "Redefining NATO's Mission in the Information Age," *NATO Review* 47, no. 4 (Winter 1999): 12.

90. Author interview, NATO Headquarters, Brussels, December 2001.

91. Ibid.

92. Somewhat ironically, the Czechs were perhaps ill-prepared for Kosovo, which occurred almost immediately following their accession to NATO, because so much attention had been devoted to NATO's political dimension. Jiří Sedivý has noted that "during the pre-accession debates NATO was presented not primarily as a war machine with a substantial out-of-area outlook, but as a traditional territorial defence alliance, as a community of shared ('Euroatlantic') values, as a safeguard of democracy and internal stability and as a means of attracting foreign investors." See Jiří Sedivý, "Are the Czechs Out?," *Newsbrief* 19, no. 6, The Royal United Services Institute, London (June 1999): 43–45.

93. *The International Position and Security of the Czech Republic: Czech Perceptions toward Security, Defense and NATO,* Gabal, Analysis & Consulting, Prague, November/December 2000, http://www.gac.cz.

94. Security Strategy of the Czech Republic, Ministry of Foreign Affairs of the Czech Republic, 2001, 4, 8. Author interview with Czech Ministry of Foreign Affairs official, Prague, September 2001.

Chapter 4

1. George W. Bush, remarks by the President in an Address to Faculty and Students of Warsaw University, Warsaw, Poland, June 15, 2001, http://www.whitehouse.gov/news/releases/2001/06/20010615-1.html (accessed June 2001).

2. Author interview with former National Security Council staff member, Washington, D.C., May 2002.

3. Bush, remarks by the President in an Address to Faculty and Students of Warsaw University.

4. On the issue of continuity between the Clinton and George W. Bush rationales for enlargement, see Philip H. Gordon and James B. Steinberg, "NATO Enlargement: Moving Forward; Expanding the Alliance and Completing Europe's Integration," Brookings Policy Brief no. 90 (December 2001): 2, http://www.brookings.edu.

5. Robert G. Kaiser, "The Alliance that Lost Its Purpose Is Europe's Most Popular Club," *Washington Post,* November 17, 2002, B1.

6. General Joseph W. Ralston, "Successfully Managing NATO Enlargement," in U.S. Department of State, U.S. Foreign Policy Agenda 7, no. 1 (March 2002): 20.

7. Lord Robertson, "NATO's Challenges: Illusions and Realities," address before the Chicago Council on Foreign Relations," June 19, 2001, http://www.nato.int/docu/speech/2001/s010619b.htm (accessed May 2003).

8. Bush, remarks by the President in an Address to Faculty and Students of Warsaw University.

9. Marc Grossman, "21st Century NATO: New Capabilities, New Members, New Relationships," U.S. Department of State, U.S. Foreign Policy Agenda 7, no. 1 (March 2002): 8.

10. Author interview with former National Security Council staff member, Washington, D.C. May 2002. Article 10 of the North Atlantic Treaty states, "The Parties may, by unanimous agreement, invite any other European State in a position to further the principles of this Treaty and to contribute to the security of the North Atlantic area to accede to this Treaty." See The North Atlantic Treaty, April 4, 1949, http://www.nato.int.

11. Bush, remarks by the President in an Address to Faculty and Students of Warsaw University. Two days earlier during the NATO summit, Bush had told NATO's North Atlantic Council that "based on the aspirants' progress to date," he was confident that they would be "able to launch the next round of enlargement" in Prague. See "Excerpted Remarks to the North Atlantic Council" at the meeting of the North Atlantic Council, NATO Headquarters, Brussels, June 13, 2001, http://www.nato.int.

12. Michael R. Gordon, "The 2000 Campaign: The Military; Bush Would Stop U.S. Peacekeeping in Balkan Fights," *New York Times,* October 21, 2000.

13. Author interview with Bruce Jackson, chair of the U.S. Committee on NATO, Washington, D.C., May 2002.

14. Author interviews with former U.S. Department of State officials and National Security Council staff members, Washington, D.C., May 2002.

15. Author interviews with U.S. Department of State and Defense officials, Washington, D.C., May 2002.

16. See, for example, James M. Goldgeier, "Not When but Who," *NATO Review,* no. 1 (Spring 2002), http://www.nato.int/docu/review/2002/issue1/english/art2_pr.html.

17. See, for example, Elizabeth Pond, *The Rebirth of Europe* (Washington, DC: Brookings Institution Press, 1999).

18. For examples of such predictions, see George Kennan, "NATO: A Fateful Error," *New York Times,* February 2, 1997. See also Michael Mandelbaum,

"Preserving the New Peace: The Case Against NATO Expansion," *Foreign Affairs* 74, no. 3 (May/June 1995): 9–13.

19. Lord Robertson, "An Attack on Us All: NATO's Response to Terrorism," remarks at the Atlantic Council of the United States, National Press Club, Washington, D.C., October 10, 2001.

20. "President Bush Thanks Germany for Support Against Terror," remarks by the President to a Special Session of the German Bundestag, Berlin, Germany, May 23, 2002, http://www.whitehouse.gov/news/releases/2002/05/print/20020523-2.html.

21. Transcript of Press Conference by U.S. Secretary of State Colin L. Powell following the meeting of the North Atlantic Council, Reykjavik, Iceland, May 14, 2002.

22. Grossman, "21st Century NATO," 8.

23. Douglas J. Feith, "NATO's Transformation: Securing Freedom for Future Generations," in U.S. Department of State, U.S. Foreign Policy Agenda 7, no. 1 (March 2002), 17.

24. Timothy Garton Ash, "A New War Reshapes Old Alliances," *New York Times*, October 12, 2001.

25. Philip H. Gordon and Steinberg, "NATO Enlargement: Moving Forward." Both Russian Defense Minister Sergei Ivanov and Putin made clear their desire for a closer relationship with NATO during meetings in Brussels with Robertson in late September. See Christopher Walker, "NATO in the Wake of 11 September," RFE/RL *Newsline* 5, no. 189, pt. II (October 5, 2001).

26. Author interview with NATO staff member, Brussels, December 2001. Similarly, the creation of the NATO-Russia Permanent Joint Council (PJC) in 1997 made NATO's first round of enlargement more palatable for Russia.

27. Jeremy Bransten, "2002 in Review: Seven New Members End 'False Balance of Fear,'" RFE/RL, December 12, 2002, http://www.rferl.org/nca/features/2002/12/12122002184027.asp.

28. Author interview with U.S. Department of State official, Washington, D.C., May 2002. See also Robert G. Kaiser, "NATO Ready to Invite in Seven from Eastern Europe," *Washington Post*, September 26, 2002, A1. Notably, the Bush administration never seemed inclined to exclude the Baltic states due to fears of antagonizing Russia. Rather, Bush had said repeatedly that no state would be left out on grounds of its history or geography. See "Eastern Europeans Urge NATO to Include Them," *New York Times*, May 12, 2001. Czech President Václav Havel had also argued in May 2001 that there was no need to "approach Russia on tiptoe" with respect to the Baltic states. Failing to admit the Baltic states, he argued, would amount to "yielding to some geopolitical or geostrategical interests of Russia." See "Czech President Calls for NATO From Alaska to Tallinn" and "NATO Must Not Include Russia Itself, but Must Include the Baltic States," RFE/RL *Newsline* 5, no. 91, pt. II (May 14, 2001).

29. Author interview, NATO Headquarters, Brussels, December 2001.

30. Philip H. Gordon, "NATO after 11 September," *Survival* 43, no. 4 (Winter 2000–2002).

31. Bransten, "2002 in Review."

32. See, for example, Strobe Talbot, "From Prague to Baghdad: NATO at Risk," *Foreign Affairs* 81, no. 6 (November/December 2002): 56. See also Michael Adler,

"NATO Stresses Western Values as Much as Military Might," Agence France-Presse, November 24, 2002.

33. See Thomas L. Friedman, "The New Club NATO," *New York Times,* November 17, 2002.

34. Author interviews with former Clinton administration officials, Washington, D.C., May 2002.

35. See Sean Kay, "The Prague Summit: Beginning or End for NATO," The Eisenhower Institute, December 2002, http://eisenhowerinstitute.org/commentary/kayoped4.htm.

36. Author interviews, NATO Headquarters, Brussels, December 2002.

37. As Juhasz recounted the conversation, Robertson told him, "You do not have any time [to fulfill military pledges]. If you don't do this you are in trouble." See Keith B. Richburg, "NATO Tells Hungary to Modernize Its Military, *Washington Post,* November 3, 2002, A22.

38. Celeste Wallander, "NATO's Price: Shape Up or Ship Out," *Foreign Affairs* 81, no. 6 (November/December 2002), 5.

39. Author interviews, Washington, D.C., May 2002.

40. Author interview, NATO Headquarters, Brussels, December 2001.

41. Ibid.

42. Goldgeier, "Not When but Who." A report issued by the Atlantic Council in April 2001 similarly concluded, "Having repeatedly assured the nine aspirant countries that the latest wave of enlargement will not be the last, the Alliance cannot, even if it wished to, renege on that commitment without severely damaging its credibility." See "Permanent Alliance? NATO's Prague Summit and Beyond," Atlantic Council Policy Paper, April 2001, 16–17.

43. Author interview, NATO Headquarters, Brussels, December 2001.

44. See Freedom House, Freedom in the World 2002, http://www.freedomhouse.org/template.cfm?page=15&year=2002 (accessed November 2006).

45. Author interview with Department of Defense official, Washington, D.C., May 2002.

46. Ambassador R. Nicholas Burns, "To Prague and Beyond: NATO's Future in a Changed World," Graduation Address, The NATO Defense College, Rome, February 8, 2002.

47. Grossman, "21st Century NATO," 7–8.

48. In the words of *Washington Post* reporter Robert Kaiser, the decision to ignore NATO's offers of assistance "sent a shiver through the alliance." See Kaiser, "The Alliance that Lost Its Purpose."

49. R. Nicholas Burns, "The New NATO: Healing the Rift," speech to the Konrad Adenauer Foundation, May 27, 2003.

50. Jennifer D.P. Moroney, "Enlarging NATO's MAP: An Expanded Membership Action Plan Can Guide Aspirants' Contributions to the War on Terrorism," DFI International Government Services, Current Defense Analyses, no. 5 (August 2002). Moroney noted that none of the nine aspirants fully met NATO's formal membership criteria, especially in the areas of defense and economic reform, and restructuring. She also argued that the first two cycles of the MAP had "shown that the military capabilities of all nine aspirants are substantially weaker than

those of the Czech Republic, Hungary, and Poland at the time they were invited to join NATO in 1997."

51. Moroney, "Enlarging NATO's MAP."

52. Patrick Quinn, "Romanian Forces in Kandahar Helping to Join NATO," Associated Press, November 14, 2002. The Red Scorpions had also participated in peacekeeping operations in Albania, Bosnia, and Kosovo through NATO's Partnership for Peace. See also Vladimir Socor, "Two NATO Aspirants Assume Strategic Roles," *Wall Street Journal,* August 23, 2002.

53. "Romanian Premier Signs Agreement on Short-Term Stationing of U.S. Troops in Romania," RFE/RL *Newsline* 5, no. 207, pt. II (October 31, 2001).

54. See Kaiser, "NATO Ready to Invite in Seven from Eastern Europe." See also Daniela Tuchel, "Romania Battles Extremists: Bucharest Hopes Its Firm Support for U.S. Action in Iraq and Strong Stands Against Suspected Extremist Groups Will Ease Its Path Into NATO," Institute for War & Peace Reporting, London, August 28, 2002, http://www.lwpr.net/index.pl?archive/bcr2/bcr2200208274 eng.text.

55. Radu Marinas, "Romania Offers Bases for U.S. Strikes on Iraq," Reuters, October 1, 2002.

56. Grossman, "21st Century NATO." Feith also observed in February 2002 that seven of the nine aspirants had "made force contributions to the NATO operations in Bosnia" and had "shown much-appreciated solidarity with the United States— through their contributions to Operation Enduring Freedom." Douglas Feith, "NATO's Transformation," 17.

57. "Lithuania to Send up to 40 Soldiers to Afghanistan," Agence France-Presse, September 1, 2002; and Moroney, "Enlarging NATO's MAP."

58. Kaiser, "NATO Ready to Invite Seven From Eastern Europe."

59. Author interviews with U.S. Department of State and Defense officials, Washington, D.C., May 2002.

60. Quinn, "Romanian Forces in Kandahar Helping to Join NATO."

61. Burns, "To Prague and Beyond.

62. Kaiser, "NATO Ready to Invite Seven From Eastern Europe."

63. Author interviews with U.S. Department of State and Defense officials, Washington, D.C., May 2002.

64. Author interview with Ambassador R. Nicholas Burns, NATO Headquarters, Brussels, May 2003.

65. Author interview, NATO Headquarters, Brussels, December 2001.

66. Author interview with U.S. Department of State official, Washington, D.C., May 2002.

67. Ralston, "Successfully Managing NATO Enlargement," 18.

68. Moroney, "Enlarging NATO's MAP."

69. Elisabeth Bumiller, "Bush Appeals to New Allies on Iraq Plans," *New York Times,* November 24, 2002.

70. RFE/RL *Newsline* 6, no. 217, pt. II (November 19, 2002).

71. For example, the United States based approximately 1,000 troops at a Romanian air base near the port of Constanta, which was described by a U.S. officials as an "air-bridge for equipment and personnel going to CENTCOM."

72. See, for example, Socor, "Two NATO Aspirants Assume Strategic Roles."

73. John Chalmers, "Enlargement Could Just Make NATO's Problems Worse," Reuters, September 1, 2002.

74. See, for example, Vernon Loeb, "New Bases Reflect Shift in Military," *Washington Post*, June 9, 2003, A1.

75. Dina Kyriakidou, "NATO Means More than War Games for Balkan Candidates," Reuters, November 11, 2002.

76. Kaiser, "NATO Ready to Invite in Seven from Eastern Europe."

77. Author interviews, NATO Headquarters, Brussels, December 2001.

78. Frederick S. Kempe, "New Europe's Hope for NATO," *Wall Street Journal Europe,* November 28, 2002.

79. Author interview, NATO Headquarters, Brussels, May 2003.

80. See, for example, Elizabeth Williamson, "Poland Cashes in by Renting Battlefields for War Games," Wall Street Journal Europe, December 16, 2002.

81. Jose Maria Aznar, Jose-Manuel Durao Barroso, Silvio Berlusconi, Tony Blair, Václav Havel, Peter Medgyessy, Leszek Miller, and Anders Fogh Rasmussen, "United We Stand," *Wall Street Journal,* January 29, 2003.

82. The Vilnius Group currently comprises Slovenia, Slovakia, Romania, Bulgaria, Latvia, Lithuania, Estonia, Albania, Macedonia, and Croatia. The group minus Croatia had first met in May 2000 in Vilnius, where they called upon NATO to fulfill its promise of a Europe whole and free and promised political and practical cooperation among themselves in preparation for NATO membership. Croatia joined the group in Bratislava in May 2001, making it the "Vilnius 10."

83. Statement of the Vilnius Group Countries in response to the presentation by the United States Secretary of State to the United Nations Security Council concerning Iraq, by the Foreign Ministers of Albania, Bulgaria, Croatia, Estonia, Latvia, Lithuania, Macedonia, Romania, Slovakia, and Slovenia, February 5, 2003, NATO Enlargement Daily Brief, February 5, 2003.

84. Alan Cowell, "A Pledge of Assistance for Bush from 8 European Leaders," *New York Times*, January 30, 2003.

85. "Secretary Rumsfeld Briefs at the Foreign Press Center: News Transcript," U.S. Department of State, Defenselink, January 22, 2003, www.pentagon.mil/transcripts/2003/+01232003_+0122.sdfpc.html (accessed May 2003).

86. Kaiser, "NATO Ready to Invite in Seven from Europe."

87. For example, Vaclav Havel, during a meeting in Washington with Bush in September 2002, had suggested that NATO needs "to re-identify itself, to find its new identity in this very changed world. And especially now, after [the] 11th of September." " I think there is a lot of a new kind of evil in this world," said Havel, "and it is necessary to face this evil and to face all who support it." Joseph Curl, "Havel Wants NATO to Target 'New' Evil," *Washington Times*, September 2002.

88. See Jeffrey Donovan, "Transcript of RFE/RL's Exclusive Interview with President Bush." Elisabeth Bumiller of the *New York Times* also noted that Bush had been known to say that he had better relations with the little countries of Europe than the big ones. See Elisabeth Bumiller, "For Bush, A Big 'Aciu' From Eastern Europe," *New York Times*, November 25, 2002.

89. Jim Garamone, "Seven Nations Bring Capabilities-Enthusiasm Mix to North Atlantic Alliance," American Forces Press Service, November 23, 2002.

90. Address by Vaira Vike-Freiberg, President of the Republic of Latvia in Prague Summit 2002: Selected Documents and Statements (NATO Public Diplomacy Division, 2003), 38–39.

91. "NATO Members-To-Be Can Help in Anti-Terror War: U.S. Military Chief," Agence France-Presse, December 5, 2002.

92. See "Czech Republic to Propose Mobile Antichemical Unit Within NATO," RFE/RL *Newsline,* 6, no. 217, pt. II (November 19, 2002); and "Czechs Close to Receiving NATO Chem/Bio Defense Training Center," CTK, December 19, 2002.

93. Author interviews with Richard Kugler and Stuart Johnson, National Defense University, Washington, DC, May 2002; and phone interview with Hans Binnendijk, June 2006. Binnendijk and Kugler had promoted the idea for the NATO Response Force beginning in early 2002 throughout the United States and Europe. See, for example, Hans Binnendijk, "A European Spearhead Force Would Bridge the Gap," *International Herald Tribune,* February 16, 2002; and Hans Binnendijk and Richard L. Kugler, "Transforming European Forces," *Survival* (Autumn 2002): 117–32.

94. Keith B. Richburg, "Czechs Become Model for the New NATO, *Washington Post,* November 3, 2002, 22. In February 2002, Robertson had said that he was again sounding his "clarion call of 'capabilities, capabilities, capabilities,'" but he added that his inclination for the Prague Summit was "to refocus on a much smaller number of absolutely critical capabilities and to commit nations to acquiring them." See Lord Robertson, "A Renewed Transatlantic Security Partnership in the Aftermath of 11 September," Remarks at the European Parliament Conference, February 19, 2002.

95. Robert G. Kaiser and Keith B. Richburg, 'NATO Looking Ahead to a Mission Makeover," *Washington Post,* November 5, 2002.

96. Peter Spiegel, "Rumsfeld Recasts Himself as NATO Believer," *Financial Times,* October 8, 2003.

97. Socor, "Two NATO Aspirants Assume Strategic Roles." See also Thomas S. Szayna, "NATO Enlargement: Forecasting the 'Who' and 'When,'" National Security Studies Quarterly 7, no. 3 (Summer 2001): 31–92.

98. Bransten, "2002 in Review."

99. Burns, "The New NATO."

100. The target goal of 2-percent growth in aspirants' defense budgets was based on the median defense expenditure in Europe per year. See Szayna, "NATO Enlargement," 31–32.

101. Author interview, NATO Headquarters, Brussels, December 2002.

102. For example, U.S. Ambassador to Slovakia Ronald Weiser warned in January 2002 that "the forming of the future government will influence whether Slovakia gets an invitation [to join NATO] or not." "Slovak Opponents Incredulous as Meciar Declares Affinity for NATO, EU, While U.S. Ambassador Warns of Isolation if Elections Usher in Non-NATO Values." RFE/RL *Newsline* 6, no. 3, pt. II (January 7, 2002).

103. Author interviews, NATO Headquarters, Brussels, May 2003. NATO diplomats note that the desire to attract foreign investors also provided incentives for the invitees to continue with reforms.

104. Author interview with U.S. Department of State official, Washington, D.C., May 2002.

105. See Ahto Lobjakas, ''NATO: Members Commit Themselves—Again—To Modernization,'' Radio Free Europe, Radio Liberty, November 2002, http://www.rferl.org/features/2002/11/21112002162242.asp (accessed May 2003).

106. See, for example Robert Weaver, ''Continuing to Build Security Through Partnership,'' NATO Review, no. 1 (Spring 2004), http://www.nato.int/docu/review/2004/issue1/english/art1.html; and Jeffrey Simon, ''NATO's Partnership for Peace: Charting a Course for a New Era'' RFE/RL East European Perspectives 6, no. 16 (August 7, 2004), http://www.rferl.org/reports (accessed January 2005). Simon suggested that the non-NATO PfP members now fell into eight distinct categories: the five ''advanced partners,'' three MAP partners (Albania, Croatia, and Macedonia), Ukraine, Russia, Moldova, and Belarus (both relatively inactive), the Caucasus states, five Central Asian partners, and two Pfp aspirants: Bosnia/Herzegovina and Serbia and Montenegro.

107. International Security Information Service (ISIS), ''Ten Years On—Is There Still a Future for the Partnership after NATO Enlargement?,'' NATO Notes 6, no. 1 (February 2004), http://www.isis-europe.org/ftp/download/partnership.pdf.

108. Author interview with NATO diplomat, December 2001.

109. Report on the Comprehensive Review of the Euro-Atlantic Partnership Council and Partnership for Peace, Prague, November 21, 2002, http://www.nato.int/docu/basictxt/b021121a.htm.

110. See Partnership Action Plan Against Terrorism, Prague, November 22, 2002, http://www.nato.int/docu/basictxt/b021122e.htm.

111. See NATO-Russia Relations: A New Quality, Declaration by Heads of State and Government of NATO Member States and the Russian Federation, Rome, May 28, 2002, http://www.nato.int/docu/basictxt/b020528e.htm.

112. Final Communique, Ministers' Meeting of the North Atlantic Council held in Reykjavik, Press Release M-NAC-1(2002) 59, May 14, 2002, http://www.nato.int/docu/pr/2002/p02-059e.htm (accessed January 2003).

113. Lord Robertson, ''NATO: A Vision for 2012,'' speech at GMFUS Conference, Brussels, October 3, 2002, http://www.nato.int/docu/speech/2002/s021003a.htm.

114. Prague Summit Declaration, Press Communique PR/CP (2002) 127, issued by the Heads of State and Government participating in the meeting of the North Atlantic Council in Prague, November 21, 2002.

Chapter 5

1. Article 4 states the following: ''The Parties will consult together whenever, in the opinion of any of them, the territorial integrity, political independence or security of any of the Parties is threatened.''

2. NATO Secretary General Lord Robertson, Farewell Speech to the North Atlantic Council, NATO Headquarters, Brussels, December 17, 2003.

3. R. Nicholas Burns, ''NATO Has Adapted: An Alliance with a New Mission,'' *International Herald Tribune,* May 24, 2003.

4. R. Nicholas Burns, ''NATO Is Subordinate to None,'' *The Wall Street Journal Europe,* Brussels, March 6, 2003, 6.

5. Quoted in Quentin Peel, "Friends More Baffling than Foes," *Financial Times,* December 4, 2003.

6. See, for example, Peter Van Ham, "Security and Culture or, Why NATO Won't Last," *Security Dialogue* 2, no. 4 (2001): 394.

7. See David S. Yost, *NATO Transformed: The Alliance's New Roles in International Security* (Washington, DC: United States Institute of Peace Press, 1998), 177.

8. See Philip Gordon, "NATO after 11 September," *Survival* 43, no. 4 (Winter 2000–2002). U.S. Secretary of Defense Donald Rumsfeld also stated after September 11 that "the mission will determine the coalition" rather than the coalition determining the mission. Jeremy Bransten, "2002 in Review: Seven New Members End 'False Balance of Fear,'" RFE/RL *Newsline,* December 12, 2002, http://www.rferl.org/nca/features/2002/12/12122002184027.asp.

9. Quoted in John Chalmers, "Born Again Ally, U.S. May Be Pushing NATO Too Hard," Reuters, December 19, 2003.

10. Peel, "Friends More Baffling than Foes."

11. James P. Rubin, "Stumbling Into War," *Foreign Affairs* 82, no. 5 (September/October 2003): 59.

12. Ronald D. Asmus, "Rebuilding the Atlantic Alliance," *Foreign Affairs* 82, no. 5 (September/October 2003): 21. Another Clinton administration official, James Steinberg, described the crisis over Iraq as the "greatest crisis since Suez." See James B. Steinberg, "An Elective Partnership: Salvaging Transatlantic Relations," *Survival* 45, no. 2 (2003): 113.

13. Author interviews with Ambassador R. Nicholas Burns and diplomats assigned to the Latvian and Slovenian missions to NATO, NATO Headquarters, Brussels, May 2003.

14. Author interviews with diplomats assigned to the Latvian and Slovenian missions to NATO, NATO Headquarters, Brussels, May 2003.

15. For example, Polish Prime Minister Leszek Miller told reporters in October, "We are strongly against the creation of any competitive structures that would be detrimental for NATO." See Paul Geitner, "EU Leaders Leave Major Decision for Later as They Wrap Up Summit, " Associated Press, October 16, 2003.

16. Peter Spiegel and Jean Eaglesham, "NATO Allies Offer Reassurance Over European Defense Plans," *Financial Times,* October 21, 2003. See also Judy Dempsey, "US Seeks Showdown with EU over NATO," *Financial Times,* October 17, 2003.

17. "Bush Reaffirms Warning Against Undermining NATO," Agence France-Presse, December 4, 2003.

18. "Divide and Fall," *The Economist,* October 25, 2003.

19. Judy Dempsey, "NATO Divided Over Separate EU Military Planning Unit," *Financial Times,* December 1, 2003.

20. Judy Dempsey, "White House Accepts Separate EU Military Planning Unit," *Financial Times,* December 14, 2003.

21. The "Berlin-Plus agreement outlines the terms under which the European Union can utilize NATO assets in non-NATO operations. The agreement paved the way for the EU to take over NATO's peacekeeping operation in Macedonia in April 2003.

22. "No Alarm for NATO," *Financial Times,* December 2, 2003.

23. John Tagliabue, "Europeans Discuss Military Plan; Try to Calm U.S. Concerns," *New York Times,* October 17, 2003.

24. Michael Ignatieff, "Why America Must Know Its Limits," *Financial Times,* December 24, 2003.

25. Timothy Garton Ash, "How the West Can Be One," *New York Times Magazine,* April 27, 2003.

26. See "To the Reader" in Timothy Garton Ash, *Free World: America, Europe and the Surprising Future of the West* (New York: Random House, 2004). Former Swedish Prime Minister Carl Bildt offered a similar assessment quoted in Thomas L. Friedman, "The End of the West?," *New York Times,* November 2, 2003.

27. See, for example, Philip Gordon, "Bridging the Atlantic Divide," *Foreign Affairs* 82, no. 1 (January/February 2003): 83.

28. William Drozdiak, "Europe and the Muscle-Bound Superpower," *Washington Post,* September 7, 2003, B1.

29. See Robert Kagan, "Power and Weakness,"*Policy Review,* no. 113 (June 2002). See also the book-length version of this essay: Robert Kagan, *Of Paradise and Power: America and Europe in the New World Order* (New York: Alfred A. Knopf, 2003), 3–4.

30. Dominique Moisi, "Reinventing the West," *Foreign Affairs* 82, no. 6 (November/December 2003): 69.

31. Friedman, "The End of the West?"

32. Van Ham, "Security and Culture or, Why NATO Won't Last," 394–96.

33. For a useful discussion of commonly cited cultural differences between the United States and Europe, see "A Nation Apart: A Survey of America," *The Economist,* November 8, 2003.

34. Asmus, "Rebuilding the Atlantic Alliance," 22–23. As Asmus describes it, "this view contends that no two parts of the world have more in common or are more integrated...The crux of the matter is not power but purpose."

35. Joel J. Sokolsky, "The Power of Values of the Value of Power? America and Europe in a post 9/11 World," http://www.ciaonet.org/casestudy/sojol/index.html.

36. Nora Boustany, "The View from Spain," *Washington Post,* January 14, 2004, A16.

37. Secretary Rumsfeld Briefs at the Foreign Press Center: News Transcript, U.S. Department of Defense, Defenselink, January 22, 2003, www.pentagon.mil/transcripts/2003/+01232003_+0122.sdfpc.html (accessed May 2003).

38. Author interviews with diplomats representing the Prague invitees, NATO Headquarters, Brussels, May 2003.

39. "Chirac Lashes Out at 'New Europe,'" *CNN.com,* February 18, 2003, http://www.cnn.com/2003/WORLD/europe/02/18/sprj.irq.chirac/ (accessed May 2003).

40. Philip Stephens, "A Divided Europe Will Be Easy for America to Rule," *Financial Times,* May 23, 2003.

41. Authors interviews with diplomats from the Prague invitees, NATO Headquarters, Brussels, May 2003.

42. Similarly, a Czech diplomat observed, "We lived on the political periphery for years, while geographically we were at the heart of Europe. Now we have the opportunity to join, we don't want to be back on the periphery again." See Michael Peel, "A Strong Penchant for Old Europe," *Financial Times,* August 12, 2003.

43. Garton Ash, "How the West Can Be One."

44. Joshua Spero and Sean Kay, "America's Precarious Trans-Atlantic Bridge," *Defense News,* August 18, 2003.

45. Jackson Diehl, "Allies and Ideology," *Washington Post,* November 24, 2003, A21. Diehl notes that a "congressional rebellion" appears to have finally prompted the waivers. In November 2003, the Senate Foreign Relations committee unanimously passed a measure exempting the six countries from sanctions.

46. Josef Joffe, "The Alliance Is Dead, Long Live the Alliance,"*New York Times,* September 29, 2002.

47. E. Wayne Merry, "Therapy's End: Thinking Beyond NATO," *The National Interest* 74 (Winter 2003–2004).

48. François Heisbourg, "A World Without Alliances," *The Economist: The World in 2004* (2003): 51–52.

49. Speech by NATO Secretary General Robertson at the Atlantic Treaty Association (ATA) 49th General Assembly, Edinburgh, November 7, 2003.

50. Jim Hoagland, "Chirac's Multipolar World, *Washington Post,* February 4, 2004, 23.

51. German troops attached to ISAF took over responsibility for the PRT from the United States on December 31, 2003. The Provincial Reconstruction Teams have been established to provide security and assist with the reconstruction effort. "NATO Expands its Role in Afghanistan," NATO Update, January 6, 2004, http://www.nato.int/docu/update/2004/01-january/e106a.htm.

52. Judy Dempsey, "NATO Widens Role with Support for German Team in Konduz, *Financial Times,* December 20, 2003.

53. "NATO to Go South in Afghanistan," NATO Update, December 8, 2005, http://www.nato.int/docu/update/2005/12-december/e1208a.htm. See also Glenn Kessler "Europeans Search for Conciliation with U.S.," *The Washington Post,* December 9, 2005, A16.

54. "To a Second Front? How Afghanistan Could Again Be Engulfed in a Civil War," *Financial Times,* November 22, 2006.

55. Following the war in Kosovo, NATO conducted a series of missions in Macedonia designed to prevent ethnic hostilities there from spreading. The EU took over the mission from NATO in April 2003.

56. Hans Binnendijk and Richard Kugler, *Dual-Track Transformation for the Atlantic Alliance* (Washington, DC: Center for Technology and National Security Policy, November 2003), 2–3.

57. Chalmers, "Born Again Ally."

58. Speech by NATO Secretary General Jaap de Hoop Scheffer at the International Institute for Strategic Studies, London, February 12, 2004.

59. Anthony Forster and William Wallace, "What Is NATO For?," *Survival* 43, no. 4 (2001): 108. See also Celeste Wallander, "Institutional Assets and Adaptability: NATO after the Cold War," *International Organization* 54, no. 4 (Autumn 2000): 714.

60. See Anthony Forster and William Wallace, "What Is NATO For?," 116.

61. "A New Job for NATO," *The Washington Post,* August 15, 2003, A26.

62. *Die Welt*/BBC Monitoring, June 4, 2003, in *NATO Enlargement Daily Brief,* June 5, 2003.

63. Interview with Ambassador Nicholas Burns, NATO Headquarters, Brussels, May 2003. See also Jim Hoagland, "Mid-Course Correction," *Washington Post,* December 11, 2003, A39.

64. Colin L. Powell, "A Strategy of Partnerships," *Foreign Affairs* 83, no. 1 (January/February 2004): 29–30.

65. Chalmers, "Born-Again Ally."

66. Judy Dempsey, "Head of NATO Has Parting Shot at 'Mean' Members," *Financial Times,* December 4, 2003.

67. Chalmers, "Born Again Ally."

68. Dempsey, "Head of NATO Has Parting Shot."

69. Peter Spiegel, "Rumsfeld Recasts Himself as NATO Believer," *Financial Times,* October 8, 2003.

70. The U.S. Senate voted 97–0 during the summer of 2003 to urge Bush to "consider requesting formally and expeditiously that NATO raise a force for deployment in post-war Iraq similar to what it has done in Afghanistan, Bosnia, Kosovo." Sean Kay, "NATO in Iraq? But Not Yet," *Globe and Mail.com,* August 26, 2003. Deputy Secretary of Defense Paul Wolfowitz had first suggested a role for NATO in Iraq in December 2002.

71. Judy Dempsey, "U.S. Asks NATO to Consider Wider Iraq Role," *Financial Times,* December 5, 2003.

72. Leon Bruneau, "NATO FORMINS to Reprise Debate on Iraq, Afghanistan," Agence France-Presse, December 4, 2003.

73. Just prior to his departure from Brussels, Robertson said, "We must, of course, not dilute our efforts in Afghanistan. But as the world's only multinational force packager, we should not stand aside if Iraq needs our special involvement." "Departing NATO Chief Urges Alliance to be Ready for Iraq Role, Agence France Presse, December 17, 2003. See also speech by NATO Secretary General Jaap de Hoop Scheffer at the International Institute for Strategic Studies, London, February 12, 2004.

74. Chalmers, "Born Again Ally."

75. Judy Dempsey, "NATO to Reinforce Military Presence," *Financial Times,* December 2, 2003. ISAF had only three helicopters until December when Robertson and Rumsfeld warned of the consequences for NATO of failing in Afghanistan.

76. Speech by NATO Secretary General Robertson at the ATA 49th General Assembly.

77. Lord Robertson, "A Global Dimension for a Renewed Atlantic Partnership," speech at the European Parliament Conference, Brussels, February 19, 2002.

78. Robertson also noted in October 2003 that "...of the 1.4 million soldiers available in theory in our standing armies, only some 250,000 are actually ready and able to deploy. And today, with 80,000 European and Canadian soldiers on the ground in the Balkans, Afghanistan and Iraq, many governments argue that their armies are overstretched and cannot do anymore." Speech by NATO Secretary General Lord Robertson at the Grandes Conferences Catholique, Brussels, October 21, 2003.

79. "NATO Officials Play out Terrorism Scenario at Colorado Talks," *New York Times,* October 9, 2003.

80. Speech by NATO Secretary General Robertson at the ATA 49th General Assembly.

81. "Former NATO Chief: Europe Must Change Military Approach, Associated Press, December 21, 2003.

82. See, for example, Garton Ash, "How the West Can Be One"; and Steinberg, "An Elective Partnership," 129.

83. Garton Ash, "How the West Can Be One."

84. See, for example, Steinberg, "An Elective Partnership," 129; and Binnendijk and Kugler, "Dual-Track Transformation for the Atlantic Alliance," 5–7.

85. See, for example, Steinberg, "An Elective Partnership," 129. See also Asmus, "Rebuilding the Atlantic Alliance," 27; and Binnendijk and Kugler, "Dual-Track Transformation for the Atlantic Alliance," 14.

86. Richard Lugar, "Nation-Building Is a Role for NATO," *Financial Times,* May 29, 2003.

87. Carl Bildt, "We Should Build States Not Nations," *Financial Times,* January 16, 2004.

88. Hans Binnendijk and Richard Kugler, *Needed—A NATO Stabilization and Reconstruction Force* (Washington, DC: Center for Technology and National Security Policy, September 2004).

89. Author phone interview with Hans Binnendijk, June 2006.

90. Department of Defense, *Quadrennial Defense Review Report,* February 6, 2006, http://www.defenselink.mil/qdr/report/report20060203.pdf.

91. Author interview with a senior member of NATO's international staff, NATO Headquarters, Brussels, May 2003.

92. "The Future Tasks of the Alliance ("The Harmel Report"), Brussels, December 13–14, 1967, http://www.nato.int/docu/basictxt/treaty.htm.

93. Strobe Talbott, "From Prague to Bagdad: NATO at Risk," *Foreign Affairs* 81, no. 6 (November/December 2002): 49–50.

94. Ministers Meeting of the North Atlantic Council, Press Release, PR/CP (2003) 152, Brussels, December 4, 2003.

95. Ibid. Ambassador Burns wrote in December 2003 that NATO needed "to accelerate efforts to apprehend the two worst war criminals in Europe since 1945 —Radovan Karadic and Ratko Mladic." See R. Nicholas Burns, "Europe and Beyond: A Broader Mission for NATO," *International Herald Tribune,* December 19, 2003.

96. See Asmus, "Rebuilding the Atlantic Alliance," 24; and Zbigniew Brzezinski, "Where Do We Go from Here?," *Internationale Politik,* Transatlantic Edition, Autumn 2003, http://en.internationalepolitik.de/archiv/2003/fall2003 (accessed January 2004).

97. Asmus, "Rebuilding the Atlantic Alliance," 24.

98. On the subject of Russia's failure to integrate with the West, see, for example, Steven Lee Myers, "Russian and the Rich Western Neighbors: A Cold Peace," *New York Times,* December 31, 2003.

99. E-mail correspondence with U.S. Ambassador to NATO Nicholas Burns, January 30, 2005.

100. Declaration on Transatlantic Relations: How to Overcome the Divisions, May 2003, http://www.cer.org.uk.

101. See, for example, Binnendijk and Kugler, *Dual-Track Transformation for the Atlantic Alliance*, 15.

102. Ivo Daalder, Nicole Gnesotto, and Philip Gordon, eds., *Crescent of Crisis: U.S.–European Strategy for the Greater Middle East* (Washington, DC: Brookings Institution Press, 2006), 2–3.

103. Comprehensive Political Guidance, Endorsed by NATO Heads of State and Government, Riga, Latvia, November 29, 2006, http://www.nato.int/docu/basictxt/b061129e.htm (accessed November 2006).

104. Garton Ash, "How the West Can Be One."

105. See the foreword to William Drozdiak, Geoffrey Kemp, Flynt L. Leverett, Christopher J. Makins, and Bruce Stokes, *Partners in Frustration: Europe the United States and the Broader Middle East*, Atlantic Council Policy Paper, September 2004.

106. FAES (Fundacion Para el Analisis y los Estudios Sociales), *NATO: An Alliance for Freedom: How to Transform the Atlantic Alliance to Effectively Defend our Freedom and Democracies*, 2005, 51.

107. Asmus, "Rebuilding the Atlantic Alliance," 25.

108. Joschka Fischer, Speech at the 40th Munich Conference on Security Policy, February 7, 2004, http://www.securityconference.de.

109. Richard G. Lugar, "NATO and the Greater Middle East," speech at the 40th Munich Conference on Security Policy," February 8, 2004, http://www.security-conference.de.

110. Binnendijk and Kugler, *A Dual-Track Transformation for the Atlantic Alliance*, 10.

111. Ibid., 11.

112. Peter Struck, "Future of NATO," speech at the 40th Munich Conference on Security Policy, February 7, 2004, http://www.securityconference.de.

113. See, for example, Steinberg, "An Elective Partnership," 114. See also Gordon, "Bridging the Atlantic Divide," 75; and Garton Ash, "How the West Can Be One."

114. Author e-mail interviews with R. Nicholas Burns, March 10 and 11, 2004. Burns suggested that "NATO does less well when we grapple with theology than when we work on a more practical basis."

115. R. Nicholas Burns, remarks at Wilton Park, Surrey, United Kingdom, February 9, 2004.

116. R. Nicholas Burns, remarks at the Opening of the Transatlantic Institute, Brussels, February 12, 2004, http://www.nato.usmission.gov/ambassador/2004/s040212a.htm (accessed January 2005).

117. Garton Ash, "How the West Can Be One."

118. Jaap de Hoop Scheffer, speech at the National Defense University, Washington, D.C., January 29, 2004, http://www.nato/int/docu/speech/2004/s040129a.htm.

119. Speech by NATO Secretary General Japp de Hoop Scheffer at the International Institute for Strategic Studies, London, February 12, 2004.

Chapter 6

1. R. Nicholas Burns, "An Alliance Renewed," *International Herald Tribune*, March 16, 2005.

2. Speech by Jaap de Hoop Scheffer, Istanbul, Turkey, April 28, 2004, http://www.nato.int/docu/speech/2004/s040428a.htm. See also Jaap de Hoop Scheffer, speech at the Munich Security Conference, February 12, 2005, http://www.securityconference.de.

3. Jaap de Hoop Scheffer, Press Statement, January 5, 2004.

4. Speech by NATO Secretary General Jaap de Hoop Scheffer at the International Institute for Strategic Studies, London, February 12, 2004.

5. Istanbul Summit Communique, PR/CP (2004) 096, June 28, 2004, http://www.nato.int/docu/pr/2004/po4-096e.htm.

6. Jeremy Druker, "NATO Club Offers No New Invitations, but Plenty of Optimism," International Relations and Security Network (ISN), January 7, 2005, http://www.isn.ethz.ch/news/sw/details.cfm?ID=9158.

7. See, for example, A. Elizabeth Jones, Assistant Secretary of State for European and Eurasian Affairs, testimony before the Subcommittee on the Middle East and Central Asia, House International Relations Committee, Washington, D.C., October 29, 2003, http://www.state.gov/p/eur/rls/rm/2003/25798.htm. See also Jim Garamone, "Central Asia, Crucial to War on Terror," American Forces Press Service, June 27, 2002, http://www.defenselink.mil/news/June2002/n06272002_200206274.html; U.S. Department of State Fact Sheet, "Frequently Asked Questions about U.S. Policy in Central Asia," Bureau of European and Eurasian Affairs, Washington, DC, November 27, 2002, http://www.state.gov/p/eur/rls/fs/15562.htm; and B. Lyn Pascoe, "Uzbekistan: The Key to Success in Central Asia?," testimony before the Subcommittee on Central Asia, House International Relations Committee, Washington, D.C., June 15, 2004, http://www.state.gov/p/eur/rls/rm/33579.htm.

8. Eugene Tomiuc, *NATO: Ten Years On; Partnership for Peace Looks Farther East*, RFE/RL, January 30, 2004; and RFE/RL *Newsline* 8, no. 230, pt. I, December 9, 2004.

9. See Ilan Berman, "The New Battleground: Central Asia and the Caucasus," *The Washington Quarterly* 28, no. 1 (Winter 2004–2005): 60.

10. Quoted in Elizabeth Wishnick, *Growing U.S. Security Interests in Central Asia*, Strategic Studies Institute, October 2002, http://www.carlisle.army.mil/ssi/pdffiles/PUB110.pdf.

11. For a useful discussion of NATO cooperation with Eurasia through PfP, see Joshua B. Spero, "Paths to Peace for NATO's Partnerships in Eurasia," in *Limiting Institutions?" The Challenge of Eurasian Security Governance*, ed. James Sperling, Sean Kay, and S. Victor Papacosma (Manchester, UK: Manchester University Press, 2003), 166–84.

12. Tomiuc, *NATO: Ten Years On*.

13. Robert A. Bradtke, Deputy Assistant Secretary for European and Eurasian Affairs, "U.S. Initiatives at NATO's Istanbul Summit," testimony before the House International Relations Committee, Subcommittee on Europe, Washington, D.C., June 16, 2004, http://www.state.gov/p/eur/rls/rm/33701.htm.

14. Bradtke, "U.S. Initiatives at NATO's Istanbul Summit"; and author e-mail correspondence with former U.S. Ambassador to NATO R. Nicholas Burns, January 30, 2005.

15. Statement by NATO Secretary General Jaap de Hoop Scheffer, Press Release (2005) 014, February 10, 2005, http://www.nato.int/docu/pr/2005/p05-014e.htm.

16. Robert Weaver, "Continuing to Build Security through Partnership," *NATO Review* (Spring 2004), http://www.nato.int/docu/review/2004/issue1/english/art/pr.htm. See also "Alliance Partnerships: Projecting Stability beyond NATO's Central and Eastern Borders," report by the NATO Parliamentary Assembly Sub-committee on Central and Eastern Europe (153 PCCEE 04 E), May 13, 2004, http://www.nato-pa.int.

17. "Alliance Partnerships."

18. Quoted in Berman, "The New Battleground," 60.

19. Ronald D. Asmus and Bruce P. Jackson, "The Black Sea and the Frontiers of Freedom," *Policy Review* June 4, 2004, http://www.policyreview.org/june04/asmus (accessed January 2005).

20. The first five states constitute the Dialogue's original membership. Jordan joined in 1995, and Algeria in 2000.

21. *NATO Public Diplomacy Division, The Prague Summit and NATO's Transformation, A Reader's Guide,* 2003, 53.

22. Istanbul Summit Communique, June 28, 2004. See also Fact Sheet on Mediterranean Dialogue, Ministerial Meeting, December 8, 2004, http://www.nato.int/med-dial/2004/041208e.pdf.

23. Lorne Cook, "U.S. Plans for NATO Meet Resistance of France, Germany," Agence France-Presse, February 8, 2004.

24. "NATO Elevates Mediterranean Dialogue to a Genuine Partnership, Launches Istanbul Cooperation Initiative," NATO Update, June 29, 2004, http://www.nato.int/docu/update/2004/06-june/e0629d.htm. The Istanbul Cooperation Initiative is officially open to all interested states in the "broader Middle East."

25. The GCC is comprised of Bahrain, Kuwait, Oman, Qatar, Saudi Arabia, and the United Arab Emirates (UAE).

26. In remarks to the American Enterprise Institute in December 2005, Assistant Secretary of State for European and Eurasian Affairs Daniel Fried asserted that "the principal theme in transatlantic relations of 2005" had been "success in defining and advancing the freedom agenda as America's national security strategy, and following from that, putting the political, economic and security assets of the transatlantic alliance to work to support it." See Daniel Fried, remarks at the American Enterprise Institute, December 14, 2005.

27. Remarks by the President at the 20th Anniversary of the National Endowment for Democracy, United States Chamber of Commerce, Washington, D.C., http://www.whitehouse.gov/news/releases/2003/11/print/20031106-2.html.

28. Philip Shiskin, "U.S. Sees NATO in Broader Role for Middle East; Washington Wants Allies in Europe to Help Reshape Region Beset by Turbulence," *Wall Street Journal,* February 11, 2004, A16.

29. R. Nicholas Burns, "NATO and the Greater Middle East," Brussels, Belgium, May 18, 2004, http://nato.usmission.gov/ambassador/2004/20040518_Brussels. htm (accessed January 2005).

30. According to a report issued by the Congressional Research Service in early 2005, while no "precise listing of designated countries" had yet emerged, the term "Greater Middle East" referred "to a large swath of Arab and non-Arab Muslim countries, stretching from Morocco in the west to as far east as Pakistan in southeast Asia." See Jeremy M. Sharp, *The Broader Middle East and North Africa Initiative:*

An Overview, Congressional Research Service Report for Congress, February 15, 2005.

31. See Sharp, *The Broader Middle East and North Africa Initiative.* For further information about the Middle East Partnership Initiative, see http://mepi.state.gov.

32. Sharp, *The Broader Middle East and North Africa Initiative.* See also U.S. Department of State. Fact Sheet: Broader Middle East and North Africa Initiative, June 9, 2004, www.state.gov/e/eb/rls/fs/33380.htm.

33. The United States Mission to the European Union, *G8 Mideast Initiative Supporting Economic, Political Reforms,* July 20, 2005, http://www.useu.be.

34. Burns, "NATO and the Greater Middle East." See also Istanbul Cooperation Initiative, NATO Policy Document, June 28, 2004, http://www.nato/int/docu/comm/2004/06-istanbul/docu-cooperation.htm (accessed January 2005).

35. Burns, "NATO and the Greater Middle East."

36. Remarks by Victoria Nuland at the German Marshall Fund, September 22, 2005, http://nato.usmission.gov/ambassador/2005/Amb_Nuland_GMF_092205.htm.

37. Jaap de Hoop Scheffer, "NATO's Evolving Role in the Middle East: The Gulf Dimension," keynote address at the Henry L. Stimson Center, June 3, 2005.

38. Jaap de Hoop Scheffer, speech at Galatasaray University, Istanbul, April 29, 2004, http://www.nato.int/docu/speech/2004/s040429a.htm.

39. Jaap de Hoop Scheffer, "NATO: Safeguarding Transatlantic Security," speech at Columbia University, September 20, 2005.

40. R. Nicholas Burns, Valedictory address before NATO's North Atlantic Council, March 2, 2005.

41. Robert Weaver, "Continuing to Build Security through Partnership."

42. Jeffrey Simon, "NATO's Partnership for Peace: Charting a Course for a New Era," RFE/RL *East European Perspectives* 6, no. 16 (August 7, 2004), http://www.rferl.org/reports.

43. Jaap de Hoop Scheffer, "NATO's Role in Gulf Security," speech at the State of Qatar/NATO/RAND Conference, Doha, Qatar, December 2005.

44. Partnership Action Plan against Terrorism (PAP-T), Prague, November 22, 2002, http://www.nato.int/docu/basictxt/b021122e.htm.

45. Partnership Action Plan on Defence Institution Building (PAP-DIB), Brussels, June 7, 2004, http://www.nato.int/docu/basictxt/b040607e.htm.

46. "The Euro-Atlantic Partnership—Refocusing and Renewal," Istanbul, June 23, 2004, http://www.nato.int/docu/basictxt/b040623e.htm.

47. Jaap de Hoop Scheffer, "Projecting Stability," speech given at the conference, "Defending Global Security: The New Politics of Transatlantic Defence Co-operation," Brussels, May 17, 2004.

48. Speech by NATO Secretary General Jaap de Hoop Scheffer during his visit to the Kyrgyz Republic, October 19, 2004.

49. Steven R. Weisman, "Rice Calls on Europe to Join in Building Safer World," *New York Times,* February 9, 2005.

50. George W. Bush, remarks by the President at Concert Noble, Brussels, Belgium, February 21, 2005, http://nato.usmission.gov.

51. Remarks at the American Enterprise Institute.

52. Bush, remarks by the President at Concert Noble. Bush reiterated this commitment during the U.S.–European Union Summit in June 2006, declaring that "the United States continues to support a strong European Union as a partner in spreading freedom and democracy and security and prosperity throughout the world." "President Hosts United States-European Union Summit," transcript of Press Conference, June 20, 2005, http://www.whitehouse.gov/news/releases/2005/06/20050620-19.html. Rice had also stressed during her visit to Brussels in February that the United States had "everything to gain from having a stronger Europe as a partner in building a safer and better world." Weisman, "Rice Calls on Europe to Join in Building Safer World."

53. Gerhard Schroeder, speech at the 41st Munich Conference on Security Policy, February 12, 2005, http://www.securityconference.de.

54. R. Nicholas Burns, "A Transatlantic Agenda for the Year Ahead," U.S. Department of State, Washington, D.C., April 7, 2005.

55. Remarks by Nuland at the German Marshall Fund. According to Nuland, Bush had "chosen to make strengthening and deepening the Transatlantic strategic consensus a signature goal of his second term."

56. See, for example, transcript of interview with Robert Hunter: Bernard Gwertzman, "Hunter: Rice Faces 'Tough Sale' to Persuade NATO Allies on Expanding Force in Afghanistan," Council on Foreign Relations, December 6, 2005, http://www.cfr.org/publication/9351/hunter.html. Burns, "NATO and the Greater Middle East."

57. Although the precise reasons for the eviction by the Uzbek government remain unclear, it followed on the heels of a brutal crackdown on antigovernment demonstrators in Andijon in May 2005 and a subsequent U.S. decision to support an airlift of over 400 Uzbek refugees from Kyrgyszstan to Romania.

58. See, for example, Wishnick, "Growing U.S. Security Interests in Central Asia"; Pauline Jones Luong and Erika Weinthal, "New Friends, New Foes in Central Asia," *Foreign Affairs* 81, no. 2 (March/April 2002): 69; and Alexander Cooley, "Base Politics," *Foreign Affairs* 84, no. 6 (November/December 2005): 79–92.

59. Quentin Peel, "America's Muddle in Central Asia," *Financial Times,* April 1, 2004.

60. See, for example, Anatol Lieven, "A Hypocritical Approach to Russia," *Financial Times,* May 31, 2006.

61. Jones, "Central Asia: Developments and the Administration's Policy," October 29, 2003.

62. Limited exceptions to this rule do exist. For example, in 1995, Kazakhstan, Kyrgyzstan, and Uzbekistan formed a joint peacekeeping union known as Centrazbat with the support of the U.S Central Command (CENTCOM).

63. Stephen Blank, "Democratic Prospects in Central Asia," *World Affairs* 166, no. 3 (Winter 2004): 139.

64. Ibid., 133.

65. Luong and Weinthal, "New Friends, New Fears in Central Asia."

66. See, for example, Berman, "The New Battleground," 67–68; Sergei Blagov, "Nay to NATO in Central Asia," *Transitions Online*, July 12, 2004; and Luong and Weinthal, "New Friends, New Fears in Central Asia," 65.

67. Geoff Dyer and Richard McGregor, "Opposition to U.S. Inspires 'NATO of the East,'" *Financial Times,* June 22, 2006.

68. Author telephone interview with NATO diplomat, July 2006.

69. NATO Parliamentary Assembly, Sub-committee on Central and Eastern Europe, "Alliance Partnerships: Projecting Stability Beyond NATO's Central and Eastern Borders," Report (153 PCCEE 04 E rev 1), May 13, 2004.

70. Laure Borgomano-Loup, *NATO's Mediterranean Dialogue and the Istanbul Co-operation Initiative: Prospects for Development* NATO Research Paper, Academic Research Branch, NATO Defense College, Rome, no. 21 (June 2005): 3–4.

71. FAES (Fundacion Para el Analisis y los Estudios Sociales), *NATO: An Alliance for Freedom: How to Transform the Atlantic Alliance to Effectively Defend our Freedom and Democracies*, 38.

72. Press Communique PR/CP(2005) 158, Ministerial Meeting of the North Atlantic Council, Brussels, December 8, 2005.

73. Partnership for Peace: Framework Document issued by the Heads of State and Government participating in the Meeting of the North Atlantic Council, Brussels, January 10, 1994, http://www.nato.int/docu/basictxt/b940110b.htm (accessed January 1997).

74. See, for example, Jim Hoagland, "Wolves in the Gulf: Arabs' Two Fears: The U.S. and Radical Islam," *Washington Post*, December 8, 2005, A33.

75. Mustafa Alani, "Arab Perspectives on NATO," *NATO Review*, no. 4 (Winter 2005), http://www.nato.int/docu/review/2005/issue4/english/art3.html.

76. See, for example, the statement of Air Vice Marshall Mohammed Al-Ardhi, Oman, "NATO's Evolving Role in the Middle East: The Gulf Dimension," Perspectives from the Gulf panel, Stimson Center Conference, June 3, 2005.

77. Zeyno Baran, "Getting the Greater Middle East Initiative Right," *The National Interest* 13, no. 9 (March 2004), http://www.inthenationalinterest.com/Articles/vol.31issue9/Vol3Issue9BaranPFV.html.

78. Ronald D. Asmus, Larry Diamond, Mark Leonard, and Michael McFaul, "A Transatlantic Strategy to Promote Democratic Development in the Broader Middle East, *The Washington Quarterly* 28, no. 2 (Spring 2005): 18–20. The authors suggest that a democracy promotion strategy in the Middle East should be based on three pillars. "First, it must aim to help strengthen the forces for democratic change and stable liberal democratic policies within these societies. Second, such a strategy must also work to create a more secure regional foreign policy context that can facilitate democratic transformation. Third, the United States and Europe need to organize themselves across the Atlantic and with partners in the region to sustain these policies effectively for a generation or more."

79. Ivo Daalder, Nicole Gnesotto, and Philip Gordon, eds., *Crescent of Crisis: U.S.–European Strategy for the Greater Middle East* (Washington, DC: Brookings Institution Press, 2006), 219.

80. Simon Serfaty, *The Vital Partnership: Power and Order, America and Europe Beyond Iraq* (Rowman & Littlefield, 2005), 140.

81. David. L. Aaron, Ann M. Beauchesne, Frances G. Burwell, G. Richard Nelson, K. Jack Riley, and Brian Zimmer, *The Post 9/11 Partnership: Transatlantic Co-operation against Terrorism*, The Atlantic Council, Policy Paper, December 2004, 12.

82. R. Nicholas Burns, "A Transatlantic Agenda for the Year Ahead," U.S. Department of State, Washington, D.C., April 7, 2005. See also Fried, remarks at the American Enterprise Institute.

83. Revised Operational Plan for NATO's Expanding Mission in Afghanistan, December 8, 2005, http://www.nato.int/issues/afghanistan_stage3/index.html (accessed May 2006).

84. Ahto Lobjakas, "NATO: U.S. Sees Global Training Role as Key to Transformation," RFE/RL, September 23, 2005, http://www.rferl.org.

85. See, for example, Gwertzman, "Hunter: Rice Faces 'Tough Sale.'"

86. Glenn Kessler, "Europeans Search for Conciliation with U.S.," *Washington Post,* December 9, 2005, A16.

87. "NATO to Assist Fellow Allies in Trouble," *New York Times,* November 29, 2006. See also "NATO Boosts Efforts in Afghanistan," November 28, 2006, http://www.nato.int/docu/update/2006/11-november/e1128a.htm.

88. Riga Summit Declaration, issued by the Heads of State and Government participating in the meeting of the North Atlantic Council in Riga, PR/CP (2006) 150, November 29, 2006.

89. See, for example, speech by Jaap de Hoop Scheffer at dinner hosted by the Turkish Minister of Foreign Affairs Abdullah Gul, Istanbul, April 28, 2004, http://www.nato.int/docu/speech/2004/s040428a.htm.

90. Gwertzman, "Hunter: Rice Faces 'Tough Sale.'"

91. Author e-mail interview with NATO diplomat, July 2006.

92. Lobjakas, "NATO: U.S. Sees Global Training Role as Key to Transformation."

93. Michael Thurston, "U.S. Plans for Mideast Reform Revive Transatlantic Strains," Agence France-Presse, March 7, 2004.

94. William Drozdiak, Geoffrey Kemp, Flynt L. Leverett, Christopher J. Makins, and Bruce Stokes, *Partners in Frustration: Europe the United States and the Broader Middle East,* 17.

95. Thurston, "U.S. Plans for Mideast Reform Revive Transatlantic Strains."

96. See, for example, Daalder, Gnesotto, and Gordon, *Crescent of Crisis,* 219.

97. "Mr. Bush Goes to Belgium, *The Economist,* February 19, 2005, 11–12.

98. Thurston, "U.S. Plans for Mideast Reform Revive Transatlantic Strains."

99. Ibid. On this point, see also Ronald D. Asmus, Antony J. Blinken, and Philip Gordon, "Nothing to Fear," *Foreign Affairs* 84, no. 1 (January/February 2005): 174–77.

100. de Hoop Scheffer, "NATO: Safeguarding Transatlantic Security."

101. Drozdiak et al., *Partners in Frustration.*

102. Michele Alliot-Marie, speech at the 42nd Munich Conference on Security Policy, February 4, 2006, http://www.securityconference.de.

103. Drozdiak et al., *Partners in Frustration,* 22.

104. Serfaty, *The Vital Partnership,* 140.

105. William Pfaff, "NATO's Future on the Line,"*International Herald Tribune,* January 11, 2006.

106. See, for example, Drozdiak et al., *Partners in Frustration.*

107. Richard Bernstein. "Merkel on Visit, Will Try Gingerly to Revive U.S. Ties," *New York Times,* January 13, 2006.

108. See, for example, Roger Cohen, "For France and U.S., a Frisson of Good Will," *International Herald Tribune,* March 1, 2006.

109. NATO Press Communique PR/CP(2005) 158, Ministerial Meeting of the North Atlantic Council, Brussels, December 8, 2005.

110. See news conference transcript, Jaap de Hoop Scheffer, December 8, 2005, at http://www.nato.int/docu/speech/2005/s051208h.htm. Press Availability with Condoleeza Rice following the meeting of the North Atlantic Council, December 8, 2005, http://www.nato.int/docu/speech/2005/s051208m.htm. U.S. treatment of terrorism suspects was reportedly also discussed during the meeting. See Kessler, "Europeans Search for Conciliation with U.S.," A16.

111. See, for example, Quentin Peel, "Merkel Leads Calls for NATO to Redefine Strategy," *Financial Times,* February 5, 2006.

112. Speech by Dr. Angela Merkel, "Germany's Foreign and Security Policy in the Face of Global Challenges," February 4, 2006, http://www .securityconference.de.

113. Dr. Franz-Josef Jung, speech at the 42nd Munich Conference on Security Policy, February 4, 2006, http://www.securityconference.de.

114. "A Secure Europe in a Better World," European Union Security Strategy, December 12, 2003, http://ue.eu.int/uedocs/cmsupload/78367.pdf.

115. Aaron et al., *The Post 9/11 Partnership,* 7.

116. Drozdiak et al., *Partners in Frustration,* 18.

117. Edward Alden and Daniel Dombey, "'Common Enemy' Speeds Transatlantic Thaw," *Financial Times,* June 22, 2006.

118. John Reid, speech at the 42nd Munich Conference on Security Policy, February 4, 2006, http://www.securityconference.de. See also speech by Merkel, "Germany's Foreign and Security Policy in the Face of Global Challenges."

119. See, for example, Owen Harries, "The Collapse of the West," *Foreign Affairs* 72, no. 4 (September/October 1993): 41–53.

120. "Mr. Bush Goes to Belgium."

121. Wolfgang Ischinger, "Pax Americana and Pax Europea" in *Beyond Paradise and Power: Europe, America and the Future of a Troubled Partnership,* ed. Tod Lindberg (Oxford, England: Routledge, 2005), 84.

122. The German Marshall Fund of the United States, *Transatlantic Trends,* 2005, http://www.transatlantictrends.org.

123. George Friedman, "The Cartoon Backlash: Redefining Alignments," Stratfor Weekly Analysis, February 7, 2006.

124. Cohen, "For France and U.S., a Frisson of Good Will."

125. Daalder, Gnesotto, and Gordon, *Crescent of Crisis,* 219–20.

126. de Hoop Scheffer, "NATO's Evolving Role in the Middle East: The Gulf Dimension."

127. See, for example, Jaap de Hoop Scheffer, speech at the 42nd Munich Conference on Security Policy, February 4, 2006, http://www.securityconference .de.

128. de Hoop Scheffer, "NATO's Evolving Role in the Middle East: The Gulf Dimension."

129. Drozdiak et al., *Partners in Frustration,* 20.

130. Blank, "Democratic Prospects in Central Asia," *World Affairs* 166, no. 3 (Winter 2004): 136.

131. Ronald D. Asmus, Urban Ahlin, Steven Everts, Jana Hybaskova, Mark Leonard, Michael McFaul, and Michael Mertes, "A Joint Plan to Help the Greater Middle East: A Transatlantic Plan for Democracy," *International Herald Tribune,* March 15, 2004.

132. Drozdiak et al., *Partners in Frustration*, 31.

133. de Hoop Scheffer, "NATO's Evolving Role in the Middle East: The Gulf Dimension."

134. NATO and Mediterranean Dialogue Foreign Ministers held their first joint meeting in March 2005.

135. Author e-mail interview with NATO international staff member, June 2006.

136. Author e-mail interview with NATO international staff members, June 2006.

137. White House Fact Sheet: The Istanbul Cooperation Initiative, June 28, 2004.

138. Author e-mail interview with NATO international staff member, June 2006.

139. For further discussion on how the ICI might potentially evolve, see Carlo Masala, "Rising Expectations," *NATO Review* (Winter 2005), http://www.nato.int/docu/review/2005/issue4/english/art1.html; and Borgomano-Loup, "NATO's Mediterranean Dialogue and the Istanbul Cooperation Initiative.

140. Nicola de Santis, panel discussion on *NATO's Role in Gulf Security and U.S. Interests*, NATO's Evolving Role in the Middle East: The Gulf Dimension, conference at the Henry L. Stimson Center, June 3, 2005.

141. Jaap de Hoop Scheffer, Speech at the Egyptian Council on Foreign Affairs, Cairo, October 12, 2005.

142. Press Communique PR/CP(2005) 158.

143. Statement of Ebtisam Al Kitbi, professor at UAE University, Henry L. Simson Center, conference on NATO's Evolving Role in the Middle East: The Gulf Dimension, Panel- "Perspectives from the Gulf—What has been the response of GCC states to the Istanbul Cooperation Initiative? What are some of the concerns regarding cooperation with NATO," June 3, 2005.

144. Author e-mail interview with NATO international staff member, June 2006.

145. Masala, "Rising Expectations."

146. Speech by NATO Secretary General de Hoop Scheffer at Galatasaray University.

147. Daalder, Gnesotto, and Gordon, *Crescent of Crisis*, 1–2.

Conclusion

1. Robert Hunter, "Europe's Leverage," *The Washington Quarterly* 27, no. 1 (Winter 2003/2004): 98.

2. FAES (Fundacion Para el Analisis y los Estudios Sociales), *NATO: An Alliance for Freedom: How to Transform the Atlantic Alliance to Effectively Defend our Freedom and Democracies* (Madrid, Spain: FAES, 2005), 19.

3. *NATO: An Alliance for Freedom*, 23–24.

4. Neyla Arnas, Hans Binnendijk, Stephen J. Flanagan, Stuart E. Johnson, Richard L. Kugler, Lee G. Michel, Anne M. Moisan, Jeffrey Simon, and Kimberley L. Thachuk, *Transatlantic Homeland Defense*, CTNSP/INSS Special Report (Washington, DC: Center for Technology and National Security Policy/Institute for National Strategic Studies, May 2006).

5. Dr. John Reid, Speech at the 42nd Munich Conference on Security Policy, February 4, 2006, http://www.securityconference.de.

6. See, for example, Condoleeza Rice's comments in Brussels following a NATO foreign minister's meeting on December 8, 2005, http://www.nato.int/docu/speech/200505051208m.htm (accessed January 2006). See also Victoria Nuland, remarks at the German Marshall Fund, September 22, 2005, http://nato.usmission.gov/Recent_speeches.htm (accessed January 2006).

7. R. Nicholas Burns, Valedictory address before NATO's North Atlantic Council, March 2, 2005.

8. Jaap de Hoop Scheffer, speech at a joint meeting between the NATO Parliamentary Assembly and the North Atlantic Council, Paris, May 30, 2006, http://www.nato.int/docu/speech/2006/s060530a.htm. See also Victoria Nuland, Op-Ed News Release: New Roles for a Transformed Alliance, December 8, 2005, http://nato.usmission.gov/ambassador/2005/Amb_Nuland_Transformed_Alliance.htm; and Nuland, remarks at the German Marshall Fund. See also Ahto Lobjakas, "NATO: U.S. Sees Global Training Role as Key to Transformation," RFE/RL, September 23, 2005, http://www.rferl.org.

9. Speech by NATO Secretary General Jaap de Hoop Scheffer at the 15th anniversary of the Atlantic Club of Bulgaria in the margins of the Sofia Ministerial, April 27, 2006.

10. Jaap de Hoop Scheffer, "Global NATO: Overdue or Overstretch?," Brussels, November 6, 2006.

11. Riga Summit Declaration, issued by the Heads of State and Government participating in the meeting of the North Atlantic Council in Riga, PR/CP (2006) 150, November 29, 2006.

12. "Afghanistan Mission," *Financial Times*, November 28, 2006.

13. Michele Alliot-Marie, *Washington Times*, October 20, 2006.

14. François Heisbourg, "Why NATO Needs to Be Less Ambitious," *Financial Times*, November 22, 2006.

15. See, for example, Kurt Volker, Principal Deputy Assistant Secretary of State for European and Eurasian Affairs, testimony before the House International Relations Subcommittee on Europe, Washington, D.C., May 3, 2006, http://www.state.gov/p/eur/rls/rm/65874.htm; and Daniel Fried, Assistant Secretary for European and Eurasian Affairs, roundtable with European journalists, Washington, D.C., October 4, 2006, http://www.state.gov/p/eur/rls/rm/73756.htm.

16. *NATO: An Alliance for Freedom*, 40. Ronald Asmus has also advocated upgrading NATO's relations with Israel, possibly culminating in full membership for Israel, although, in this case, the stated intention would be to address the nuclear threat posed by Iran. See Ronald D. Asmus, "Contain Iran: Admit Israel to NATO," *Washington Post*, February 21, 2006, A15.

17. Ivo Daalder and James Goldgeier, "Global NATO," *Foreign Affairs* 85, no. 5 (September/October 2006): 110.

18. Ibid., 111.

19. "Czech President Does Not Consider Russia to be a Viable Candidate," RFE/RL *Newsline* 5, no. 224, pt. II (November 28, 2001). See also RFE/RL *Newsline* 5, no. 93, pt. II, May 16, 2001.

20. Timothy Garton Ash, *Free World: America, Europe, and the Surprising Future of the West* (New York: Random House, 2004), 176–77.

21. Jaap de Hoop Scheffer, Speech at the Australian Defence College, Canberra, April 1, 2005.

22. Ivo H. Daalder and James M. Lindsay, "An Alliance of Democracies," *Washington Post*, May 23, 2004, B7.

23. Daalder and Goldgeier, "Global NATO," 113.

24. Quoted in Ian Q. R. Thomas, *The Promise of an Alliance: NATO and the Political Imagination* (Lanaham, MD: Rowman & Littlefield, 1997), 145.

Selected Bibliography

Albright, Madeleine. "NATO Expansion: Beginning the Process of Advice and Consent," Statement before the Senate Foreign Relations Committee, U.S. Department of State *Dispatch,* October 17, 1997.

Asmus, Ronald D. *Opening NATO's Door: How the Alliance Remade Itself for a New Era.* New York: Columbia University Press, 2002.

———. "Rebuilding the Atlantic Alliance." *Foreign Affairs* 82, no. 5 (September/October 2003): 28–40.

Asmus, Ronald D., Larry Diamond, Mark Leonard, and Michael McFaul. "A Transatlantic Strategy to Promote Democratic Development in the Broader Middle East." *The Washington Quarterly* 28, no. 2 (Spring 2005): 7–21.

Asmus, Ronald D., Richard L. Kugler, and F. Stephen Larrabee, "Building a New NATO." *Foreign Affairs* 72, no. 4 (September/October 1993): 28–40.

Axworth, Lloyd. "NATO's New Security Vocation." *NATO Review* 47, no. 4 (Winter 1999).

Baker, James. "A New Europe: A New Atlanticism: Architecture for a New Era." (Current Policy no. 1233), December 12, 1989.

———. *The Politics of Diplomacy: Revolution, War and Peace, 1989–1992.* New York: G.P. Putnam's Sons, 1995.

Bebler, Anton, "The Evolution of Civil-Military Relations in Central and Eastern Europe." *NATO Review* 42, no. 4 (August 1994): 28–32.

Berman, Ilan. "The New Battleground: Central Asia and the Caucasus." *The Washington Quarterly* 28, no. 1 (Winter 2004–2005): 59–69.

Binnendijk, Hans, and Richard Kugler. *Dual Track Transformation for the Atlantic Alliance.* Washington, DC: Center for Technology and National Security Policy, November 2003.

———. *Needed—A NATO Stabilization and Reconstruction Force.* Washington, DC: Center for Technology and National Security Policy, September 2004.

Blank, Stephen J. *Prague, NATO and European Security.* U.S. Army War College, Strategic Studies Institute, April 17, 1996.

Booth, Ken, ed. *The Kosovo Tragedy: The Human Rights Dimensions.* Portland, OR: Frank Cass, 2001.

Bring, Ove. "Should NATO Take the Lead in Formulating a Doctrine on Humanitarian Intervention?" *NATO Review* 47, no. 3 (Autumn 1999): 24–27.

Buckley, William Joseph. *Contending Voices on Balkan Interventions.* Grand Rapids, MI: Wm. B. Eerdmans Publishing Co., 2000.

Buergenthal, Thomas. "Copenhagen: A Democratic Manifesto." *World Affairs* 153, no. 1 (Summer 1990): 5–8.

Bush, George. "Proposals for a Free and Peaceful Europe." Speech at Mainz, Federal Republic of Germany (Current Policy no. 1179), May 31, 1989.

———. "Security Strategy for the 1990s." Address at the U.S. Coast Guard Academy (Current Policy no. 1178), May 24, 1989.

Bush, George, and Brent Scowcroft. *A World Transformed*. New York: Knopf, 1998.

Buzan, Barry, Morten Kelstrup, Perre Lemaitre, Elzbieta Tomer, and Ole Waever. *The European Security Order Recast: Scenarios of the Post–Cold War Era*. London: Pinter Publishers, 1990.

Daalder, Ivo H., Nicole Gnesotto, and Philip Gordon, eds. *Crescent of Crisis: U.S.–European Strategy for the Greater Middle East*. Washington, DC: Brookings Institution Press, 2006.

Daalder, Ivo H., and Michael E. O'Hanlon. *Winning Ugly: NATO's War to Save Kosovo*. Washington, DC: Brookings Institution Press, 2000.

Daalder, Ivo, and James Goldgeier. "Global NATO." *Foreign Affairs* 85, no. 5 (September/October 2006): 105–113.

de Hoop Scheffer, Jaap. "Projecting Stability." Speech by the Secretary General, Brussels, May 17, 2004.

Deutsch, Karl W. *Political Community and the North Atlantic Area: International Organization in Light of Historical Experience*. Princeton, NJ: Princeton University Press.

de Wijk, Rob. *NATO on the Brink of the New Millennium: The Battle for Consensus*. London: Brassey's, 1997.

———. "Towards a New Political Strategy for NATO." *NATO Review* 2 (Summer 1998).

Drozdiak, William, Geoffrey Kemp, Flynt L. Leverett, Christopher J. Makins, and Bruce Stokes. *Partners in Frustration: Europe the United States and the Broader Middle East*. Atlantic Council Policy Paper. Washington, DC: The Atlantic Council, September 2004.

Duffield, John. "NATO's Function after the Cold War." *Political Science Quarterly* 109, no. 5 (Winter 1994/95): 763–87.

Evans, Gareth, and Mohamed Sahoun. "The Responsibility to Protect." *Foreign Affairs* 81, no. 6 (November/December 2002): 99–110.

FAES (Fundacion Para el Analisis y los Estudios Scoiales). *NATO: An Alliance for Freedom: How to Transform the Atlantic Alliance to Effectively Defend our Freedom and Democracies*. 2005.

Feith, Douglas J. "NATO's Transformation: Security Freedom for Future Generations." U.S. Department of State, *U.S. Foreign Policy Agenda* 7, no. 1 (March 2002).

Finnemore, Martha, and Kathryn Sikkink. "International Norm Dynamics and Political Change." *International Organization* 52, no. 4 (Autumn, 1998): 887–917.

Flanagan, Stephen J. "NATO and Central and Eastern Europe: From Liaison to Security Partnership." *The Washington Quarterly* (Spring 1992): 141–51.

Forster, Anthony, and William Wallace. "What Is NATO For?" *Survival* 43, no. 4 (2001): 107–22.

Garton Ash, Timothy. "Europe's Endangered Liberal Order." *Foreign Affairs* 77, no. 2 (March/April 1998): 51–65.

———. *Free World: America, Europe and the Surprising Future of the West.* New York: Random House, 2004.

Gheciu, Alexandra. *NATO in the "New Europe": The Politics of International Socialization after the Cold War.* Stanford, CA: Stanford University Press, 2005.

Glennon, Michael J. "The New Interventionism." *Foreign Affairs* 78, no. 3 (May/June 1999): 2–7.

Goldgeier, James M. "Not When but Who," *NATO Review,* no. 1 (Spring 2002).

———. *Not Whether but When: The U.S. Decision to Enlarge NATO.* Washington, DC: Brookings Institution Press, 1999.

Gordon, Philip, "NATO After 11 September." *Survival* 43, no. 4 (Winter 2001–2002): 89–106.

Gordon, Philip, and James Steinberg. *NATO Enlargement: Moving Forward.* Brookings Policy Brief, no. 90. Washington, DC: The Brookings Institution, December 2001.

Grossman, Marc. "21st Century NATO: New Capabilities, New Members, New Relationships," U.S. Department of State, *U.S. Foreign Policy Agenda* 7, no. 1 (March 2002).

Harries, Owen. "The Collapse of the 'The West.'" *Foreign Affairs* 72 (September/October 1993): 41–53.

Havel, Vaclav. "A Call for Sacrifice: The Co-Responsibility of the West." *Foreign Affairs* 73, no. 2 (March/April 1994): 2–7.

———. "A New European Order?" *The New York Review of Books,* March 2, 1995.

Holbrooke, Richard. *To End a War.* New York: Random House, 1998.

Hunter, Robert. "Enlargement: Part of a Strategy for Projecting Stability into Central Europe." *NATO Review* (May 1995): 3–8.

Hutchings, Robert L. *American Diplomacy and the End of the Cold War: An Insider's Account of U.S. Policy in Europe 1989–1992.* Washington, DC: The Woodrow Wilson Center Press, 1997.

Kagan, Robert. *Of Paradise and Power: America and Europe in the New World Order.* New York: Alfred A. Knopf, 2003.

———. "Power and Weakness." *Policy Review,* no. 113 (June 2002).

Kaldor, Mary, and Ivan Vejvoda, eds. *Democratization in Central and Eastern Europe.* London: Pinter, 1999.

Kaplan, Lawrence S. *The Long Entanglement: NATO's First Fifty Years.* Westport, CT: Praeger, 1999.

———. *NATO Divided, NATO United: The Evolution of an Alliance.* Westport, CT, 2004.

Katzenstein, Peter J. *The Culture of National Security.* New York: Columbia University Press, 1996.

Kay, Sean. *NATO and the Future of European Security.* Lanham, MD: Rowman & Littlefield, 1998.

Kennedy, Robert. "Educating Leaders for the 21st Century—A Snapshot of the Marshall Center for Security Studies." *NATO Review* 46, no. 4 (Winter 1998).

Lindberg, Tod. *Beyond Paradise and Power: Europe, America and the Future of a Troubled Partnership.* New York: Routledge, 2005.

Linden, Ronald H.. "Putting on Their Sunday Best: Romania, Hungary, and the Puzzle of Peace." *International Studies Quarterly* 44, no. 1 (March 2000): 121–46.

Lunak, Petr. "Security for Eastern Europe: the European Option." *World Policy Journal* 11, no. 3 (Fall 1994): 128–32.

Lunn, Simon. "NATO's Parliamentary Arm Helps Further the Aims of the Alliance." *NATO Review* 46, no. 4 (Winter 1998).

Luong, Pauline Jones, and Erika Weinthal. "New Friends, New Foes in Central Asia." *Foreign Affairs* 81, no. 2 (March/April 2002): 61–70.

Mandelbaum, Michael. "A Perfect Failure." *Foreign Affairs* 78, no. 5 (September/October 1999): 2–8.

———. "Preserving the New Peace: The Cast Against NATO Expansion." *Foreign Affairs* 74, no. 3 (May/June 1995): 9–13.

McCalla, Robert. "NATO's Persistence." *International Organization* 50, no. 3 (Summer 1995): 445–75.

Mearsheimer, John. "Back to the Future: Instability in Europe After the Cold War." *International Security* 15, no. 1 (Fall 1990): 5–56.

Meeting the Challenges of Post–Cold War World: NATO Enlargement and U.S.–Russia Relations. A Report to the Committee on Foreign Relations, submitted by Joseph R. Biden, Jr., in *The Debate on NATO Enlargement,* hearings before the Committee on Foreign Relations, 105th Congress, 1st session, October/November 1997.

Michta, Andrew A., ed. *America's New Allies: Poland, Hungary, and the Czech Republic in NATO.* Seattle, WA and London: University of Washington Press, 1999.

Moisi, Dominque. "Reinventing the West." *Foreign Affairs* 82, no. 6 (November/December, 2003): 67–73.

Moroney, Jennifer D.P. *Enlarging NATO's MAP: An Expanded Membership Action Plan Can Guide Aspirants' Contributions to the War on Terrorism.* DFI International Government Services, Current Defense Analyses, no. 5 (August 2002).

Newman, Edward. "Human Security and Constructivism." *International Studies Perspectives* 2, no. 3 (August 2001): 239–51.

Owen, John. "How Liberalism Produces Democratic Peace." *International Security* 19, no. 2 (Fall 1994): 87–125.

Pond, Elizabeth. *The Rebirth of Europe.* Washington, DC: Brookings Institution Press, 1999.

Powell, Colin L. "A Strategy of Partnerships." *Foreign Affairs* 83, no. 1 (January/February, 2004): 22–34.

Ralston, Joseph W. "Successfully Managing NATO Enlargement," in U.S. Department of State, *U.S. Foreign Policy Agenda* 7, no. 1 (March 2002).

Reiter, Dan. "Why NATO Enlargement Does Not Spread Democracy." *International Security* 25, no. 4 (2001): 41–67.

Risse-Kappen, Thomas. *Cooperation Among Democracies: The European Influence on U.S. Foreign Policy.* Princeton, NJ: Princeton University Press, 1995.

Robertson, Lord. "NATO in the New Millennium." *NATO Review* 47, no. 4 (Winter 1999).

Rose, Charlie. "Democratic Control of the Armed Forces: A Parliamentary Role in Partnership for Peace." *NATO Review* 42, no. 5 (October 1995): 15–19.

Ruggie, John Gerard. *Winning the Peace: America and the World Order in the New Era.* New York: Columbia University Press, 1996.

Rühe, Volker. "Shaping Euro-Atlantic Policies: A Grand Strategy for a New Era." *Survival* 35, no. 2 (Summer 1993): 129–37.

Rupp, Richard E. *NATO After 9/11: An Alliance in Continuing Decline*. New York: Palgrave Macmillan, 2006.

Shea, Jamie. *NATO 2000: A Political Agenda for a Political Alliance*. Brassey's Atlantic Commentaries. London: Brassey's, 1990.

Simon, Jeffrey. *NATO Enlargement and Central Europe: A Study in Civil-Military Relations*. Washington, DC: National Defense University Press, 1996.

———. "NATO's Partnership for Peace: Charting a Course for a New Era," RFE/RL East *European Perspectives* 6, no. 16 (August 7, 2004).

Sloan, Stanley R. *NATO, The European Union, and the Atlantic Community: The Transatlantic Bargain Reconsidered*. Lanham, MD: Rowman & Littlefield, 2003.

Solana, Javier. "A Defining Moment for NATO: The Washington Summit Decisions and the Kosovo Crisis." *NATO Review* 47, no. 2 (Summer 1999).

———. "NATO in the 21st Century: An Agenda for the Washington Summit." *Congressional Digest* (April 1999).

Steinberg, James B. "An Elective Partnership: Salvaging Transatlantic Relations." *Survival* 45, no. 2 (2003): 113–46.

Szayna, Thomas S. "The Czech Republic." In *America's New Allies: Poland, Hungary, and the Czech Republic in NATO,* edited by Andrew A. Michta. Seattle: University of Washington Press, 1999.

———. *NATO Enlargement 2000–2015: Determinants and Implications for Defense Planning and Shaping*. Santa Monica, CA: RAND, 2001.

Talbott, Strobe. "From Prague to Baghdad: NATO at Risk." *Foreign Affairs* 81, no. 6 (November/December 2002): 46–57.

Thomas, Ian. *The Promise of Alliance: NATO and the Political Imagination.* Lanham, MD: Rowman & Littlefield, Publishers, Inc. 1997.

U.S. Commission on Security and Cooperation in Europe. *Report on Human Rights and the Process of NATO Enlargement*. Washington, DC: U.S. Commission on Security and Cooperation in Europe, 1997.

U.S. Mission to NATO, *Report to Congress on Enlargement of the North Atlantic Treaty Organization: Rationale, Benefits, Costs and Implications—Executive Summary,* February 24, 1997.

Wallander, Celeste. "Institutional Assets and Adaptability: NATO After the Cold War." *International Organization* 54, no. 4 (2000): 705–35.

Weaver, Robert. "Continuing to Build Security Through Partnership." *NATO Review,* no. 1 (Spring 2004).

Yost, David S. *NATO Transformed, The Alliance's New Roles in International Security.* Washington, DC: United States Institute of Peace Press, 1998.

Index

About the Author

REBECCA R. MOORE is Associate Professor of Political Science at Concordia College in Moorhead, Minnesota, where she chairs the Global Studies program. She teaches courses in U.S. foreign policy, international relations, and international security, and she has published previously on NATO, U.S. human rights policy, and the promotion of civil society in China. She held a NATO-EAPC Fellowship from 2001 to 2003.